D0777208

33914

DATE			

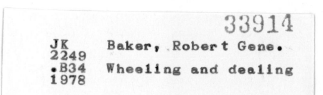

Wheeling
and Dealing

CONFESSIONS OF A CAPITOL HILL OPERATOR

Wheeling and Dealing

BY BOBBY BAKER

WITH LARRY L. KING

 W·W· NORTON & COMPANY · INC · NEW YORK

FIRST EDITION

This book is typeset in photocomposition Baskerville with Deepdene display. Manufacturing is by The Maple-Vail Book Manufacturing Group. Book design is by Marjorie J. Flock.

Library of Congress Cataloging in Publication Data
Baker, Robert Gene.
    Wheeling and dealing.
    Includes index.
    1. Corruption (in politics)—United States.
2. Baker, Robert Gene. 3. United States. Congress.
Senate—Officials and employees—Biography. I. King,
Larry L., joint author. II. Title.
JK2249.B34 1978   973.923′092′4 [B]   78-5740

ISBN 0 393 07523 0

1 2 3 4 5 6 7 8 9 0

For my old friends, Etta and Emery Inman,
Scotty Peek, Glenn Troop, John Paleologos,
and Bob Thompson; for my loyal children,
Bobby, Jr., Jimmy, Sissy, Lynda, and
Lyndon; and my faithful siblings—
especially Mimi—and to those who never
waivered: Edward Bennett Williams,
Boris Kostelanetz, Milton Hoffman,
Mike Tigar, and, of course, Doris Myers.
Last, but not least, for my fellow inmates
and pals, Jake Ursini, Don Plotnick, and
Frank (Blinky) Palermo.

Contents

Wheeling
and Dealing

Chapter One

In Jail with Jimmy Hoffa

"Bobby, watch your ass. Don't trust anybody but me and my boys."

I HAD never believed that I would go to jail.

Even during sensational congressional hearings fueled by some senators who loved to see their names in print (while others may have feared that same fate, should I tell all I was presumed to know), even though countless investigations by FBI and tax agents, even through federal grand jury proceedings culminating in my indictment on nine criminal counts, even through the long trial, my subsequent conviction, and the endlessly complex appeal processes, I simply had not believed that I would be sent to jail.

Certainly I had not believed it on that October day in 1963, when—not a little angry and drunk—I had impulsively resigned as secretary to the majority of the United States Senate. I had done so in preference to facing what I considered star-chamber quizzings from Senator John J. Williams, the fiesty Delaware Republican who enjoyed billing himself as the "Watchdog of the Senate," and by scholarly, pipe-sucking Senate Majority Leader Mike Mansfield of Montana, who abhorred controversy almost as much as Williams thrived on it.

Nor had I believed it, seven years later almost to the day, when the U.S. Court of Appeals handed down a decision unanimously affirming the findings of my trial judge, Federal Judge Oliver Gasch of the District of Columbia.

In my secret parts I refused to accept that I was jail-bound, even after the Supreme Court of the United States, just before Christmas in 1970, denied my petition for *certiorari*. This meant that my legal appeals were exhausted and that I must prepare to live in prison for a maximum period of three years.

Three years may not sound ominous if you are breathing free air and no one is trying to take it away from you. Time is relative, however, as anyone who ever sat down on a hot stove can tell you. Three years works out to 1,095 days, and for every day there's a night. Veteran convicts routinely advise newcomers to serve their sentences "one day at a time." You learn that this is excellent advice, there being no other way to do it and no shortcuts.

I had not dwelled on the dismal mathematics of three years in prison—3,285 mandatory trips to the mess hall whether or not one wanted to eat; countless shakedowns and numberless work details and the hundreds of little humiliations—for I had refused to face the realities. In time I would learn about time. Later, when I heard people express contempt for the "light sentences" given John Dean, Charles Colson, Egil Krogh, and others of the Watergate gang, I would know they had never counted the days or the hours while living behind locks.

This knowledge lay in the future, however, on the night of January 13, 1971, as I climbed into my car while icy sleet pinged against it and Washington's roadways were covered with a treacherous glaze. Even then I still held to a stubborn belief in unspecified miracles. Somewhere, somehow, someone—the Supreme Court or God or Santa Claus—would step forward to say, "Bobby, there's been a horrible mistake. You don't belong in jail." Only fleetingly had I considered the dismal alternatives, including suicide. But always such dark thoughts quickly were chased to the backlots of my mind by whiskey or by force of will.

As the family car pulled away from my home in the Spring Valley section of Northwest Washington, where I'd once been a neighbor to Lyndon B. Johnson, I was obliged at last to reexamine my faith in miracles. It dawned with a physical finality that only a serious car wreck could prevent my surrendering the next morning to U.S. marshals in Lewisburg, Pennsylvania, there to begin my term in federal prison.

It would be convenient to the art of storytelling if I could claim that during that long ride over hazardous highways I mused on how Bobby Baker had fallen so far and so fast. Bobby Baker—pal of presidents, advisor to the mighty, a political mover and shaker, hailed as the "101st Senator" by, among others, John F. Kennedy. "The last man I see at night," Lyndon Johnson often had said, "and the first man I see every morning."

Bobby Baker—who'd been rumored as a possible future governor or senator from his native South Carolina, and who had not been entirely innocent of that rumor's good taste. Bobby Baker—who had cavorted with lobbyists and show folk and athletic heroes as well as the political biggies, and whose country-boy heart perhaps had enjoyed it a shade too much. Bobby Baker—who had been at least a paper millionaire, a kid up from scratch, and a compulsive hustler. Bobby Baker—who had assisted senators in their well-intended public programs as well as in their less noble, if entirely human, ambitions of money and the flesh.

The truth is, however, that on that night ride toward Lewisburg Prison I was alternately morose and pointlessly manic. Not for a long time would I become introspective about my life; not for longer still would I begin to understand much of what had happened to me, or why, or be able even marginally to sort out which portions of the blame might accrue solely to me or which portions might properly be assigned to other men or institutions. It is an ongoing process, and probably shall continue throughout my life.

I sat in the back seat with Dorothy, my wife of twenty-three years. Though we had shared five children, and high times as well as low, all we now seemed to share was a bottle of scotch and long, brittle silences. You might think there might have been much to say, but I do not recall that we said it. I kept thinking, *It's happening, it's really happening, I'm going to jail!* I didn't have any idea of what jail life might be like, for I'd never permitted myself to dwell on it.

Dorothy's brother, Robert Comstock, hunched over the wheel and peered through the storm to keep the car on the glazed road; her sister, Jean, sat beside Robert and gazed out into the sightless night. I thought Robert appeared ill-at-ease and evasive when I attempted conversation, though this may have been the paranoia of one long hounded and soon destined to give up his freedom. Though I had placed my financial affairs in Robert Comstock's hands, even to giving him my power-of-attorney, we did not talk business that night. Perhaps we should have: within mere days Robert would fire my employees at the Carousel Motel in Ocean City, Maryland, and then sell what the newspapers called "the celebrated playground of the *Advise and Consent* set"—without having consulted its owner. (I must admit, however, he turned a neat capital gains profit. This somewhat lessened my original frustration at not having been consulted.)

The time or two I reluctantly had talked to Dorothy about the prospect of prison, I had papered it over with optimism, and generally that suspect optimism had been watered with a cocktail or two. I told Dorothy that I would do my time with dignity, that I would read and try to keep a positive attitude and attempt to grow, that whatever period of time I was in prison would be overcome if we didn't let it defeat us. The most important thing, we agreed, was keeping our family together and seeing that three of our children remained in college. I also had said, "I'm a realist. I don't expect you to live an unnatural life if I go away. Just try not to fall in love." All that seems a little naive, now.

As the car slipped toward Lewisburg there seemed nothing else to say. We checked into a motel room and continued our drinking. To tell the truth, I don't remember much else about it; as always, in times of adversity I tend to numb myself with liquor. I suppose it was about two

"I had never believed that I would go to jail. . . ." The senior marshal said, "I'm sorry, Mr. Baker, but we've got to handcuff you now." (*United Press International*)

o'clock in the morning when I took the last drink remaining from the two fifths of scotch we'd started with from Washington. I recall thinking that I'd better enjoy it because it would be the last for a long time.

I knew the boys and girls of the Fourth Estate would be out in full cry, cameras at the ready, blinding me with their kleig lights, shouting rude or inane questions. Just doing their jobs, yes; I understood that. I didn't see any profit, however, in Dorothy's being forced to witness yet another circus. And so, a couple of blocks before reaching the Post Office Building in Lewisburg, I asked Robert Comstock to pull the car over.

I didn't linger over good-byes, just quickly kissed my wife and began to mush through the packed snow toward the reporters. They came running in a pack, microphones extended; one of them asked the penetrating question, "Mr. Baker, how do you feel?" I've often wondered, had I responded "This is the greatest day of my life," where the dialogue might have gone from there. I was in no flippant mood, however. To all questions I said only, "Gentlemen, I shall do my duty and do it with honor."

A small covey of U.S. marshals awaited me inside. We shook hands and exchanged uneasy pleasantries. I recall being surprised that the marshals appeared nervous: this was the first time I had participated in such a ritual, but I had presumed it to be old-hat among them. After a certain shuffling, and appearing a little embarrassed, the senior marshal said, "I'm sorry, Mr. Baker, but we've got to handcuff you now. It's a regulation we don't always think is necessary, but . . ."

Handcuffed? I had never owned a gun, robbed a bank, or been charged with any act of violence. Probably sounding calmer than I felt I said, "That's all right, gentlemen. I probably understand the ways of the bureaucracy better than you do." The marshal cuffed my hands together in gentle movements, and then folded an overcoat over them. "They'll have cameras downstairs," he said.

The reporters were not fooled by the folded overcoat; there was a great surge and crush when the marshals led me out of the Post Office Building, photographers fighting for footholds on the ice and snow. Though I attempted to hold my head up and not cringe, I felt like something in a zoo. The cameras were still rolling and clicking when we drove out of sight. I remember thinking that I hoped my aged parents wouldn't see it on television in South Carolina that night. I'd had enough experience to know that Bobby Baker going to jail handcuffed would make the national news, and sure enough it was played big on all three networks. Many of my friends would later tell me they had been shocked or outraged at seeing me hauled away in handcuffs, because they thought it an unnecessary humiliation. It was, I am sure, a calculated humiliation. Just as the military services make certain their basic training programs are brutal and dehumanizing, in order to break down individuality and teach the soldier he is dependent upon the group, so too prison officials adopt measures to quickly inform the new arrival just who is boss and who a faceless number possessed of few rights.

Lewisburg is an old prison, an undistinguished pile of dingy brick buildings and dim corridors and thick bars constantly reminding you where you are. I had not expected a country club, but Lewisburg was more dismal and depressing than I had anticipated. I knew that I was a jailbird for sure, that no miracle would snatch me out, as I heard metal doors slamming behind me, the grating of keys in locks, the scraping of shoes on concrete floors. Yet, I recall feeling detached from it: as if I stood back watching myself going through the motions of processing. The impersonal faces and impersonal tones of the prison guards, as they routinely processed me, added to the sense of detachment.

About a half dozen of us went through the dismal rites that cold morning, shuffled along like cattle from dingy room to dingy room and down endless hall after endless hall. Our attempts at conversation were hushed and halting. We were not in the greatest of moods, and, frankly, I found little in common to discuss with my new colleagues, most of whom were black, came from a different culture, and had not known the benefits of much education. Later, I would learn from one of the prison authorities that the psychological tests they administered on that first day showed that I felt "superior" to my fellow convicts and to the guards themselves. Maybe so, but as I shuffled along in cheerless gray prison pants, which failed to fit me at any point and which I had to hold up with one hand, I felt like a character in a Donald Duck cartoon.

Throughout the day, as I sat on hard, bare benches awaiting the next uncertain ritual, I gave myself silent lectures. Pep talks. It was a way of cutting down on the despair that crept into my bones, a way of holding on, a way of getting through it, a way of reminding myself that nothing is forever. *Don't be mad at the world,* I told myself. *Be a positive thinker. Don't feel sorry for yourself or think the system screwed you. Read. Improve your mind. You've just got to make the best of this mess.* A few minutes later, with a fresh sinking spell coming on, I would do it again: *You've got a legal education, you've had an unusual career and more of the good things than most, you've proved you can hold up your end while working with the best.* I also recalled something my father had often told me: "Son, a good run is better than a bad stand." Well, I had made my legal stand against the federal government, had lost, and now I would run with the system. I would blend in, make no waves, be a model prisoner. I vowed to come out undefeated by the experience.

I lived most of that first day in my head, going through the orientation program as if in a daze or sleepwalking through a bad dream. That night, after eating only a few bites of supper, I sat with thirty or forty other prisoners and felt very much alone. Suddenly, the television news came on and there was Bobby Baker in handcuffs and in living color. Some of my new pals snickered or catcalled when my electronic image said, "Gentlemen, I shall do my duty and do it with honor." Among the cynics and callused souls of that place, the words sounded hollow and perhaps a touch grand.

Just before lights out, a prisoner I'd never seen before sought me out to say, "Baker, Jimmy Hoffa wants you to join him for breakfast tomorrow morning. Be there."

The command puzzled me. It also made me uneasy, being another unknown factor in a strange experience. Scuttlebut had it that the Teamsters Union's former president "ran" Lewisburg Prison, that his word was law among the inmates, and that he had the clout to back up his words.

I had only met Jimmy Hoffa once in my life, at a social function in Washington, where we'd exchanged perfunctory small talk. A New Orleans businessman rumored to be well connected with the Mafia had once sought me out to inquire whether President Lyndon Johnson might be willing to pardon Hoffa in exchange for one million dollars. "Don't do it," I had advised him. "LBJ would be petrified at the possibility of discovery, and whoever made the offer would find his ass in jail.

"Lewisburg is an old prison, an undistinguished pile of dingy brick buildings and dim corridors and thick bars constantly reminding you where you are."   (*Wide World Photos*)

And it wouldn't help Jimmy Hoffa at all." Now I wondered whether Hoffa knew of that incident, and what his temper might be with respect to my advice.

I was a long time finding sleep that first night in my narrow prison cot. My thoughts tumbled and jumbled like clothing buffeted about in a washing machine; none could be kept in sight. I suppose, in retrospect, I was for the first time tentatively attempting to sort out what had happened to me since I'd fallen from power more than seven years earlier, shortly before John F. Kennedy's assassination had elevated Lyndon Johnson to the presidency, and less than a year after the death of my closest friend in high places, Oklahoma Senator Robert Kerr. *Bob Kerr. If Bob Kerr had lived, I might not be in jail . . . I don't belong here,* I thought. *I'm here for something that never happened.* Somewhere in those reveries, fatigue caught up with me and I slept a dreamless sleep.

The next morning, in the mess hall, I went to find Jimmy Hoffa among two thousand men identically garbed. Knowing something of the habits of power, I began by checking the four corners of the huge room. Sure enough, I spotted Hoffa presiding at a large corner table. As I approached with my tray, several tough-looking customers sitting with Hoffa rose and disappeared as if in response to some silent signal.

A politician first, last, and always, I began with the usual small pleasantries. Hoffa, a more direct man, cut them short and came straight to the point. "Bobby," he said, "you're in great danger here." Before I could digest that along with my oatmeal he went on, "We have about a murder a month in this place. There are tough bastards here and crazy bastards and bastards who don't give a shit about anything. They're goddamn animals. The human life isn't worth a nickle to them."

"My God!" I said. "I never dreamed it was like that. You mean in a prison run by the government there's that kind of anarchy?"

Jimmy Hoffa's laugh was short and mirthless. "You ain't anybody in here, Bobby," he said. "Your ass belongs to the gypsies. Uncle Sam couldn't care less what happened to it."

"But why me?" I managed. "Why am I in danger?"

"You were a big shot," Hoffa said. "You represent the Establishment to these guys. Some of these goddamn animals, they'll be looking to snuff you just to make a rep. You represent authority to them, goddammit. You represent the enemy."

"Look," I said, "I'm not breathing free air. The government put *me* in here."

"Listen to me, Bobby," Hoffa growled. "You're a babe in the goddamn woods here. You don't have any idea how it is or how these goddamn animals think. You just be quiet and listen to me."

"I spotted Jimmy Hoffa presiding over a large corner table. 'Bobby,' he said, 'you're in great danger here . . . watch your ass.' " (*Wide World Photos*)

I nodded, dazed and uncomprehending. It was getting through to me, however, that Jimmy Hoffa was trying to do me a great big favor.

"Be seen with me at every opportunity," Hoffa said. "At church. In the prison library. On sick call at the infirmary. I'll send word when and where you're to meet me. Got it?"

I said I had it.

Hoffa said, "I'll see that my guys get the word out. 'Bobby Baker is Hoffa's friend. If you fuck over Baker than you're fucking over Hoffa.' Maybe that way you'll stay alive—if you're careful. Don't go anywhere with strangers. Stay out of isolated places. Don't trust anybody but me and my boys. I'll see to it that you get to know them. If anybody but them asks you to meet me somewhere, don't go. Got it?"

I tried to articulate my thanks, but Hoffa gruffly interrupted. "Ah, what the hell? We gotta stick together in here. There's not anybody much, you know, to talk to among these animals." Then, as if embarrassed at implying that he might be lonely, he said abruptly, "Walk out of here with me." We left the mess hall by what seemed to be a circuitous route, until I realized Hoffa was parading his friendship for me so that others might see it.

Just before we parted he said, "They'll probably assign you to Allenwood after you finish processing here. You oughta tell 'em to go fuck theirselves. Tell 'em you wanta stay here."

I had heard that the nearby Allenwood was a better prison. Not so many locks and bars, more like a military barracks. I wasn't looking for a place to pull hard time. I told Hoffa this.

The stocky Teamster boss scowled. "Ah, Allenwood, it's a goddamn old-folks home. Nothing but pussies over there."

I said, "Jimmy, I thank you for your help. But I think I'll go to Allenwood if I get the chance."

"If you do," he said, "I'll have my boys over there look after your best interests and get you a good job. You'll be hearing from me. Watch your ass, Bobby." With that he abruptly walked away, nodding to a couple of guards as if they might be his footmen.

I took the man seriously. I watched my ass, and I slept with one eye open.

Chapter Two

From Pickens to Washington

"Son, it's a chance for a start."

I WAS born the first of eight children, in the village of Easley, South Carolina, on November 12, 1928, the son of a mill-hand father and a mother who had clerked in Rich's Department Store in Atlanta before becoming an eighteen-year-old bride. My father, Ernest Baker, only twenty when I was born, was not without ambition. He was an excellent student, who never lost a lifelong thirst for learning, and who had grandiose notions—for the day and his circumstance—of attending college. As so often happened in those hard-scrabble times, he was forced to leave high school in his senior year and go to work as a millhand after his own father had been fired from the mills for trying to organize a labor union among the workers.

My father was a popular man; I was always proud to be singled out as "Ernest Baker's boy." Despite his paucity of education, he became one of the most successful high school football coaches that Pickens, South Carolina, ever had; later, Dwight D. Eisenhower would appoint him as postmaster of Pickens.

It was a fitting appointment. When I was a small child, my father ran the seven miles from Easley to Pickens in order to take a postal examination as a city mail carrier. He was always fond of remembering that he won the job by posting the highest score, and that be became the first door-to-door mailman in Pickens. The town then was home to about 1,400 people.

One of my earliest memories, it must have been when I was about five, is of my father coming home worried that Franklin D. Roosevelt would cut his pay. It's not generally remembered now but "Dr. New Deal" originally campaigned against Herbert Hoover on a platform of cutting back government spending. He said in a campaign speech that he would reduce the federal payroll by at least five percent. I recall hearing my father tell my mother that he didn't know how in hell he would

survive if FDR cut his pay by five percent, because he only made $100 a
month. I'm not sure that I understood what a pay cut portended, due to
my tender years, but I recall my mother being upset and that the general
tensions scared me. The incident impressed me enough, obviously, to be
among the earliest memories stored in my young mind.

My first job was as cleanup boy at the Rexall Drugstore in Pickens.
Dr. Byrd Lewis, a pharmacist, hired me at the princely sum of ten cents
an hour. It seemed a sizeable beginning to an eight-year-old boy who
had it in him to hustle. I've read, in press reports of my well-advertised
troubles, that Dr. Lewis once said he'd hired me as a cleanup boy and it
wasn't long until I was doing everything but filling prescriptions. I won't
argue with him. I did hustle, and rose through the ranks to delivery boy
to soda jerk to become something of a general all-purpose—if unofficial—store manager, even before I had reached my teenage years. In
the summertime, I opened the drugstore in the morning and often
closed it after the day's receipts had been counted.

I thrived on the job and enjoyed it more than home or school. On my
first day at school, indeed, I had conned my way out of the confinement
of the classroom. One of my classmates was a little girl who was slightly
retarded. The excitement of school proved too much for her and she
wet her pants. The teacher told her to go home. It was a beautiful day
and I thirsted to enjoy it, so I held up my hand and said, "Teacher, her
mother doesn't let her cross streets by herself." As I had hoped, the
teacher sent me along as her escort and I didn't come back that day.
Anytime the little girl experienced adversity, I usually managed to escape the classroom by acting as her escort and protector.

The drugstore offered not only gainful employment and a sense of
belonging, it was also a social center and a fascinating place to learn the
town's people and its secrets. I had the opportunity to observe the
human frailties, and to witness the practice of hypocrisy in Pickens.
Though the townsfolk paid court to a severe religious fundamentalism
holding that drinking liquor qualified one for hellfire, a high percentage
of the local prohibitionists preferred a patent medicine high in alcoholic
content. Early on I discovered that when the devotees of the patent medicine sang its praises and told of how much better they felt, they were
probably just high—and I figured that in their secret hearts they knew it
and covered up their guilt by prattling of their improved health.

I also observed that while a man had to be brought in from Georgia
to operate the local movie house, because the reigning fundamentalism
preached against Hollywood's products as sinful and no local person was
willing to wear the taint, the movie house was one of Pickens's more successful businesses. I learned, too, that leading citizens with reputations

for generosity demanded more ice cream in their sodas than was the norm, that others paid their bills only when backed against the wall, and that some few might conveniently forget to pause by the cash register after they'd chosen an item from the drugstore shelf. As a delivery boy, I witnessed secret drinkers and occasionally found a strange man in another man's house. Very early I concluded that things are not always what they seem.

Attending church in Pickens was obligatory among all respectable families. I honored this demand and its attendant Baptist rituals until I left my father's house to work in Washington. My parents were not among the community's religious zanies: they spoke in no tongues, rolled in no sawdust, ran no spiritual fevers. They did, however, honor a basic code loosely based on the Ten Commandments and what others might expect of them. Though they would occasionally take a social drink—after carefully lowering the shades against the disapproving eyes of their more straitlaced neighbors—my mother cried all one Christmas Day when, in my early teens and freshly strutting newfound sophistications I learned in Washington, I stayed out all night drinking and carousing with my former high school classmates.

I knew troubles with the law only on two occasions as a youngster. One of these was the result of teenage mischief, when the boys of Pickens and the boys of Easley met by appointment in a neutral cornfield to establish territorial superiority through a gang fight. The other side, however, flashed guns and we fled in a panic through the cornfields. The farmer complained that we'd ruined about forty acres of his corn; once the participants had been identified, we were required to pay the damages.

The other incident was far more traumatic. I was home from Washington during a congressional recess on the Fourth of July weekend in 1944, proudly driving an old 1937 yellow Buick convertible with red wire wheels. It was quite a cock wagon for a teenage boy in Pickens in those years, and it was the envy of many of my contemporaries. The car was flashier than it was stable. To start it, one employed a piece of surgical tape, a fifty-cent piece, prayer or profanity, and two loose electrical wires. All my friends in town knew how to start the car, and more than once, while I slept, they took it out for joyrides. This was fine with me.

On the weekend in question, a physician in Pickens, Dr. Jack Gravelly, asked me to go about seven miles from Pickens to the backwoods countryside around Alice Mill to pick up a little holiday whiskey from a bootlegger. I started out with three companions. The road was rough and not well engineered; when I drove the heavy old Buick across a particularly washboardy intersection, my jack fell out of the back. I stopped to retrieve it. As I alighted, a city officer of the town of Easley, where I was born, grabbed me by the belt and said, "You're under arrest." I asked why. "For reckless driving." I said, "Well, I'm sorry, I wasn't speeding over this rough road and I don't understand."

The officer said, "You know what I'm talkin' about. You came through Easley last Friday night doin' a hundred miles an hour."

I knew that one of the football stars of Pickens had gone out in my car that night; although I didn't personally know whether he'd been speeding, I didn't want to squeal on him. So I said, "Officer, I swear to you, I wasn't anywhere near Easley last Friday night." The officer said, "Well, somebody damn sure was and they tore up the roads in this car. It's your car and it's your responsibility, so you're going to jail."

He placed me in his police car, much to my anger and embarrassment, and drove me to jail. My friends started back to Pickens to raise the money for my fine; we only had eight dollars among the four of us, two dollars less than the speeding fine. I said to the arresting officer, "This isn't right. It's a miscarriage of justice for you to put me in jail over something I didn't do." The officer turned a deaf ear and locked me up.

This was wartime, remember, and since decent tires were impossible for civilians to attain, my old Buick operated on inferior tires with boots in them. My friends, returning home for money to spring me from the hoosegow, had two flat tires; the short round trip required almost three hours. Pacing the small jail cell, I had no way of knowing why they took so long to return. I envisioned multiple disasters: my mother would be shamed and my father disappointed in me; I might lose my job in the Senate; I would have a police record that might follow me to the ends of the earth. From that day on I've had an absolute horror of jails; probably that youthful experience was at the root of my being unable or unwilling in later years to admit that I might go to prison.

(Years later, when I was riding high as Lyndon Johnson's right-hand man and was being honored in my home precincts on one of several such occasions, I chanced upon the officer who had arrested me. He then was chief of police in Easley. I could not help saying to him, "That was a terrible thing you did. You wouldn't listen to me, you accused me of lying when I wasn't lying, and you put a green kid in jail without giving him a chance." The chief was embarrassed and stuttered out an apology, but as far as I was concerned the damage long had been done, and I felt no quick rush of forgiveness.)

But it would be unfair to dwell excessively on my youthful personal disappointments, or to brand the good people of Pickens as any weaker than human beings elsewhere. The times may have been hard and the people sometimes may have matched the times, but I have far more good memories than bad. Indeed, when I reflect on my formative years there seems more often than not to be an improbably idyllic, Tom Sawyerish quality about them. I was personally popular and early assumed among my peers the role of a leader; I was the first freshman elected a cheerleader, and though my grades were spotty—I did well in mathematics and history, because I cared about them—I was among those favorites our teachers looked to for evidence that they had not wasted their lives on ungrateful hicks.

My ambitions, if I had thought about them, would not have blinded onlookers. I had no great dreams. It was not, really, a time or place for dreaming. I believed that you got ahead by hard work and hustle. Had I paused to examine my potential, I suppose I might have liked one day to own the drugstore where I worked. Anything beyond that would have seemed excessively grand or unattainable.

I pretty much accepted the local mores, and did so without calling them into question. I did not wonder why those making up the ten percent black population of Pickens—a mere scattering of blacks when compared to the usual racial ratio found in other sections of South Carolina and the South—had to sit in the balcony of the local theater, or why they visited segregated restrooms, or did not enjoy the run of such restaurants as Pickens provided. Only after a few years in Washington, itself a Southern-oriented city at the time, did I note that the black residents of Pickens lived on unpaved streets, that they might receive short shrift in our courts or schools or other tax-supported institutions, or that they had no chance to claim the town's better jobs. Not that I recall any vitriolic racism, or even any discussion of racial injustice, temperate or otherwise. I simply accepted things as I found them.

My pleasures were those of the small-town boy: there was the legendary ol' swimming hole, the high school gang hanging out on the corner or in the pool hall, a few soirees to Greenville to attend movies or dances or beer busts as one grew up. My favorite youthful recreation was serving as batboy for the Pickens Mill Textile team, which competed in an industrial league. The millhands played their games in the late afternoon, after their workaday shifts had ended, and they were fiercely competitive. My particular hero was a lanky outfielder known as "Woolly Bugger" Adams, whom, I was convinced, could spot Ted Williams ten points and hit for the higher average. I was crushed when Woolly Bugger caught a strain of religion that convinced him God disapproved of his playing baseball, and quit the game. I loved taking the players their favorite bats, fetching them ice water, and performing other services which made me feel a part of the team.

Because money was so scarce, my father one day announced that in addition to my drugstore job I would become the delivery boy for the Greenville *News-Piedmont*. I uncharacteristically did not want the job, despite the opportunity to add to my earning power, because I so hated the idea of giving up my batboy duties. My throwing the afternoon paper to about fifty families in Pickens coincided with those hours in which the baseball team played its games. On my first day as a newsboy, I could not bring myself to tell the team manager of my defection; I later learned that the team had waited for me at a gasoline station long past the normal hour of departure. They waited so long, indeed, that they had to forfeit the game, and I felt some vague guilt because I'd let the team down.

Boys in my circumstances were expected to contribute to the family coffers; my mother charged me about half of my earnings for rent. I learned to bypass this involuntary tax by, in compensation, charging Pepsi-colas, Moon Pies, peanuts, and other snacks to my father's account at Finley's Meat Market. My father, more indulgent than my mother, kept it a secret from her.

I was happy in Pickens and not at all prepared when my father told me he wanted me to leave there to become a page boy in the United States Senate in far-off Washington. Senator Burnett Maybank had offered the job to a son of Harold Holder, the local political boss. By Pickens standards the Holders were wealthy, and I so enjoyed the surroundings that I spent almost as many nights with the Holder boys as I did in my father's home. But my friend Dwight Holder did not want the page boy job, so his father offered the job to me through my father— who accepted it in my behalf without consulting me. Once he had done so, it was a foregone conclusion that I would accept it: one did not cross one's father in so major a matter.

Far from being excited at the prospect of Washington, I shrank from it. I did not know what a page boy was and found little condolence in the dictionary: a page boy seemed to be a mere messenger; I preferred to remain among my friends—where I had status as a cheerleader and flashy soda jerk—rather than to walk among strangers in a job of no particular merit.

My father, however, saw the opportunity. "Son," he said, "it's a chance for a start." Though I did not argue with him, I'm not sure I grasped his meaning. Later, of course, I came to appreciate my father's understanding of the career limitations in Pickens. He knew a caste system was in effect, that if one came from a working family one was almost certain to remain in that category. The major money in the town was controlled by a handful of old first families, people who had gotten in on the ground floor and had continued to accumulate; they were not eager to share the wealth. My father knew, too, that in those days not five children of every one hundred would leave Pickens for college. Being young, I had not thought of that, and might not have cared if I had. I had my eye on owning that drugstore, you see, and couldn't care less about toting messages for senators in Washington.

My page boy appointment came through about December 1, 1942, less than a month after I'd reached my fourteenth birthday. After it became absolutely certain I would be going to Washington, I rode the Southern Railroad train from nearby Easley to Greenville—a distance of twelve miles—at a cost of twenty-five cents, in order that I might say on arriving in Washington that no, the trip to the nation's capital had not been my first train ride. As it turned out, after all my preparation, my family chose to send me to Washington on the Greyhound. I remember being served potatoes for breakfast in the bus station cafe in Richmond, Virginia, and thinking that with such curious eating habits being observed I surely must be up to my ass in blue-bellied Yankees.

Before the leave-taking, however, my friends and associates showered me with presents at a surprise party held in the American Legion hall. It was an emotional leave-taking. I truly did not want to go. Maybe because I sensed, even then, that though I might return I never truly would go back.

Chapter Three

New Boy on Capitol Hill

From Japanese spies to FDR's missing silver

I ARRIVED in Washington full of trepidation. On January 1, 1943, I reported to the office of Les Biffle, who then held the job I later would hold as secretary to the Senate majority. Biffle was a gentle man from Arkansas I later would know as a friend, but I do not recall whether I reported to him or to some faceless subordinate. Perhaps this is because I was worried about Japanese spies.

A hoary old merchant seaman, recognizing a gullible kid when he saw one, told me in the boarding house we newly shared (at First and Constitution, where the Dirksen Senate Office Building now stands) that fifteen Japanese spies had sneaked up the Potomac River in submarines and were thought to be somewhere in the bowels of the Capitol Building. They were not idle, according to my craggy informant, but even then were working to place explosives which would blow the Capitol to smithereens.

This was not difficult to believe if you not only didn't know anything but didn't even suspect much—and if you had seen through wide eyes the antiaircraft guns, and the military men with bayonets at the ready, which guarded the Capitol grounds. I had heard, too, that only those in possession of security passes—with, I guess, the obvious exception of Japanese spies—were permitted admittance to the Capitol Building. There had to be a reason for that.

Government propaganda, and the messages of potboiler war movies cranked out in Hollywood, had conditioned my mind to the dangers of sabotage; I thus had no cause to doubt the presence of Japanese agents on Capitol Hill. Remember, this was in a time when Uncle Sam had taken his lumps in the Pacific; the memories of Pearl Harbor and the horrors of the Bataan Death March remained fresh. I did not feel any patriotic stirrings to go into the catacombs of the Capitol Building in search of Japanese spies, but I kept a wary eye out in case they saw me first.

Washington represented the frozen northlands to a Southern boy, and so I reported for work wearing old-fashioned long-handle underwear under my outer garments. When I was suffering a beating with brooms from other pages during my initiation rites, these long-handle woolies were discovered by my tormentors amid much laughter and much to my own humiliation.

I was miserably unhappy and homesick during those first weeks on Capitol Hill. My education in Pickens perhaps left something to be desired and so I found myself having to struggle to keep up academically in the Capitol Page School, which met for daily classes conducted under the big dome.

One of my letters home admitted to my loneliness and disenchantment. This word filtered back to a former teacher of mine, Miss Lucille Hallum, who wrote from Pickens to urge me to reach for the best in myself. Unfortunately for those who love the correct uses of grammer, my letter of response has been preserved and it surfaced some years later during my highly publicized troubles. "Bobby Baker don't quit," I assured my old teacher.

There were times, however, when I wanted to. Pickens, whatever its limitations, had been a warm cocoon where I was nurtured by family and friends. I was accepted there, permitted to grow at my own pace; perhaps, as a budding big duck on a small pond, I had received more praise than was good for me. It was a shock to discover that in Washington I might be just one among the many. In the early months I did not find much camaraderie among my more sophisticated fellow page boys or among the rag-tags with whom I shared a boarding house. I was physically smaller at fourteen than almost all of my associates, I was green, and I was scared. This often caused me to be the target of rough humor and the butt of jokes.

The uniform of a Senate page boy, alone, was hateful to me in the extreme. The knickers we wore implied that we were juveniles, of low rank, less than full citizens. Girls giggled at them and adults often teased us about them. I hated them with a passion difficult to fully measure. Years later, when I had the power, I ordered that page-boy knickers be replaced by long trousers.

The work of a rookie Senate page boy is mundane enough. We filled the traditional inkwells and snuff boxes on each senator's desk, though by the 1940s few senators were snuff addicts. We filled the senatorial water tumblers. We brought the senators public documents, newspapers, telephone messages, or anything they desired. To call us, they'd snap their fingers and we'd scurry to them in a half trot.

I realized early on that the key to being efficient and well liked in the Senate was learning to anticipate what each senator might require. I noted each senator's special preferences: Senator X might prefer Kalak water, a soda-water-like beverage, while Senator Y might insist on Mountain Valley spring water; I did not confuse their tastes. When I learned that a given senator would be making a speech on a given day, I stationed myself nearby to quickly fetch some documents or materials or fresh water as he might need. It was not long until many senators asked for me by name. I took pride in my good reputation among the senators, because it meant that I was successful in what I was being paid to do.

In lax times I enjoyed roaming the Senate chamber to read the names of former senators (many of whom had been only dead figures of history for me) which they had burned or carved inside their desk drawers—a tradition still honored to this day. I recall running my fingers over the names—Daniel Webster, Stephen Douglas, Andrew Johnson—and marveling that I stood where they had stood.

One of my big thrills was hearing the great figures of World War II— Winston Churchill, Madam Chiang Kai-chek—when they came to address the United States Senate. I hustled to the front of the chamber to sit on the carpeted step where alert and ambitious page boys posted themselves; so great was my enthrallment that I even forgot for a few moments that I wore those hated little-boy knickers.

I very early became fascinated with the give and take of Senate debate. Each day I contrived to find an advantageous position from which to listen to the senators, while keeping an eye and an ear open for the sight or sound of snapping fingers calling me to work. I took an early interest in mastering the parliamentary rules. When I did not understand a particular rule, or why something had been done, I sought out Mr. Charles Watkins, the Senate parliamentarian. He was a kindly, gracious man from Arkansas and he patiently educated me. I learned, too, to anticipate how long each individual senator would be likely to talk and to read from the visible parliamentary signs just when an adjournment for the day might come. My favorite pastime was counting noses: long before my job would require that I tell Senate Majority Leader Lyndon Johnson how many votes he might expect for a given bill, I made private tallies and predictions for my own amusement. In retrospect, I suppose one might say that I had a little of Sammy Glick in me. Ambition was honorable in the society I had been raised in, however; I tried constantly to learn, to serve, to improve myself.

One learned, too, the human frailties harbored by each United States senator. Senator Bennett Champ Clark of Missouri, when sober, was a kind and gentle man. When drunk, however, he became an abusive tyrant, one who railed and cussed at his subordinates. Consequently, I danced attendance upon Senator Clark in the early part of the day and then, as the hours passed and he began to show signs of inebriation, I

"So many souvenir-hunters among the page boys had pocketed so much of the best White House silver that not enough remained for a state dinner that night. . . . What would the President and Mrs. Roosevelt think of such ruffians?" (Baker is in profile, second row, fifth identifiable face from the right.) (*Wide World Photos*)

made myself scarce. I learned that Republican Senator Charles McNary of Oregon, an Irishman with a twinkle in his eye and a man I much admired for his friendly countenance and ability, simply could not see a skirt pass by without compulsively chasing it. For a while I distrusted Senator Robert Wagner, Sr., of New York—a truly nice man—because, as part of the normal initiation rites, he once sent me to the Senate Document Room to fetch a nonexistent "bill stretcher." One of my favorites was old Senator Tom Connally of Texas, one of the great characters of American politics. He was so pigeon-toed it was unreal, and we pages sometimes mimed the way he walked across the floor. He was a kind man at heart, though in debate he could become the most partisan, caustic man I would know until Oklahoma's Bob Kerr came along. With long curly hair that flowed over his collar, his old-fashioned high-top shoes, and his bombastic oratorical style, Connally may have been a caricature of Senator Claghorn; to me, however, he was a better show than any Shakespearean actor.

Of all the senators in my early Washington years, my favorite was a small, unassuming man from Missouri. Harry Truman was the most genteel man I ever met. Not once did I see him act imperiously toward lowly page boys. "Young man," he would say—not "Sonny" as so many called us—"Young man, when it's convenient, could you please get me a glass of water?" Or, "Young man, would you mind calling my secretary and asking her to send me such-and-so?" In any popularity contest, among page boys or senators, I think Truman would have won in a land-slide.

A minor scandal occurred among Senate page boys in September of 1943, and in recent years I've sometimes had the feeling it portended the darker side of my future. It began well enough—indeed, it began as the biggest thing that had happened to me in Washington—when Mrs. Eleanor Roosevelt invited the congressional page boys and the Supreme Court page boys to the White House for a Saturday luncheon to be fol-lowed by a movie. The splendor of the White House dazzled the country kid from Pickens.

After lunch came a surprising bonus. Mrs. Roosevelt escorted us up-stairs to the First Family living quarters. I vividly recall her knocking on the door of the president's second-floor office—not the Oval Office, but a secondary one in the living quarters—and saying in that high half-yodel of hers, "Franklin, Franklin, I have some guests for you." Presi-dent Roosevelt received us with a warm smile and pleasantries I no longer remember. He exhibited a German helmet captured in the North African campaign, and I recall that he spoke at length of America's and of freedom's stake in the war. The remainder of the visit he spent in cor-dially asking each of us our home states and personal questions. He talked inordinately long of my sponsor, Senator Maybank, saying how much he personally appreciated the senator's having quit the governor-ship of South Carolina to assist the New Deal in Washington. Perhaps it was merely the practiced prattle of the consummate politician, but it caused me to feel pride and to get the impression that my sponsor might be a bit special. I went back to my boarding house to dash off a letter home describing my big day, and I was delighted when excerpts from it later appeared in the Pickens weekly newspaper.

The Monday morning following our White House visit, however, proved to be embarrassing and scary. Shortly after Capitol Page School convened, Secret Service men appeared to consult with our agitated headmaster, a Mr. Kendall. Soon a general school assembly was called. Mr. Kendall, angry and humiliated, stated the problem: so many souve-nir hunters from among us had pocketed so much of the best White

House silver that not enough remained to meet the requirements of a state dinner scheduled that night. School would be dismissed and we would return to our homes, on the double, to return the pilfered silver. I felt as embarrassed as Mr. Kendall did; I was not a souvenir hunter to begin with, and, had I been, I would have considered it a breach of good manners to pocket my host's silver. This lack of good manners among my peers caused me to feel a collective guilt and shame. What would President and Mrs. Roosevelt think of such ruffians?

When I became one of the few page boys not to leave the room to return home, Mr. Kendall asked me, "Bobby, hadn't you better be running along?"

"No sir," I said. "I wasn't raised to steal silver, and I didn't steal silver. I've got better manners than that."

I may have said it with a sting in my voice; I'd resented Mr. Kendall since he'd written my parents, shortly after my arrival in Washington, that I might not be high school material. My improving grades, as I advanced through Capitol Page School, were, I imagine, attained by way of showing Mr. Kendall up for a bad prophet.

Not long after Congress adjourned and I returned to Pickens feeling much a man of the world, I attended a South Carolina political ritual known simply as "The Speaking." It was a command performance for all political candidates and officer holders, and each county annually held one. It was obligatory for everyone from the lowliest constable to the congressman to appear and give the voters an account of themselves. I was astonished when Mr. Julien Wyatt, the Democratic county chairman, suddenly said, "Ladies and gentlemen, we are honored to have all these distinguished people on our platform, candidates for many important offices, but we're proudest of a young man who comes from us, is one of us, and belongs to us. He's now making a name for himself in Washington—our own Bobby Baker. Bobby, we'd like to hear you say a few words."

I could not have been more astonished had he asked me to tap dance or announced my engagement. Groping toward the microphone, I was shaking so badly that I only vaguely heard the rustle of applause; I had no more idea than a fencepost of what to say. Somehow it flashed in my mind that someone had once said that if you really wanted to make a good speech you should say: "To be seen, you must stand up. To be heard, you must speak out. To be appreciated, you must sit down." So I recited it and quickly sat down, basking in the laughter and applause greeting my first public speech. It may not have ranked with the best of Churchill, but for a few days you might have had trouble convincing me otherwise. If the political bug hadn't already fatally bitten me, that was the day it did.

Chapter Four

Meeting Lyndon B. Johnson

"Mr. Baker, I understand you know where the bodies are buried . . ."

T HE drawling voice on the telephone said, "Mr. Baker, I understand you know where the bodies are buried in the Senate.
I'd appreciate it if you'd come to my office and talk with me." I think I
recall those first words Lyndon B. Johnson ever said to me because of
the colorful language, and because it signified that here was a man who
understood political shorthand. In a few words he had paid tribute to
my expertise, asked me to share it with him, and invited—or rather com-
manded—me to appear.

This happened in December 1948; I then was just twenty years old, a
six-year veteran of the Senate, and had risen to become chief telephone
page. The title actually was a misnomer; the job had been created especially for me so that I might remain on the Senate payroll even when
Congress had adjourned. As a common page, and then later as chief
page, my pay had ended with the adjournment gavel. As I became more
immersed in the business of the Senate, knowing more of its day-to-day
operations than many of its members, Senate Democrats decided to
create a new post giving me a more professional staff status. The title of
chief telephone page was merely a handy peg on which to hang my full-
time salary and duties.

The position had been created for me in 1945; I kept that job for
eight years, until elected assistant secretary to the Senate minority during a brief period when Republicans controlled the chamber thanks to
the 1952 Eisenhower landslide. As the years went by I had become an
unofficial part of the leadership among key Senate employees: the secretary to the Senate, the sergeant-at-arms, the secretary to the majority,
and so on. These made the wheels go around at the staff level, and—as I
would come to understand—Senate staffers who proved reliable had
more to do with the day-to-day operations of that body than did all save
a handful of senators themselves.

I've often been asked how a kid could come out of the South Carolina backwaters and within a relatively short period gain the reputation of being one of the most powerful men in government. There wasn't any magic in it. I was industrious, hard-working, ambitious, and I cared about my job. I very early grew to love the Senate: its air of excitement and sense of making history, its aura of power. Extraordinary men there occupied themselves with extraordinary events, I felt, and it was heady to be a part of it: this was in a time, remember, when young men in America were not yet afraid to admit to heros and assumed that their government existed to promote the common good. Cynicism had not yet descended. Down home it might simply have been stated, in the wry humor attending that region, that my work was "mainly indoors and beat heavy lifting." But to me it meant much more.

I knew early on that I had the opportunity to be tutored by the best political brains this country had to offer, and so I was not bashful in seeking senators out to ask their views on bills and issues, to learn who influenced who. It was simply a matter of watching, listening, and doing one's homework to understand that while all senators were theoretically equal and that many were men of talent, some would rise to the top like cream while others would sink to the bottom of the institutional churn. The trick was in learning *why*. What made these character studies so fascinating was that the success or failure of each man was a different case unto itself; no neat answer could be applied across the board.

I learned, for example, that while Henry A. Wallace, as vice-president, might preside over the Senate, he was no real power and that one should not waste much time in cultivating him. It was more than that Mr. Wallace, as a member of the executive branch, did not belong to the inner circle in a legislative body. His problem was one of personal eccentricities. He was seen by hard-nosed, pragmatic senators as an impractical dreamer, something of a poet and a mystic, one who failed to understand those trade-outs and compromises and alliances of convenience necessary to the doing of the nation's business. "You simply cannot do business with that damn fool," I heard my original sponsor, Senator Maybank, say. "He just doesn't understand the processes." I also heard through Senator Maybank and others that President Roosevelt often cried out his vexation at having a vice-president who seemed incapable of grasping the realities of politics, and so I was not surprised in 1944 when the president dumped him in favor of Missouri's senator Harry S. Truman. An ambitious young man thus served Vice-President Wallace politely when called upon, but did not seek him out as a helpful ally.

I was well served by being a Southern boy. Southern senators, from one-party states, were returned time and again by the electorate and be-

"Southerners on Capitol Hill stuck together in those days. As I rose in the ranks, I became close to Felton (Skeeter) Johnston whom I one day would succeed as secretary to the Senate majority." *(Wide World Photos)*

came powerful as they attained seniority and advantaged positions. Though a mere employee, I was welcome in their circles. Southerners stick together. Perhaps it's because we lost a war together or perhaps it's because the Southern culture places a high value on civility and good manners, but for whatever reasons we feel set apart from others and thus easily find a common ground. Many of the Southern senators I knew had started life in hard-scrabble circumstances, as I had, and this, too, caused them to identify with me and to take a special interest in my career. The average senator, when I first arrived in Washington, was probably about sixty years old; among Southerners, it may have been more. I found those courtly old gentlemen of another era to harbor a great respect for energetic and ambitious young men and to assist and encourage them when they could. They were like surrogate fathers. Had I not been a Southern boy, I firmly believe, my rise in the Senate might not have been half so rapid. Southern staffers were no less clannish. These, too, held powerful positions out of proportion to their numbers.

This clannishness was applied across the board, and was applicable to the lowest employee. Once my initial hazings had been accomplished, and I lost some of my fear of the big world into which I'd suddenly been thrust, it dawned that I had dozens of geographical and spiritual cousins eager to help me. These proved invaluable in making connections. Through the namesake son of a supporter of Senator Alben Barkley of Kentucky—Barkley Blagg, a Senate doorkeeper—I became friendly with Flo Bratten, the senator's top secretary, and, in turn, with the senator himself. One of the better political tricks is learning what someone enjoys or is obsessed with, and then playing to it. Senator Barkley, I soon learned, was a randy old goat who for all his Bible-spouting rhetoric was unusually preoccupied with sex. He had a great fixation on breastworks. The bazooms of a particular Senate secretary occupied much of his mind, and when the senator was not trying to get his hands on her, he was talking about it. I saw to it that Senator Barkley and I talked a great deal about mammary glands and exchanged risqué jokes.

The distinguished and dignified senior senator from Georgia, Walter George, required quite another approach. A gentleman of the old school who enjoyed being thought of as an elder statesman, he responded to elaborate courtesies. "Bobby," he said shortly after I had turned twenty-one, "you've got a boy's name and now you're a man. It doesn't have enough decorum or dignity. I'd strongly advise you to change it." My sports-minded father had named me Bobby Gene after two of his special idols—the golfer Bobby Jones and the boxer Gene Tunney—and he was offended when I took Senator George's advice and changed it to the more formal Robert G. Baker by the simple act of going to the proper South Carolina courthouse and writing it on my birth certificate. Senator George, however, was flattered and delighted and thereafter treated me in the warmest possible fashion.

Senator Dick Russell of Georgia was an aging bachelor with no family of his own. But he put a great stock in kinship and often seemed to stray far afield in search of it. When he discovered that my parents had both been born in his native Georgia, Senator Russell demanded the family names of all my Georgia ancestors and then, with all the dedication of a dowager seeking credentials among original passengers on the good ship *Mayflower,* he attempted to find matching names in his own line. When we were not talking Senate business or Democratic politics, we talked kinfolks.

All in all, my tactic was to out-politic the politicians.

I also learned how to sell, not only myself but the products of others. When a given senator or a lobbyist or a Senate staffer asked for my help in passing legislation, I asked them—or their proclaimed experts on the bill—to give me both written and oral information as to its particulars. "Tell me simply," I'd say to them, "so I can sell your product. Tell me

what your bill will do, what it will cost, what it will yield. Keep it simple."
This often enabled me to say to senators—who could not possibly be familiar with all the thousands of bills to be acted upon—"This is a vote to
spend $10 billion dollars to put a man on the moon. The experts say they
can do it within four years." Some senators might ask for a little more:
"What would it accomplish?" I'd say "Well, senator, in addition to giving
us a possible military advantage and enhancing national prestige and
writing large history, our scientists say blah-and-so and our environ-
mentalists say this-and-that and we may learn how to control the weather
and spy on our enemies unbeknownst to them, and get closer to God,"
and so on and so forth. If I could not satisfy a senator's reservations, I
then arranged for the expert proponents of the bill to seek the senator
out and supply stronger or more detailed ammunition.

The Senate Democratic cloakroom didn't look like much with its
cracked old black leather couches, a dingy rug which might have been
bought at a rummage sale, its scarred tables and stacks of newspapers
and a dozen phone booths insuring privacy. I early learned to make it
my outpost when I could, however, even after I'd been awarded a spa-
cious three-room office with impressive chandeliers, a marble fireplace,
mahogany bookcases, and rich silk drapes of gold with matching couch
and chairs. The Democratic cloakroom might be called the Central Intelligence Agency of the Senate, because it was the place where interested spies could learn what was going on. The cloakroom is not so much
a place to keep coats or shawls as it's a private retreat for senators, where
no one save other senators and select Senate officials may reach them.
No prying newsmen, constituents, or general worrywarts need apply for
admittance behind those sacrosanct doors: most senators discourage
even their staff employees from disturbing them there.

Safe among partisans, in the cloakroom senators may read, sleep,
drink, bullshit, make deals, tell lies, gossip, or whatever—and no one's
the wiser. Many National Football League locker rooms host signs saying
"What you see here, what you hear here, let it stay here when you leave
here." No such signs were posted in the Democratic cloakroom, but everyone knew the rule of silence prevailed. One became the sum total of
the three monkeys who saw, heard, and spoke no evil. Any breach of
that rule would have been dealt with almost as quickly as the Mafia en-
forces its similar code.

Consequently, when safe in the cloakroom, senators opened up their
heads and their hearts—especially as the day wore on and flasks were
nipped. An eager observer had no trouble telling the workers from the
players, who might become increasingly powerful and who likely would
remain obscure. It was here I first heard direct from the horse's mouth
what senators were considered to be for hire, and to what extent, and to

whom; I learned one could not presume that just because two senators shared a common ideology or a common state that they were soul mates. Jealousies played a part, and all the other human factors entered in: competing wives, distaste for another's lifestyle, class differences, clashing personal goals. Where I may have been different from my peers was in keeping careful mental book on the individual dislikes and preferences.

One had to be a social tactician in the matter of handling egos, and one learned that favors begat favors. Anytime that I could perform a service for a senator, whether getting him a free ride on a military aircraft or helping his pet legislation along or stalling a vote or hiding a drunk (too far gone for the cloakroom) in a small hideway called the Senate Reading Room—where, strictly, senators *only* might enter, save those helping them in the door—I did it. If there were tricks to rising quickly, I did not perform them with mirrors but with the usual tools of the political trade: hustle, service, hard work, public rleations, gathering intelligence and then acting on it. To me this has always been the most natural and simplest of formulas, and I just don't understand those who don't understand it.

I did not understand, either, my peers and colleagues who seemed apathetic in their work. They seemed merely to go through the motions, to be unaware that they were engaged—however peripherally—in the making of history, and that the opportunity existed to do more. They did not seem to thrill to the ebb and flow of power as I did, to want to be on the inside and help make things happen. Until a given point, when I perhaps grew too big for my britches—a common danger among power seekers—no legislative sparrow dropped from the tree, if I could help it, but that I knew about it. I constantly read committee hearings on major bills, discussed their merits and demerits with the legislative technicians, and carefully read the committee reports. I counted noses after testing all possible sources of information. I paid particular attention as human beings to unsung Senate staffers who often felt misused and neglected in quietly doing the necessary trench work credited to their more famous employers. In short, I worked to insure that everyone knew I could be counted on, that I could be trusted to come through or to keep my mouth shut, and that I would not always play to the grandstand. In time, as LBJ flatteringly suggested the first time he telephoned me, I came to know where the Senate bodies were buried.

I had no special inkling, on that December day in 1948 as I walked toward Congressman Lyndon Johnson's office in the Cannon House Office Building, that I would rise almost to the heights of American power with him, and then fall while he went to the top, or that almost exactly twenty-six years later I would listen to a dying Lyndon Johnson complain of how his presidency had been sold out and had gone sour. On that first day I knew only that he originally had come to the House of Representatives in 1937, that he'd been something of a protégé of President Roosevelt and of House Speaker Sam Rayburn, and he'd lost a close race for the U.S. Senate in 1941, and that now—in 1948—he was a senator-elect from Texas after a contested and disputed eighty-seven-vote victory that bequeathed him the hated nickname of "Landslide Lyndon." He was just another incoming freshman to me, and by then I'd seen a number of them.

Congressman Johnson never was much for small talk; he came directly to the point. "I want to know who's the power over there, how you get things done, the best committees, the works." He solicited opinions of, and thumbnail sketches of, senators little known to him; he peppered me with keen questions for a solid two hours. I was impressed. No senator ever had approached me with such a display of determination to learn, to achieve, to attain, to belong, to get ahead. He was coming into the Senate with his neck bowed, running full tilt, impatient to reach some distant goal I then could not even imagine. It was, as I came to know, wholly characteristic of Lyndon Johnson and close to a typical performance. Politics simply consumed the man.

Nearing the end of our conversation, during which Johnson had prowled the room and waved his arms and poked me on the chest in that frenetic manner of his, he finally sat at his desk, calmed his fevers, cocked his head, and told me what I might expect of him. "Now," he drawled, "I know your job is to assist the Senate Democratic leadership. I know you count noses and maybe you lobby a little bit to help the Democratic program. Fine. But I gotta tell you, Mr. Baker, that my state is much more conservative than the national Democratic party. I got elected by just eighty-seven votes and I ran against a caveman." He toyed with a pencil, drumming it on the desk, and said, "I cannot always vote with President Truman if I'm going to *stay* a senator. I am a Texan and I've got a Southern constituency and so I'm going to be more conservative than you would like me to be or than President Truman would like me to be. President Truman's about as popular as measles in Texas, and you'll waste your time trying to talk to me when I know it would cut my own throat to help him."

I asked the senator-elect what issues likely would give him the most trouble.

"Well," he said, "I'm committed to the continuation of the Taft-Hartley Act. Labor's not much stronger in Texas than a popcorn fart, and so I can't vote to repeal it. I'm for the natural gas bill and for the tidelands bill. Frankly, Mr. Baker, I'm for nearly anything the big oil boys want because they hold the whip hand and I represent 'em. Yeah, I represent farmers and working men and when I can help President Truman help 'em, I'll do it. But you tell the president for me, and you tell your leaders in the Senate for me, that the New Deal spirit's gone from Texas and I'm limited in what I can do. Hell, half the people from Texas are against me! If I go to voting for the Fair Employment Practices Commission and so on, they've got a good start toward forming a lynch mob. I need time to mend my own fences, and then I'll worry about President Truman's."

Though this doubtlessly represented the political realities, it startled me. I recalled Congressman Johnson as an early supporter of the New Deal and, since he seemed so eager to become a factor in the Senate, I felt he might be handicapping himself by so quickly announcing his inability to support his party on many key issues. I murmured something to this effect. LBJ said, "I know my own pasture better than my neighbor knows it." Later, when I indeed lobbied Senator Johnson on a key issue he found too liberal for Texas tastes, he grew very stern: "Mr. Baker, you've already been told that you're wasting your time and mine. And you've been told why."

Johnson would later tell a staff aide, Booth Mooney, that he'd made a big political mistake during World War II by voting against a bill which would have raised the ceiling price on oil. "The oil people have hated me since then," he gloomed. LBJ now set out to please them.

He did not, however, neglect his wider constituency. If you had a mailbox or a street address anywhere in Texas, likely Lyndon Johnson would keep it filled with everything from his periodic newsletter reporting on his actions in Washington to bulletins directed toward specific groups: farmers, ranchers, small businessmen, veterans, you name it. Staff aides searched Texas newspapers, large or small, to find people who might deserve congratulations from their junior senator: win a local Pillsbury bake-off or sponsor the fattest hog at a Future Farmers of American whingding or simply get married, and here would come a letter from Lyndon Johnson noting your accomplishment; one year, he attempted to send a contratulatory note to every graduating high school senior in Texas. Other senators availed themselves of these tools of incumbency, but LBJ did it with a vengeance. I felt sorry for his staff aides who worked from can until can't, and especially for the loyal, harried Walter Jenkins who was on call twenty-four-hours per day. Senator Johnson thought nothing of waking Walter at 3 A.M. should the notion strike him, and he might rattle off a dozen things to be done before breakfast. Jenkins, who learned shorthand in order to keep up with the many Johnson utterances, slept with pen and pad at bedside.

It was not long until I noted that the freshman from Texas was pressing an ardent courtship on Senator Richard Russell of Georgia. Russell was a powerful Senate insider: chairman of the Armed Services Committee, chairman of the Southern Caucus, and, unofficially, as much a part of the Senate leadership as those who held the leadership titles. It benefited LBJ in the Senate, and in Texas, to be known as a special friend of the powerful conservative.

Senator Russell was a bachelor, though getting along in years, and perhaps LBJ sensed that for all his power he was lonely. Though it isn't well known, Dick Russell did a great deal of solitary reading and drinking—the mark of a lonely man. Lyndon Johnson took pains, therefore, to make his family Dick Russell's family. Soon, Russell took most of his weekend meals with the Johnsons; afterward, LBJ would take him for long drives and pick his brains. The Johnson daughters were encouraged to call the Georgia senator "Uncle Dick," and Lady Bird Johnson—always charming and gracious—went out of her way to make him feel at home in her home. There were some who snickered behind their hands at LBJ's obvious courtship of the powerful Georgia senior, but there's absolutely no doubt that his campaign worked. (I learned something in watching LBJ and considering his career: he always aligned himself with powerful sponsors. First there was FDR, then Sam Rayburn, and finally Senator Russell. I had my own powerful sponsors, in time, in LBJ and Senator Bob Kerr.)

Though LBJ voted with Senator Russell's Southern bloc much of the time, he shied away from formally joining the Southern Caucus. "I think," he said in declining membership, "that I can be more effective by not putting any regional label on myself." Senator Johnson received a great deal of publicity for his refusal; it may have jumped him in popularity with blacks and chicanos in Texas, though in those years the minority vote there was a small minority indeed. I've always thought that Johnson's stubborn refusal to be labeled as anything close to Dixiecrat constituted the earliest evidence of presidential ambitions lurking in his head.

My first conversation with Lyndon Johnson about the presidency occurred in 1956, the year Adlai Stevenson was nominated to oppose President Eisenhower for a second time. My impression was that LBJ thirsted to run for president; he insisted, however, that his "favorite son" candidacy was exactly that and no more, an opportunity to receive the plaudits of his home-state politicians on national television. By early 1960, however, LBJ had White House fever—although he often took pains, both publicly and privately, to disavow it. For a couple of years, I had urged support of LBJ's candidacy with Governor Bufford Ellington of Tennessee, Senator Carl Hayden of Arizona, Senator Kerr, and others who were political powers in their respective states.

Late one afternoon, shortly after John F. Kennedy had won the Wisconsin primary, Senator Johnson sent for me. We were in the Senate chamber, and Johnson walked me not to his majority leader's chair but back to the old desk he'd occupied as junior senator from Texas. "Bobby," he said, "you've never had a heart attack. I had a bad one in 1955, and every night when I go to bed I'm afraid I'm not going to wake up. When I get tired, I have terrible chest pains and I really live on an hour-to-hour basis. Few people understand it but I really am not competent to run for president because of my health problems. You are doing me and the country a great disservice, you know, by leaking stories to the press and telling people I'm going to be a candidate. It's just not true, and I wish you'd quit it."

I'm certain that at the moment Senator Johnson believed what he was saying; I'd seen him alternately hot and cold on the presidential notion. Sometimes he appeared to want it like a sixteen-year-old teenager smitten by puppy love might want to get married; at other times he seemed to have little or no interest in the White House or the chase for it.

I knew, however, that Johnson's closer political advisors—John Connally, Speaker Rayburn, Walter Jenkins, and Booth Mooney among them—had been operating a "Johnson for President" effort for more than a year. Connally and Oscar Chapman, who'd been secretary of interior under President Truman, were co-chairman of a Citizens for Johnson committee operating out of the old Ambassador Hotel in Washington; it had both salaried and volunteer workers, and was under the indirect supervision of Walter Jenkins, LBJ's chief of staff in his Texas office on Capitol Hill. I personally had met with Jenkins to discuss strategy and tactics; I had seen him hand wads of $100 bills to Johnson loyalists as they fanned out to many states to round up delegates. I knew LBJ well enough, and the tight control he exercised over his political empire, even to the smallest detail, to know that the presidential operation never would have gotten off the ground without his consent.

I had also been involved in a big effort to obtain the endorsement of Governor David Lawrence of Pennsylvania and other political bosses in that state. John Connally and I once met with Congressman Bill Green of Philadelphia, who had excellent relations with Speaker Rayburn. Congressman Green told us that he couldn't endorse LBJ because the Catholic vote in Philadelphia was for Jack Kennedy so strongly that he faced a runaway situation. "Frankly, gentlemen," he told us, "I'm not about to get trampled by the mob." We finally made a deal with Green, who had been harassed for years by the Internal Revenue Service: he could choose Lyndon Johnson's Secretary of the Treasury if he would switch Pennsylvania to the Johnson banner, provided Jack Kennedy failed to be nominated on the first ballot. That, of course, did not happen—but we had a handshake deal in case it might have.

LBJ did wind up with a few Pennsylvania delegates because of a deal made with Albert Greenfield, a wealthy Pennsylvanian with tax problems. Greenfield's accountants somehow had failed to contribute enough of his money to charity to enable the wealthy Pennsylvanian to take maximum advantage of the tax laws. Consequently, the Internal Revenue Service was demanding about $10 million in back taxes.

A politician, then high in Democratic councils, called to tell me of the Greenfield situation. He strongly hinted that although Mr. Greenfield had been a staunch Adlai Stevenson man, he might switch to LBJ should relief be obtained on the tax matter. I did not pause, in my enthusiasm for my leader's cause, to consider that this might be improper, or that it might constitute a bribe or the next thing to it, in that we were being asked to trade away a possible $10 million in potential tax revenues for a political endorsement. I held a luncheon for Mr. Greenfield and there introduced him to Senator Kerr. Kerr in turn took him to see Lyndon Johnson. I never followed up on the details, but I do know that the IRS dropped its case—and that Greenfield delivered a handful of votes for LBJ from among the Pennsylvania delegates despite great pressure from Governor Lawrence and other Kennedy men.

Knowing of the many schemes and manipulations in operation in behalf of a Johnson candidacy, I couldn't take LBJ's periodic disavowals at face value and I did not. I simply pretended to agree, and then went on wheeling and dealing in his behalf as did others—including, quite often, himself. It was, however, a frustrating experience. Often LBJ's advance men would telephone or come in mad enough to stomp snakes because they thought his pious declarations hurt him in the field. "You're out there bustin' your ass and eatin' sorry food and stayin' in third-rate motels while you kiss the butts of some of the most boring bastards in America," one man shouted. "About the time you've half-convinced somebody LBJ is a viable candidate, you pick up the newspaper or turn on television and there's Johnson saying 'Ah jes' wanna be the very best Senate majority leader and Texas senator that God ever allowed to draw air.' It pulls the rug out from under you." About all one could do in such cases was to pour the outraged a drink and try to soothe him with clucking noises.

I think the problem was LBJ's fear of being defeated. He always was petrified by that notion. On his up days—and Johnson may have been the classic manic-depressive, with all the wide swings of the emotional pendulum typical of the breed—LBJ saw himself as a potential president who would govern better than Jack Kennedy. Privately, in such moments, he bragged of knowing ten times as much about running the country as did the young senator from Massachusetts. "That kid needs a little gray in his hair," he would say; he also sneered at Kennedy's playboy proclivities, and considered him a lightweight. "He's smart enough," LBJ said, "but he doesn't like the grunt work." As one who lived and breathed the Senate, Lyndon Johnson could not understand a rival who used it merely as a way station and utilized its trappings without deeply caring for it.

When on the down side, however, LBJ complained of friends who pushed him toward a race his health wouldn't permit, and of conspiracies among the "red hots"—labor bosses, limousine liberals, the big-city political bosses—to embarrass him or worse, just because he happened to be "a Texan rather than a Harvard." I believe, however, he was really reacting in such moments to fear of defeat.

This fear kept him out of some primaries in which he might have successfully challenged John F. Kennedy; I'm also convinced that this same fear prompted Lyndon Johnson to retire in 1968 rather than face embarrassment at the polls. When counting noses for LBJ during his reign as Senate majority leader, I was often cautioned never to overestimate our strength because Johnson feared losing on the Senate floor. His insistence on not bringing up any bill for voting action until he could be assured of maximum strength often enraged more adventurous Democrats. Liberal senators such as William Proxmire, Paul Douglas, and Wayne Morse often cried out to me against LBJ's timidity which, they felt, deprived them of making a fighting record in behalf of their causes. Pyrrhic victories were not Lyndon Johnson's cup of tea, however, and he saw no value in glorious defeats. Since childhood—as he would reveal in retirement—Lyndon Johnson had been haunted by fears of failure; throughout his life his nightmares centered on his being rooted and immobile, unable to act in times of great crisis.

Lyndon Johnson covered these insecurities well, however, when I knew him in his political prime. I'll admit that I found him fascinating from that first talk in 1948, and—though we would several times fight and suffer strained relations over the years—I was, indeed, beguiled by him. With the exception of Senator Kerr, I felt closer to him than to any other public man—probably, indeed, any other person—and I named two of my children—Lynda and Lyndon—for him. This, of course, was long before I knew that on the day I would need him he would not be there.

Chapter Five

Learning the Political Ropes
"Money talks and bullshit walks."

I ORIGINALLY arrived in Washington innocent in my half-
formed belief that Congress comprised a collection of nature's noblemen come together to form a more perfect union. The scales
eventually would drop from my eyes.

From my earliest days as a knickers-clad page boy I had heard whis-
pers of what senator might be entertaining his secretary on the office
couch, which senator's legs had betrayed him in chambers or in a hideaway office after a five-martini lunch, and what senators had their hands
out. These originally were little more than rumors, the prattle of subordinates spying on their masters, and sometimes may have been suspect
in the specifics. As I climbed in the Senate hiearchy, however, I would
find them true in a general sense and come to know my own secrets.

One of my earliest discoveries was that the storied Capitol Building—
so massive and awesome to the eye with its grand expanses of marble,
impressive columns, burnished desks, silk drapes, and general aura of
polish—contained dozens and dozens of hideaway nooks and crannies
not visible to the naked eye; it was as if the original architects had anticipated that legislators might require a special solitude, though I'm uncertain as to whether they knew the extent to which many senators would
utilize the hideaway nests for their private recreations. These spaces
were highly coveted by the powerful, and particularly by the playful.

I learned early on that, should one be asked to seek out one of the
hidden offices and gently rap on the door as a signal that the senator
locked away there should hurry to the legislative chamber, one should
not assume that the senator would be alone. Such senators as Dennis
Chavez of New Mexico, Tom Hennings of Missouri, Burnett Maybank
of my home state, Pete Williams of New Jersey, or Clair Engle of California might be discovered with no more company than old friend John
Barleycorn. Old or new lady friends, however, might be found in the
company of the Alben Barkleys, Estes Kefauvers, Jack Kennedys,

George Smatherses, Lyndon Johnsons, or Bob Kerrs, among others. (Senator Kerr was not, strictly speaking, a compulsive skirt-chaser: for years he carried on what amounted to a monogamous love affair with one of his secretaries, who later was paid—according to what she told me—$50,000 to *not* write her memoirs.)

Though I partied with certain senators, and made informal introductions of others to eager young ladies who'd let it be known they were out for a good time, I drew the line at furnishing professionals. Only once was I literally badgered to produce a woman for a senator's gratification. He was a deep-dyed Southerner, a real mushmouth whose name I do not intend to use because he's still alive, still in the Senate, and probably needs no more problems.

The senator telephoned my office one afternoon, sounding as if he'd been locked up in a bourbon distillery for about three days, to insist that I find a lady to accommodate his passions. I said, "Senator, I just wouldn't know how to go about that." He called a second time a few minutes later to insist that I bring a woman to his suburban home. "My wife's away and my dick's so hard a cat couldn't scratch it," he said. "I'll pay real good." Again, I demurred. The third time the legislator called he said, "Bobby, I'm gonna keep on callin' you 'til pussy shows up on my doorstep. And if you don't bring me pussy, I ain't bringing you no more votes." I said I'd see what I could do.

I walked to a hotel bar near the Senate side, where I knew a young cocktail waitress rumored to do a little minor-league hustling in her spare time. Wayne Bromley, a lobbyist friend, went with me. "I don't want to know anything about the arrangements," I told the cocktail waitress, "but I know where there's a horny senator with money in his pocket." She said to give her a few minutes to find someone to replace her on the shift. Bromley, the girl, and I drove out to a well-appointed home about twenty minutes from Capitol Hill. When we arrived, the randy senator stood in the center of his dining room, holding onto the table with both hands; despite such support, he was swaying and weaving in invisible breezes. "Senator," I said, "this is Miss Smith and she's your date for the afternoon." The senator looked past me, squinted at the woman and said, "Honey, le's me and you fuck." The girl later told a friend of mine that she'd extracted $100 and cab fare. The Southern senator in question tended to avoid me for a while after he'd sobered up, but I found that his vote was easier to obtain than previously.

If you can't always tell a book by its cover, then the same may be said for some senators. When Estes Kefauver of Tennessee died, after establishing his public image as a war maker against organized crime and corporate gougers or bilkers, many were shocked to learn that he owned

$300,000 worth of stock in drug companies he had been charged with regulating.

I was not the least bit shocked. For one thing, I'd long heard stories that Senator Kefauver was among those senators who more willingly put themselves up for sale; he didn't particularly care whether he was paid in coin or women. What always amazed me was that the press didn't stumble onto this story. More than once Senator Kefauver skated on the thin ice of trouble by attempting to seduce women, one of them a comely newswoman, through tactics bordering on the strong-armed. I recall the fretting within Democratic circles, after he'd been nominated for vice-president in 1956, that such dangerous news might become public.

I once delivered $25,000 in cash for Senator Kefauver. I handed the money over to a Kefauver staff man in his committee office in the old Senate Office Building. This in itself was a violation of the law: it's forbidden even to hand over a legitimate campaign contribution on federal property, to say nothing of an out-and-out bribe.

I can't say that the staffer knew what the money was for, but *I* certainly knew it was for the purpose of the Kefauver subcommittee's finding that George Preston Marshall, owner of the Washington Redskins football team, held an illegal monopoly with his so-called Redskin Television Network. This network profitably televised the Redskins games throughout the Southern states.

The money to influence the Kefauver decision had been paid by Texas interests and was delivered to me by an employee who knew his way around the back rooms of power; I in turn handed it over to Kefauver's staff man. More is implied than stated in such transactions. As I recall, I handed him the money in a briefcase the courier had given me and simply said, "I hope you'll get this to the senator with the compliments of some Texas friends." He nodded, accepted the briefcase without comment, and launched into a discussion of Democratic politics.

People who wonder why the Dallas Cowboys–Washington Redskins football rivalry seems to be among the most bitter in the National Football League may better understand after hearing this story. A group of Texans palpitated to gain a profitable National Football League franchise. They ran into trouble in the form of stiff opposition from Marshall, the Redskins' owner, who as one of the founding fathers of the NFL claimed unusual power and influence.

Marshall was by then an old man, and an old-fashioned racist who wouldn't hire a black player until Secretary of the Interior Stuart Udall forced it by a political power play in 1961. Udall simply told Marshall that his lily-white football team would not be permitted to play in the new D.C. Stadium, built with tax funds, unless blacks joined the squad.

The Redskins then signed Bobby Mitchell, the fleet running back who'd been an All-American at the University of Illinois.

Marshall long had considered the South to be his team's natural territory, and his personal preserve. He was adamant against sharing the South with a Texas-based team certain to divide regional loyalties at the expense of his pocketbook; until Dallas came into the league, the NFL had no Southern-based team. Marshall's proprietary instinct, wholly robber baron in character, may well have been rejected by an honest subcommittee. With millions at stake, however, the Texans were taking no chances.

I was approached by the operative whom I knew as a fellow reveler and high roller in Washington.

"Bobby," he said over drinks in my office, "my job and my ass are on the line. I've got to lock up that damn football franchise for Texas, and I've been told to leave no stone unturned."

I remember that it was after hours, and my office—with the employees gone—was as hushed as a corporate lawyer's on Wall Street. In the quiet I said, "Have you got any money to spend?"

"Sure," he said. "But how much?"

I said, "I don't have any idea. But you need to see Senator Kefauver. Explain your problem. If I know Estes Kefauver, he'll play the ball once you put it in his court."

Webb said, "Can you arrange the appointment?"

I said, "No sweat."

I arranged the appointment. The next thing I knew, the operative brought a briefcase in my office, handed it over, and said, "There's $25,000 cash in there. Will you get it to a fellow named such-and-so?" And I did.

Clint Murchison, Jr., applied whimsical thumbscrews to George Preston Marshall as well. In company with my law partner, Ernest Tucker—and at Clint's suggestion—I brought from composer Barnee Breeskin the rights to the Redskins' official song, "Hail to the Redskins." Barnee, fortunately for our cause, found himself in financial straits at the time we approached him and eagerly accepted our offer without knowing why we wanted the song—which Marshall, generally a shrewd businessman, had astonishingly neglected to buy. You couldn't make that sort of basic boo-boo when engaged in a pissing contest with the Murchisons. Anyhow, Ernest Tucker and I bought the song for $2,500. Our price for the Redskins' being able to continue to use the song: withdrawal of Marshall's opposition to the Dallas NFL franchise. Since Marshall's band was left only with "Dixie" as an alternate fight song, we got what we asked. The Murchisons, naturally, had provided the $2,500 to buy the song. They thus assured themselves of a franchise now probably worth $20 million if you could buy it.

The Murchisons understood how business sometimes was done in the hardball world of Washington politics. Though in 1960 the Murchisons backed Richard Nixon for president, and gave him Lord knows how much money, they had Tommy Webb, a former FBI agent, bring a bet-copping $10,000 in cash for the Kennedy-Johnson ticket. The loyal courier Webb and I flew to New York City where, outside an office building owned by the Kennedy family, we traded handshakes with Bobby Kennedy and then handed him the money in a white envelope. He whisked it to the safety of his inner coat pocket and, as with so many people to whom I made cash deliveries, seemed eager to see our departing dust. Bobby Kennedy and I were regarding each other warily in those days, having almost come to blows at the Democratic National Convention in Los Angeles a few weeks earlier, in the heat of prenomination tensions.

The Murchison brothers, John and Clint, Jr., spent several years in attempting to gain control of a giant holding company, the Allegheny Corporation. Allegheny owned the New York Central Railroad and a big banking institution, Investors Diversified Services. Charges flew back and forth between the competing interests, and the Murchisons long had trouble with the regulatory staff at the Securities and Exchange Commission; the SEC staff was very anti-Texas and anti-oil, and its rulings continually thwarted and frustrated the Murchison efforts. In one of the dark moments Clint Murchison, Jr., sought my advice on how to obtain more favorable treatment. I said to him, "Clint, if you don't hire Abe Fortas to represent you then you're out of your mind. Fortas has the most successful SEC practice in America. Go hire the man." He did, and soon his SEC staff problems disappeared. *Time* shortly ran the Murchison brothers on its cover and said they were on the verge of the largest takeover in the history of American corporate finance.

Over the years I carried a lot of water for the Murchisons, at no great profit to myself, though I did accept their hospitality to parties in Washington, Dallas, and Miami, as I recall. I also enjoyed helling around with a couple of their employees, Bob Thompson and Tommy Webb. Once I fell from grace, however, the Murchisons were as difficult to locate as hen's teeth; Washington is, after all, a place of alliances of convenience and temporary associations. When the king is dead there, he's dead for good and all: I've noticed that when a senator or congressman is defeated, his colleagues shy away from him and act as if there is a death in the family or some secret shame attached to his rejection. In forgetting they'd ever known Bobby Baker, John and Clint Murchison belonged to a long line of what I might call—borrowing from Tom Paine—"sunshine patriots and summer soldiers."

Money flew fast and loose on Capitol Hill in the 1950s and 1960s. As we learned in the later Watergate investigations, and in more recent scandals involving the buying of congressmen by the government of South Korea, it still does. There's another verse to that song: so long as men and women in politics, or in the business world, thirst for power and the good life, it always will. No matter how many Ethics Committees or Codes of Conduct or Campaign Expenditure Laws are passed, the eager and the greedy will find ways to get theirs. "Money talks and bullshit walks," my father used to say; I've never found a reason to disagree with him.

Gentlemen may find ways to do each other favors. Take the example of Senator Olin Johnston of South Carolina, and *Reader's Digest*. Senator Johnston, as chairman of the Senate Post Office and Civil Service Committee, had tremendous power over the postage rates to be paid by newspapers, magazines, and other periodicals; *Reader's Digest* was, and is, among the big users of the mail in distributing its product. Obviously, accommodations were in order.

About every six years—when he came up for reelection—the senator's by-line appeared in their magazine over stories tending to do great credit to his public record. One of my old Capitol Hill roomies, Jimmy Leaver, wrote most of the stories attributed to Senator Johnston. Leaver, as a speechwriter on the South Carolina senator's staff, was in turn paid by tax funds. Everyone's itch got scratched. It was very cozy, and it was far from atypical.

I do not mean to indicate that you couldn't get things done in Washington without money changing hands, nor that good motives failed to attend the legislative processes. I did favors for people for many reasons, and I'm sure that held true for the senators themselves. I was a "doer," and, if you want to call it that, a "fixer." Sometimes I was a bag man. Indeed, when I was elected secretary-treasurer of the Democratic Senatorial Campaign Committee, I suppose you could say I was the official bag man for my party. It was my job to solicit, collect, and distribute funds among deserving senatorial Democrats; I can guarantee you that very few disinterested parties go around giving money away to politicians. The assumption of the *quid pro quo*—something for something—is there, and make no mistake about it.

Looking back, I think I made a major mistake in accepting the job as the money comptroller for the Senate Democratic election apparatus. It was dumb from the standpoint of personal politics, because when you're participating in decisions on how much money to give a senator for his political race, you'll never entirely satisfy him. If you occasionally please one, you'll automatically alienate three others.

Fifteen thousand dollars going into a New York senator's campaign would be a mere drop in the bucket, while in sparsely populated states such as Montana or Wyoming it might be the deciding factor. Senators looking to their own problems, however, do not make allowances for the realities. The New York senator will be angered that the cowboy-state senators got as much money as he did, when his cost is greater. Give the New Yorker an additional $10,000 to assist his expensive campaign, however, and the cowboy-state senators will scream of favoritism and howl that good money is being poured down the bottomless maw— money they might use more effectively. Back will come the New Yorker to charge that X percent of the senatorial campaign kitty came from his state's sources, while the cowboy states contributed only small change. There's no end to the bickering and whining and jealousies. I think that when my big troubles came along, some senators whom I'd angered or disappointed in the money department were not unhappy at that turn of events.

Those personal considerations aside, no public employee paid from tax funds—as I was—should be placed in the position of being expected to raise money from special-interest sources. A conflict of interest exists, no matter how well intended the objective; it is built in. As an example: say the Senate passed a bill beneficial to the housing industry—as we did, when I was instrumental in convincing Senator George Smathers of Florida to sponsor a bill requiring only a three-percent down payment on FHA homes up to about $15,000; you could build a pretty good little bungalow for that price in those days, though now it wouldn't build a chicken coop. I urged that bill because I thought that if Congress made it possible for more Americans to own a home, then it would help make a better country. Nobody paid me to do it; I had no ulterior motives. I could not then know, of course, that greedy builders and developers would perform shoddy work and would overbuild in many towns to their own personal profit—not caring that the government would be forced to reclaim the houses and lose money on them as they sat idle, unwanted, and deteriorating. That point aside, however, and even had the program worked perfectly, I was put in the position of saying to home builders and contractors, "Well, we passed this bill to help your industry and now it's election time and elections cost money." Perhaps we should play a little light hijacking music here . . .

I mindlessly imitated the common practice of many senators, and the prevailing institutional mores, in accepting the more subtle forms of bribery. I realize that now; had I stopped to examine the original values instilled in me, I would have realized it then. Like many a country boy exposed to the bright lights and the good life, however, I enjoyed it and wanted more. More wine. More women. More song. More money. More power.

My social friends, from the time I reached my mid-twenties, were almost all powerful men, whether senators or businessmen. They had far more money than I, enjoyed more perks, lived better. Not only did I want to share the good life with them, it was a point of pride to carry my financial weight in their company. I did not want to accept their charity by having them pick up my checks or consider me to any degree a moocher or a deadbeat. In short, I faced the old problem of keeping up with the Joneses—and these Joneses could not be kept up with on a government salary ranging at various times between $10,000 and $19,000 annually.

Consequently, I established a law partnership in conjunction with a friend who also had been a Senate employee, Ernest Tucker. We had been classmates at American University Law School. I did not actually practice law before government agencies, but I was useful to the firm in other ways. Before long, people who wanted things done in Washington among the federal agencies, as well as on Capitol Hill, learned that it might profit them to get in touch with me directly or with the firm of Baker and Tucker. Naturally, there was profit in it for the partners of the firm, too.

I received fees from my partner for "referrals"; in turn, I helped to open the political and bureaucratic doors. This was (and to some extent still is) a practice common among senators and congressmen who hold law degrees, and there are more lawyers in Congress than anything else. The Baker-Tucker firm once received a handsome referral fee from a firm in which Congressman Manny Celler of Brooklyn was a partner. Celler was chairman of the House Judiciary Committee. We referred a client who had problems with the Immigration Service. The Judiciary Committee—Congressman Celler's committee—had primary legislative jurisdiction over Immigration Service functions and operations. It was in the best interests of that Service to keep Congressman Celler happy. *Q.E.D.*

I also entered into business deals with senators, lobbyists, a JFK cabinet member, and other public officials or former politicians. I have no doubt that these opportunities would not have come had I been anyone but who I was. I have no doubt that the hundreds of thousands of dollars I borrowed from banks, and the generous lines of credit they extended to me, often through the intervention of Senator Kerr—who was, after all, chairman of the Senate Finance Committee and thus was influential in tax matters—might not have been so readily available had I not been Bobby Baker and well connected at the top. No question about it! Remember that Washington is, above all, a back-scratching town—and that the business community knows it as well as it knows the tax laws. Take a Humpty Dumpty fall, however, and suddenly the money stops and the credit lines dry up. As the old advertising slogan used to say, "Ask the man who owns one."

I have always been fond of money and of making it. I like, too, the wheeler-dealer aspects of business: putting people and deals together, creating something, watching an idea spring from the drawing board to become reality and, hopefully, a paying reality. Without thinking much about it, I suppose my attitude was kin to that of Huey Long when he said, "I took no vow of poverty when I came to public office."

My inclination to stay busy, to hustle, and to accumulate did not abandon me when I moved from Pickens to Washington. In those early days, during World War II, after voting its war appropriations and regulations Congress put aside its social programs. (President Roosevelt said, "Dr. New Deal has become Dr. Win-The-War.") With wartime prosperity having put the Great Depression to flight, the nation's tax dollars were spent on guns rather than butter. Thus, Congress attended its wartime appropriations and little else; its sessions were not as lengthy as they had been during New Deal pump-priming days, or as they would become in the postwar years. As a consequence, I had much spare time and decided to again take up the drugstore trade; I worked as a counter man at a drugstore lunchroom near the Supreme Court building and drove a taxi-cab part time.

Driving a taxicab part time, however, did not appear to be a quick way to riches. For some years I scuffled along, a young husband whose bride—Dorothy Comstock, whom I'd married in 1949—worked directly for Rosemary Wood on the staff of Senator Dick Nixon of California. We shortly began to produce babies, of which ultimately there would be five, and even at the height of our combined Capitol Hill earning power we totaled only a bit over $30,000 per year. It was much less for a long time, believe me.

By 1948 I had been chief telephone page for three years and was a Senate insider. My basic function was to know precisely every bill or amendment being considered by the Senate, what the parliamentary status of each bill was, when a vote might be anticipated on each of them, when the Senate was likely to recess or adjourn, and dozens of other details. In short, I was the head technician in the legislative business of the Senate and something of a traffic cop in regulating its daily flow.

It became commonplace for senators to call me for accommodations of one sort or another: "Bobby, I'm having a rubdown in the gym. Can you hold the vote for a half hour?" Or, "Bobby, I've got the worst hangover since Jesus turned the water into wine. You've got to postpone the calling up of amendments to S.R. 1234."

I then would go to another senator, explain the situation, and ask him to request a time-consuming quorum call so that Senator Jones might enjoy his rubdown or so that Senator Smith might have time to wash his face after he'd regurgitated. Everything you've heard about the Senate's being a clubby place is borne out by the rapidity with which such requests were honored. Senators cooperated with me, too, in my attempts to arrange "pairs" for the convenience of their colleagues.

The "pairing" of Senate votes is a device by which absentee senators may get on record their sentiments toward a given bill. Suppose Senator X is to make a speech in his home state to the powerful Goat Ropers Association, or simply wants to go to Las Vegas to get drunk, but fears to be shown absent when an important issue is voted on. He would ask me to find another senator, of the opposite persuasion on that particular bill, and dissuade him from voting on the bill but, instead, "pair" his vote with that of Senator X. The record then would show how each of the senators would have registered themselves had they been present and voting. When accused of nonaction on the bill by some future opponent, they could bluster of how they'd "been recorded" on the bill—either for or against—no matter that they'd had absolutely no influence on it. It would take the poor opponent six days to explain the parliamentary deceptions involved, by which time he'd be speaking to empty chairs or dark television sets. Such tricks are important in the political game, and politicians do not forget those able to arrange them.

Just as alert employees judged senators, so did alert senators evaluate their employees. Once one proved reliable, one almost became a part of the family. Invariably, as one became trusted by senators and then friendly with them, there would be opportunities to get in on the ground floor: to make investments or buy stock in cases where maybe somebody knew a little something nobody else knew. Like what specific ruling might soon be expected from a regulatory agency. Or what parcel of land just where might be going up in value because of a new highway or housing development or military base. Sometimes the young employee offered such opportunities didn't know whether his sponsor knew anything or not, or what he might know if he did, but you didn't ask questions in the absence of volunteered details.

My original investments did not immediately excite Dun & Bradstreet, though I made money at a more rapid clip than I'd been accustomed to. As the years passed I had become increasingly friendly with Senator Bob Kerr of Oklahoma, the wealthy co-owner of Kerr-McGee Oil Company, as well as blooded cattle, ranches, real estate developments, banks, blue-chip stocks, and you name it; there's no doubt he was the richest man in the Senate when he died on January 1, 1963. Money was Senator Kerr's god; given our budding friendship, and his preoccupation with money, it only seems natural that he would have given me my first investment opportunity.

In 1949, Senator Kerr offered me the opportunity to buy one hundred shares in Kerr-McGee Oil Company. "It's a growing company, Bobby," he told me. "Nothing's a sure shot unless you've got a gun, but this is the next thing to it." That was good enough for me. Though I was going to George Washington University at night, and then to law school classes; though my salary was only about $6,500, and my net worth, including furniture, could not have been more than $5,000; I rushed home to Pickens to borrow the necessary $3,800 from an attorney named Julien Wyatt. He let me have it on my signature. Before long, I'd made about a $10,000 profit on Senator Kerr's advice.

Then I gambled and lost. On $3,000 borrowed from a Pickens bank—with my oil stock backing the loan—I set out to become the real estate czar of my own home territory. I first bought a credit bureau in Easley, where my sister, Betty Baker Chapman, was employed. I next made a $10,000 investment in the Blue Ridge Development Company of Pickens, $8,000 of which was borrowed from banks and individuals; our idea was to develop a middle-class housing project. The project failed, however, because Pickens just wasn't a going concern. I had become blinded by my desire to make my mark back home, I guess, and I paid dearly for the mistake. The loss in the ill-fated Pickens project almost exactly negated my profits in the Kerr-McGee venture. Perhaps it began to dawn on me that tips from well-connected senators, who knew what they were doing, might be worth more than my own sentimental fly-by-night schemes.

George Smathers, the urbane and handsome junior senator from Florida, offered my next investment opportunity. Smathers, his assistant Scotty Peek, and I shared a high appreciation for the good life. We all had a little high roller in us; we'd reveled together a bit by the time Senator Smathers offered me stock in the Winn-Dixie company in the amount of $2,100. I bought in and made a small profit. A bit later, Smathers permitted me to buy into a land deal near Orlando—a housing development in Florida has to be better than one in Pickens, right?—and I eventually made about $7,000 as my end of the profits. As Secretary to the Majority, I inquired as to the status of the postal rate bill from

"There's no doubt Oklahoma Senator Bob Kerr was the richest man in the Senate. Money was his god." (*United Press International*)

"George Smathers, the urbane and handsome junior senator from Florida, offered me investment opportunities." (*Wide World Photos*)

the staff of Senator Olin Johnston's Post Office and Civil Service Committee. I learned that low mass mail postal rates would continue, and I therefore bought stock in the Spiegel Mail Order House at ten cents on the dollar and made more than $10,000. Other and bigger investments would come later, and these would cause me grief in time, but at the moment I was satisfied with my connections and felt that at last I might be on my way.

Chapter Six

Climbing the Ladder with LBJ

*"Hubert can't win, but I don't want him gumming up
the works for me."*

T HE coattail effect of the Eisenhower-Nixon landslide in the
1952 election brought a Republican rarity—control of the
Congress—for only the second time in twenty years. It also wiped out the
Senate Democratic leader, Ernest McFarland of Arizona, who lost to a
young rightist firebrand named Barry Goldwater. Senator McFarland
was an affable soul, but, frankly, I did not see his loss as any great disaster for the Democratic party. I had learned he did not have the touch or
feel for leadership, or any great appetite for it. I knew someone who did,
however.

Lyndon Johnson had impressed me in his first four years in the
Senate, despite spending much of his time fence-mending in Texas and
concerning himself with problems attuned to that state more than to national themes. I had found him a quick study, a man who could instinc-
tively grasp the essence of a complex bill, one who might drawl in a
twang and scratch himself but who had a keen mind. I was impressed,
too, by his astonishing energy and by the way he had managed to become an effective insider in the Senate. Though his support for Adlai
Stevenson in 1952 had been tepid and perfunctory—largely because Ike
was so venerated in Texas—Johnson had a good to moderately good
Democratic record. These were the conservative postwar and Cold War
years, remember, and LBJ's record was more in the mainstream than
not. I thought I saw unique qualities of leadership in him. I believed that
once he'd won reelection by a safe margin (as he would do in 1954, getting seventy-two percent of the vote) and felt his home base to be more
secure, he would blossom. On several occasions I'd suggested to Lyndon
Johnson that he might be a future Democratic leader; I don't recall his
ever throwing up his hands in horror or walking away.

Johnson had been in the Senate only two years when he climbed on
the first rung of the leadership ladder. A vacancy for Democratic whip

occurred when Senator Lister Hill of Alabama resigned the job. Hill did so because his state was up in arms against Harry Truman's FEPC legislation, the alleged "No Win" policy in Korea, and a general dissatisfaction with Democrats. "I'm far too liberal for Alabama tastes," Senator Hill told me, "and I've got to do everything I can to move away from the national Democratic party. If I'm to be reelected, I have no choice but to quit as whip." Quietly, before Senator Hill's intentions became general knowledge or reached the newspapers, I began to line up support for Lyndon B. Johnson. Senator McFarland, the Democratic leader—and at least nominally my boss—was opposed to LBJ on the grounds that an Arizona-Texas combination made for a bad geographic balance in the leadership and he was put off by the Texan's lust for power. The fact is, however, that those of us promoting Lyndon Johnson had pretty much locked it up for him before Senator McFarland knew what was going on. He dropped his opposition when faced with the inevitable. A year later, McFarland would lose in the Republican landslide made possible by Ike's popularity.

On the morning after Senator McFarland's defeat, I was called out of law class at American University to take a call from Senator Johnson, who was on his Texas ranch. "How do things look for me?" he asked. "It looks like you're the new leader," I said. He said, "I don't know. The Democratic party's in disarray. The Senate 'red hots' probably wouldn't go for me. Even if I get elected, it might be like getting caught in a nutcracker." I received the impression that Lyndon Johnson was eager to be persuaded otherwise, and I was happy to accommodate him. "The math's in your favor," I told him. "All you've got to do is convince one man and you're home free."

"You're talkin' about Dick Russell," he said.

"Sure. We're gonna have forty-seven Democrats in the Senate. And Senator Russell will pretty much control half or more."

"If he's got that many peckers in his pocket," Lyndon Johnson said, "then why does he need to look around for somebody else to support?"

"Dick Russell doesn't want the job, in my judgment."

"Why in hell not?" he asked.

"I simply don't think he wants the grief or aggravation of national leadership. I think he found out at the national convention that the libs won't accept him." (Senator Russell, in 1952, had waged an abortive campaign for the presidential nomination and had fallen far short.)

"He may be smarter than both of us," LBJ said.

"No, your situation's different. You can draw support from a broader spectrum than Senator Russell can, and I think he knows it. Who else is he gonna support? Hubert Humphrey?"

"I'll have to think about it," Johnson said. I had the feeling he'd been thinking about it full time, and would think of little else.

I went to my original sponsor, Senator Maybank of South Carolina, and asked him flatly to endorse LBJ. "I'm a Dick Russel man first, last, and always," he said. "If he wants it." I said there was no way in hell Senator Russell would seek the job: "It will be a headache trying to hold these divided Democrats together, and I really don't believe Dick Russell is interested in being caught in the middle. He's got it made in Georgia and among his Southern colleagues. He'll be a big factor no matter who's the official leader, and he knows it. I can't see him volunteering for trouble when he's already got a bird's nest on the ground."

Senator Maybank agreed. Shortly afterward, I presented for his approval a draft of a telegram; it was sent to Lyndon Johnson and it pledged to support him should Senator Russell decline to become a candidate. I saw to it that word of this endorsement got around among other Southern senators and friendly newsmen. Lyndon Johnson himself was delighted; over the years, especially when he'd been mellowed by a few drinks, he several times mentioned that I had come through with his first official endorsement for the leadership job.

Sure enough, Senator Russell told LBJ he had no interest in being minority leader and was quick to pledge his support to the Texan. This was a cause for alarm among the Americans for Democratic Action crowd—what LBJ called "the red hots"—and soon liberals attempted to unite behind Hubert Humphrey. "Hubert can't win," LBJ said, "but I don't want him gumming up the works for me. If he fights to the bitter end, then I won't have a cut-dog's chance to be an effective leader. We can't have everybody squabbling. The Republicans would eat our lunch and the sack it came in."

Johnson set about courting Humphrey. Despite their ideological differences—and, remember, HHH then was perceived as being miles to the left of LBJ—the two senators had maintained a warm relationship. "Hubert," Lyndon Johnson told him, "let's not permit our followers and our disciples to destroy our friendship. When this thing's over we're gonna have to work together for the good of the party and the country. We must not permit the misguided zealots on either side to come between us or cut each other up." He received Senator Humphrey's assurance that no crippling animosities would be permitted.

I, too, talked to Senator Humphrey. I'd always found him eminently approachable, and did in this case. As delicately as possible, for I knew that most senators were as sensitive as small children when faced with rejection, I told him that in my opinion Lyndon Johnson had the votes to win. Then I offered him the promise of candy: "I know that Senator

Johnson will be looking to you as the spokesman for Senate liberals, and for the national constituency you're building. I wouldn't be surprised if he brought you into the leadership circle." Humphrey decided not to contest LBJ, after Johnson had told him he would be his "ambassador" to the liberal camp and promised to place him on the leadership ladder in the near future. Years later, in 1961, when Johnson became vice-president, Humphrey became whip, or assistant majority leader, under Mike Mansfield.

In 1953, once it became clear that LBJ had enough pledges to become leader, I attempted to win the whip's job for my friend George Smathers of Florida. LBJ was amazingly receptive; I had expected to encounter opposition. I now think—with the benefit of hindsight—that LBJ knew Senator Smathers wouldn't be willing to do the daily ditch-digging work that might make a rival of him in future years when the Democrats would again be the majority party in the Senate. Smathers in the mid-1950s had a more liberal image than he would retain. He was young, handsome, and was thought to represent the "New South." He also was well connected among young Eastern liberals; Jack Kennedy was his close friend. I was elated when it appeared that LBJ would agree to Smathers.

My elation was short-lived. I was working in my office one day when LBJ telephoned me from Page Airways Terminal in Washington. "Scratch Smathers," he said. "Sam Rayburn says he won't do."

I was stunned; I'd already been peddling pro-Smathers sentiment among Senate Democrats and had told several that he was LBJ's personal choice for whip. "What's happened?" I sputtered. "What in the hell—?"

"I'm gonna miss the goddamn airplane," LBJ growled. "Sam Rayburn made me get off and call you and tell you to scratch Smathers. Do it. I'll talk to you when I get back."

As Johnson later told the story, old Sam Rayburn had gone up in flames when Johnson told him he was considering Smathers to be his whip. "Once a son-of-a-bitch always a son-of-a-bitch," Rayburn had snapped. "When Claude Pepper was in the Senate, he made George Smathers an assistant U.S. attorney in Florida. The next thing you know, Smathers turned around and ran against him and defeated him. He's an ingrate and he's not to be trusted. He'll cut your throat as quick as he cut Claude Pepper's." This was an early-dewline warning to LBJ's sensitive political radar, and I'm not so sure Speaker Rayburn had to shove him out the door to call me. Johnson instead selected an old friend, Senator Earl Clements of Kentucky, who would be unlikely to cut his throat. Smathers received a consolation prize: he was chosen as secretary to the Democratic Conference Committee.

Once he had the Democratic leadership cinched, Lyndon Johnson began to tinker with the Senate staff machinery. For reasons I never understood, he seemed to have an antipathy for the then secretary to the Senate minority, Les Biffle; perhaps it was simply that Biffle was not his man and had been in the Senate years ahead of Johnson. At any rate, LBJ moved to place Felton (Skeeter) Johnston in that post, and he selected me to be assistant secretary to the Senate minority. LBJ had always been aware of what went on around him, and he was frank with me: "Skeeter likes whiskey too much. I'll be counting on you more than on him." Though I was careful to observe the formalities, and to show good manners toward Skeeter Johnston, the fact is that we bypassed him in many matters.

Lyndon Johnson's first statement upon becoming leader (he refused to use the official title "Minority Leader," and saw to it that his stationery referred to himself as Senate Democratic Leader) was one of conciliation. "We will not oppose President Eisenhower and his party merely for the sake of opposing," he said, "but will work together when we can, for the good of the country. It shall be out goal to make divided government work." Immediately, of course, the kamikaze liberals began to grumble. Johnson privately snarled of damned fools who'd rather piss into the wind than with it. For the record, he resorted to such homelies as "Any jackass can kick down a barn, but it takes a carpenter to build one," or "If you can't get the whole loaf, a slice is better than crumbs."

I like to think that I had something to do with what became known as the "Johnson Rule." For years, I'd watched the senior senators grab all choice committee assignments and leave junior members with the dregs. I thought this unwise for a couple of reasons: (1) it discouraged some good men from doing their best work in places where they might most naturally contribute, and (2) it was short-sighted in that Democrats with good committee assignments, and the resulting attention they might receive, would be easier to reelect.

I proposed that LBJ spread the honey around. "Not only is it right and would be good for the party," I argued, "but you'll make new allies among the freshmen and the junior senators. They'll be in your debt." LBJ liked the idea, but was fearful the crusty old seniors of the Senate might revolt against him; he knew that to tamper with tradition, especially the hallowed seniority system, might invite wrath. "It's a way to divide the liberals in their loyalties," I said. "In the end, the senior senators and committee chairmen will work with you because they have to and because it will be instinctive with them. On the other hand, it's the younger liberals who are more disposed to give you trouble. You can disarm them by improving their stations." Johnson was persuasive with Senators Russell and Humphrey, and he got the divided Democratic camps to agree to the Johnson Rule. It provided that senior senators might select one major committee assignment rather than two, as had been the case, thus opening up major slots to the junior members.

While the Johnson Rule had been adopted under the guise of offering more opportunities to more Senate Democrats, and did have that effect, Lyndon Johnson made certain that he controlled what opportunity each senator was offered. Those loyal to him received the better posts or, at least, what LBJ perceived as the better posts for his own purposes.

The new leader pleased both organized labor and oil by certain shufflings he arranged. John F. Kennedy and Herbert Lehman of New York went to the Labor Committee; Lehman was replaced on the Interior and Insular Affairs Committee by Price Daniel of Texas. That committee had jurisdiction over the tidelands bill, and Daniel's well-advertised position that the oil-rich offshore tidelands should be deeded to the states— rather than to the federal government—was the opposite of Senator Lehman's stance. Oilmen were dizzy with gratitude over the swap. They also were delighted when Russell Long of the oil state of Louisiana, and himself a holder of oil properties, was placed on the Finance Committee. They knew he would be friendly to their tax legislation.

Senator James Murray of Montana was in Johnson's pocket, an echo who would do LBJ's slightest bidding. I usually passed the word to his son and administrative assistant, Charlie Murray, as to what the leader desired; it soon was done. Senator Murray thus was placed on the Senate Democratic Policy Committee, where his rubber stamp vote could be employed to solidify Lyndon Johnson's control in party matters.

Senator Warren Magnuson of Washington, an LBJ drinking buddy and a staunch team player, was placed on the powerful Appropriations Committee. This helped LBJ gain more control over the pursestrings. Dissidents might not so easily attack Johnson if they knew a word from him might determine whether their pet projects would be funded.

The leader shared his thinking as to Judiciary Committee assignments going to Olin D. Johnston of South Carolina and Tom Hennings of Missouri. "Olin won't yell 'nigger' any more than he has to. He'll vote against us, of course, but Tom Hennings will offset his vote when he's sober enough to function." These assignments also made it possible to tell Senator Albert Gore of Tennessee that no vacancy existed for him on Judiciary. LBJ feared that Gore, a liberal who saw himself as presidential timber, if not a first cousin to God, would play to the grandstand if given a glamorous assignment. He therefore placed him on the Public Works Committee, there being little charisma in the matters of roads, dams, and public buildings.

Freshmen Hubert Humphrey and Mike Mansfield were flattered to be assigned to Foreign Relations, where few first-termers landed. This gave Humphrey a forum from which to bolster his national ambitions. Mansfield was not a compulsive seeker of power, nor was he wildly ambitious. LBJ took this into consideration in awarding him the plum.

George Smathers of Florida was persuaded to take Interstate and Foreign Commerce. This committee had jurisdiction, among other things, over radio and television legislation. LBJ was building a broadcasting empire, which eventually would make him the richest president in history; Smathers was perfectly positioned to assist him.

Freshman Senator Stuart Symington of Missouri, who'd been President Truman's secretary of the air force, was assigned to Armed Services. Later, LBJ would complain that Stu Symington had been his biggest disappointment among the new men. "He's not a team player. All he's done is run for president and try to appease Marquis Childs and the St. Louis *Post-Dispatch*." This was another way of saying that Symington was an independent loner who refused to let LBJ get a grip on him. Johnson felt that Symington was an ingrate, because one of his own intimates—John Connally—had raised so much campaign money for Symington that Connally had found it expeditious to leave the country during publicity about it. LBJ's personal code was violated when someone accepted favors and then refused to stay hitched.

The Symington disappointment aside, however, I thought Lyndon Johnson had played Senate Democrats like a violin; I had been fascinated by his explanations of why he'd acted as he had in each case. "We've got a real leader," I enthused to my friends and staff members. "He knows what makes the mule plow."

Liberals soon were angered, however, by LBJ's "unanimous consent rule" as applied to the Democratic Policy Committee. "It makes sense," he said in arguing that Democratic bills should not be called up for voting unless one hundred percent—or at least ninety percent—of the Policy members had endorsed them. "If we can get our team solidly behind a bill and pick up scattered Republicans, we'll win. Otherwise, we'll lose. We're a *minority* party, remember."

The argument did not much impress liberals. They saw the Democratic Policy Committee as Johnson's private rubber stamp—which it was—and they accused LBJ of using the unanimous consent doctrine as a ploy to place on the back burner those bills he did not want called up. They were not entirely wrong. "I don't see any profit," LBJ told me, "in calling up bills so that Jim Eastland and Herbert Lehman can insult each other, or so that Paul Douglas or Albert Gore can exercise their lungs. Why should we cut each other up and then lose after the bloodshedding?" Johnson's cautious pragmatism, as opposed to making a partisan record by forcing Republicans to go on record against bills which might be considered popular by the public at large, would always remain a bone in the throat of liberals. They wanted confrontations and campaign issues; he wanted victories and accomplishments to stress.

Senator Paul Douglas of Illinois was one of Johnson's more vocal critics. One afternoon LBJ beckoned me to his Senate desk with a grin. "I think I've gound a way to defuse Paul Douglas. He was an economist, you know. I think he taught economics in college. Well, I'm gonna name him chairman of the Joint Committee on Economic Reports. It can't do a damn thing. Hell, a joint committee's usually as useless as tits on a bull. But it'll give Professor Douglas some papers to shuffle and a headline or two and maybe it'll keep him off my neck."

Lyndon Johnson loved to manipulate people, to control events, to feel he'd put something over on somebody. He loved the processes—the flanker movements, pincer movements, the deployment of troops—almost as much as he savored the victories. Sometimes, high on liquor or simply on himself, he tended to brag. Occasionally a sensitive colleague would be outraged when word leaked back that LBJ had too publicly boasted of having bested him.

Though Senator Johnson publicly spoke of responsible cooperation with the Republican administration—and, indeed, often pulled the presidential chestnuts out of the congressional fire—he privately appeared astonished at how little Ike knew of the particulars of some legislation, or of the political realities on Capitol Hill. "You have to explain a lot to him," he griped. Sometimes he made denigrating remarks about Ike's naive approach, and imitated him. Johnson was a good mime in private, a talent the masses never suspected in him, and he would adopt a bland look while speaking in the flat, choppy manner of the president: "Now, fellows, I don't know all the details on this bill, but I'm *sincere* in believing it would be good for the country." I think in retrospect that Ike, one of the better political generals the army has produced, may have sometimes out country-boyed Lyndon Johnson when Johnson didn't know it. Ike, too, was a fine actor and not a bad manipulator of men.

Lyndon Johnson and I operated on a simple mathematical formula to get legislation passed. Given the makeup of the Senate as then constituted, we knew that on almost any given issue that body would produce about forty votes that might loosely be considered as "conservative" and about the same number that might be construed as "liberal." Though a few senators in each camp sometimes crossed the ideological line on a given issue, they tended to cancel each other out. It was amazing how often those eighty senators split exactly even; thus we always were looking for the eleven votes that would give us no worse than a 51–49 advantage.

"It's not like a football game," Lyndon Johnson once told me. "I don't care about winning sixty to nothing on most bills. Get us our bare majority, except when I tell you to the contrary, and then let senators who need to vote against us go ahead and do that if it causes no harm. That way, we'll have a little something in the bank for future uses. If we'll be understanding when senators are in a bind and have to go against us for the record, then we can press 'em a little harder on another issue when the going is really tough."

It was often said of LBJ, and of myself, that we employed unusual powers of persuasion to attain our thin majorities. I'd like to think that sometimes we were eloquent or clever or both, but most of the time we employed no magic—just plain common sense. I would go to a senator and say, "Would it embarrass you to try and help the leadership on this one?" If the senator gave me reasons why that would be impossible, I'd say, "Well, could you possibly find it handy not to vote at all?" For every vote that I could take away from the other side, I had to come up with one less vote for the leadership: a 47–46 vote is just as final and binding as one of 50–49.

Much of the work of putting together a simple majority consisted of logistics. A senator who's for your cause down to his toenails is of no help if you can't produce him when the vote is taken. My first goal always was to produce one hundred percent of those senators who'd promised to help us; if I did that, no way in hell we'd lose—because LBJ was not one to call for a vote until he knew he had the horses. It was not always as simple as it sounds to keep senators in the corral, however; they had a way of suddenly straying as they fanned out over the country to make speeches, attend ceremonies, politic, and so on. One had to be particularly careful that a Hubert Humphrey, Wayne Morse, Paul Douglas, Jack Kennedy, or other big names did not disappear into Oshkosh, on the eve of a big vote, to further their national ambitions or to pad their pocketbooks by accepting generous fees for speaking engagements. When they did so disappear, it was up to me to locate them and get them back. When we had a Democratic president in the White House, I had Air Force One available to fetch them on short notice. Even when Republicans ruled the White House we could command police cars and wailing sirens to round up the strays. I remember once that Senator Fulbright was flown back from Arkansas for a key vote and then was rushed from Friendship Airport at near supersonic speeds by Baltimore City police. I was waiting on the senate steps when he arrived, pale and shaken: "To hell with it," he snapped. "I'd rather you lose a vote than lose my life. That damn fool drove me back at ninety-five miles an hour and ran every red light we came to." A few moments later, however, the senator was beaming and smiling as his Democratic colleagues stood to applaud his entrance into the Senate chamber; they knew his presence would insure another cliff-hanging victory. Of course, some senators enjoyed being rushed back to cast a deciding vote. It gave them a sense of importance and often reaped the headlines on which they nurtured themselves.

Some senators who had an antipathy toward LBJ might tell me, "I won't go along to help the leader, but if you say the word I'll go along to help you." These included Paul Douglas, Gaylord Nelson, Quentin Burdick, and an occasional caveman Southerner such as Strom Thurmond. Conversely, I learned never to approach certain senators who seemed to resent my asking them how they expected to vote; Margaret Chase Smith of Maine was one of these. She truly liked Lyndon Johnson, however, from their days together on the Armed Services Committee, and often would give him a private indication of how she planned to vote. LBJ would then tell me, so I'd know how to list her in our head count. Johnson had a special way with Mrs. Smith; she responded well to his flatteries, and sometimes he fed her so much Southern candy I almost feared she'd choke on it.

Occasionally I'd get caught in the middle. This happened most frequently when LBJ and Senator Bob Kerr found themselves on opposite sides of an issue—as happened on much health legislation, some tax legislation, and, particularly, with respect to repealing Section 14b of the Taft-Hartley Act: the "right to work" proviso. When LBJ and Bob Kerr found themselves at loggerheads, they'd wave their arms and argue until it became apparent that neither would give an inch. Soon they would individually slip around to enlist my support in their campaign to convince the other. Naturally, neither would take no for an answer and I had to employ a great deal of fancy dancing to waltz out of the danger zone; often, I felt, their sense of competition—their instinct to top or outhorsetrade the other—was more the motivating factor than any deep ideological conviction. As surely as I approached one of them in the service of the other—or begged that I didn't want to—I was certain to be accused of "ganging up" on one or the other of them.

One night the three of us were in the majority leader's office when the two senators began to argue about an upcoming issue. I've forgotten what it was, but they waxed hot and heavy at each other; though both fired their best oratorical guns, the battle wound up in a dead heat. Soon they turned to me and began to argue their respective cases, each of them imploring me to bring the other to his senses.

I said, "Senators, I'm gonna tell you a little story that Herman Talmadge tells on himself. Senator Talmadge says that shortly after he was elected he was called upon by three members of the Georgia legislature.

Naturally, he wanted to impress them so they'd go back to his state and talk him up. Well, they all filed in and sat down and the first legislator said, 'Senator Talmadge, the worst problem this country faces is the niggers.' And Senator Talmadge took the cue and declaimed against this threat at great length. Then the next legislator said, 'No, senator, the biggest problem is communism.' So Herman Talmadge laid into the Communists for ten minutes, saying he'd fight them without sleep or food if need be. Then the third legislator said, 'Senator, I'm amazed that you'd think that race or communism is the biggest problem America faces. Our main problem is one of a healthy economy, of getting people to work and keeping them there.' So at this point Senator Talmadge rared back in his chair, looked up over his eyeglasses, and said, 'Gentlemen, if you wish for me to agree with every one of you then you've got to learn to come in here one at a time.' "

While Johnson and Kerr laughed I said, "So please, gentlemen—come see me one at a time." I then made a rapid exit before they could collect their thoughts and start lobbying me again.

I was always on the lookout to gain information that might one day secure a key vote. Certain Senate junkets were highly prized and the competition to be named to them was brisk and fierce. If I happened to hear a certain senator's wife say that she loved South America or had a special thing for Africa, I filed the information away and at the proper time worked to get her husband named to official trips going that way—and made certain, of course, that not only the senator but also his lady knew who'd taken care of the matter; since senators' wives were permitted on most such junkets, I often made valuable new allies. If for sentimental or historical reasons a senator had an urge to be assigned to a certain desk—as new Senator Ted Kennedy wanted to occupy his brother Jack's old spot—I did everything possible to help. One did not merely go looking for votes when they were needed on a given bill, but constantly did the mule work—some of it dull and bothersome—that might store up residues of goodwill for the future.

Sometimes I found myself having to do a bit of freelancing to help the Democratic program, as when Lyndon Johnson couldn't get out front on statehood for Alaska and Hawaii because of opposition to the statehood bill in Texas. Many Southern senators, indeed, opposed statehood for Alaska and Hawaii because of their concern over having four new senators who might favor civil rights legislation, and cloture—(limiting debate on any issue).

I went to Hawaii's nonvoting delegate to Congress, Jack Burns, and told him, "Jack, if you'll go see Senator Russell of Georgia and pledge that if you're elected U.S. senator you will never vote for cloture, and if you will agree to having the Hawaiian statehood bill split off from the Alaskan statehood bill, I'll give you my word that Hawaii will get statehood within one year from the time Alaska is admitted. The Southerners just aren't gonna swallow four new senators at once. It scares them. Make it right with Dick Russell and you're home free." Burns did so, and the strategy worked. Though Burns never became a U.S. senator, he passed word of my assistance to the four senators from the new states and I drew on that deposit of goodwill for years.

I grew closer each day to Lyndon Johnson. Soon I was one of the guests he often took to his Northwest home, on 30th Place and across the street from J. Edgar Hoover's house, to share dinner on short notice. Poor Mrs. Johnson! Nightly she telephoned the office, at about 6:30 P.M., to urge her husband to come home for dinner and to rest. Likely he'd promise to be home in an hour. An hour later she'd call and he'd ask for thirty minutes more. By ten o'clock, perhaps, he'd telephone to say "We're on the way. And I'm bringing a few folks with me." He might bring two or he might bring five.

Mrs. Johnson bore these invasions of guests, who'd already sampled the grape during late sessions in her husband's office, with patient grace; her cook, Zephyr Wright, often grumbled of late meals and of not being given an earlier and reliable head count. Perhaps after arriving home, full of talk and liquor, LBJ would want another scotch and soda or two before going to the table. Once seated, however, he ate like a starving dog. I've seen him wolf down God-awful platters of the heavy Southern cooking he preferred; it's little wonder that he suffered massive heart attacks, the way he drove himself and given his habits of food, drink, and cigarettes.

It was after such a late, heavy meal one night in 1954 that Lyndon Johnson talked to me of the Supreme Court's decision to integrate the nation's public schools. *Brown v. Board of Education of Topeka* had been decided in the plaintiff's favor a few months earlier; already the diehards among Southern politicians were shaping their massive resistance policy.

"It's the most significant Supreme Court decision in a hundred years," LBJ said, "but it's likely to play hell with my leadership role. Dick Russell's basically endorsed this massive resistance policy, and the yellers and the screamers like Strom Thurmond are gonna stir everybody up." I poured another light scotch and soda for the leader as he prowled the room thinking out loud. "I'm damned if I do and damned if I don't. The Dixiecrats, and a lot of my people at home, will be on me like stink on shit if I don't stand up and bray against the Supreme Court's decision. If

I *do* bray like a jackass, the red hots and senators with big minority blocs in the East and the North will gut shoot me."

Lyndon Johnson was not yet the civil rightist he became; indeed, he had—as he'd explained to me in 1948 he would do, to appease his Texas constituency—voted against repealing the poll tax; in the House he had voted against an antilynching bill; he had spoken out against the FEPC bill. After the *Brown* decision, he attempted to walk a tightrope.

"I'm not gonna sign that Southern manifesto," he said of a firebrand document espoused by massive resisters. "I'm gonna have to do a lot of fancy tap-dancing to survive. Price Daniel, he's whooping and hollaring for Earl Warren to be impeached and stirring 'em up in Texas. Thurmond and Eastland and the rest of the old plantationers are going crazy. Well, I can't run around here being a goddamn bandit. I'm the *leader,* and I can't lead Democrats over a cliff. It would preclude me being thought of as anything more than just another Southern mushmouth." On another night in his office, glumly reading Texas mail from segregationists giving him what-for, he said, "Everything's been turned upside down. All the law-and-order nuts are the lawless people now."

In later years, Johnson would boast that in 1957 he passed the first civil rights bill since Reconstruction. He had, and though the bill didn't have all that many teeth in it—as we later would come to understand—its worth as a breakthrough act cannot be too highly appreciated. Johnson would later tell of how and why he increasingly came down on the side of human rights: "Once when my black cook and her husband were driving a car back to Texas for me, I asked 'em to take along a dog I wanted to get to the ranch. He said to me, 'Mr. Johnson, when black people ride through the South we have to go to the backside of town to find anything to eat and a place to sleep, and sometimes we have to pee in a ditch. We've got enough troubles without having to drag a dog along.' Well, that absolutely astonished me. I hadn't really thought about it. But what a shame that people who worked for the vice-president of the United States had to live that way, be treated that way, in a free country. I decided to do something about it." Johnson had not yet become, but was merely becoming, the civil rights champion he ultimately would be; otherwise, he would not have injected the elitist phrase about "people who worked for the vice-president of the United States." While it's true that LBJ never would have become vice-president or president had he joined the Southern Bourbons back in the mid-1950s, I have no doubt he was sincere in his hopes and his efforts to end racial discrimination. I like to remember that the last speech he made on earth was a ringing declaration for human rights.

Though Johnson wanted smooth waters among Senate Democrats,

and made much of "responsible bipartisanship" in behalf of making divided government work, he loved to bait and tease his GOP counterpart, Bill Knowland of California. Senator Knowland was a bull-in-a-china-closet type, a rightist who perhaps did not own the best mental equipment. LBJ did not consider Knowland very quick or bright, and seemed to enjoy subjecting him to ridicule; something of the playground bully came out in him when he'd defeated Knowland and he couldn't help but rub it in. After I had supplied Johnson with my head count on a given bill, he often would lean across the Senate aisle and say, "Bill, you know you don't have the votes, don't you? You just don't have 'em! I can tell you what the vote's gonna be if you'd like to know." Poor Knowland would offer a grimace that passed for a smile and busy himself with paperwork.

Senator Knowland had succeeded Robert Taft of Ohio as Republican leader, when Taft was forced to resign because he was terminally ill with cancer. LBJ greeted the news with a hoot and a chortle: "Goddamn, Bill Knowland will give Ike twice the problems he'll give me." Johnson liked to tweak President Eisenhower because Knowland's Old Guard instincts often placed him in opposition to GOP programs which Lyndon Johnson supported. "I don't have any trouble supporting you, Mr. President," he'd say to Ike. "Wonder why Senator Knowland does?" In relating such scenes, following White House conferences, Lyndon Johnson would laugh in recalling how Speaker Rayburn had frowned at him in disapproval while the president flushed red under Johnson's needling.

Frankly, I felt as sorry for the opposition leader as a good party man could; matching Bill Knowland against Lyndon Johnson was like pitting an unlettered teenager against Tolstoy. LBJ danced around his Republican counterpart on the Senate floor like a matador toying with a wounded bull and then, after the kill, often verbally cut off his ears. I don't think LBJ disliked Knowland, despite his often imitating him with heavy-footed lumbering walks and indistinct mumblings. Actually, he had as warm a relationship as was possible with a rather strange man who in later years would go on to kill himself. Johnson simply enjoyed parading his superiority, a thing he often did even with his staff people.

Lyndon Johnson could alternately be warm and kind or cold and mean to his staffers. I saw both sides of him. It appeared to me that he took particular delight in humiliating George Reedy, the intellectual who would become his most abused press secretary in the White House, and I've seen the loyal Walter Jenkins grow pale and pop out in sweat during an LBJ tirade. I've heard it said that only John Connally and Bill Moyers could talk back to LBJ, or say him nay, without suffering horrid consequences. I'd like to amend the record to include Bobby Baker in that select group occasionally.

Though the press often referred to me as "Little Lyndon," remarking on our similiarities in dress and mannerisms—perhaps with some merit; LBJ *was* a compelling figure and a big influence on my life—I was no mindless sycophant. For one thing, while LBJ was my sponsor I was not, strictly speaking, his employee alone. The entire Democratic membership of the Senate formally elected me, I had many friends among them, and technically I was the employee of all of them. I had my own office rather than working in one for Lyndon Johnson. These factors caused him to treat me with more deference than was his normal wont, though LBJ wasn't bashful about complaining even to God should the mood be on him. I never silently endured torrents of abuse, however, because the Baker nose was as capable of getting out of joint as was the Johnson nose—a characteristic that later would cause me grief, and expose me to some danger, in prison.

Our most memorable dispute occurred during the 1960 presidential campaign. I was in charge of a campaign train taking Senator Johnson—the vice-presidential nominee—from Washington through the Southern states; the press referred to it as the "Cornpone Special." Throughout the South I had goaded and prodded and cajoled politicians to come aboard the train so as to present LBJ to their home folks and permit their popularity to rub off on him. Many, because of John F. Kennedy's Catholicism, and because the Kennedy-Johnson ticket was perceived as so much more liberal than the Nixon-Lodge ticket, were reluctant in the extreme. They reminded me of old fat hogs being driven to the slaughterhouse, squealing at the first sniff of blood. Senator Herman Talmadge of Georgia sent his wife, and personal excuses. Senator Russell urged LBJ to be silent: "You may carry Georgia if you don't say anything, but you'll lose it if you talk issues." I knew if the trip aboard the Cornpone Special flopped, I'd be a marked man; I thus worked under great tensions.

I had worked unusually hard to cap the Cornpone Special's trip with a tremendous turnout in New Orleans. I had persuaded the mayor, DeLesseps Morrison, to spend thousands of dollars receiving LBJ and to give him a gracious party of welcome. "I want a sea of people to greet Senator Johnson," I told the Louisiana politicians. Senator Russell Long, Congressman Hale Boggs, and Mayor Morrison utilized their political machines to produce a gigantic crowd; each of these politicians, and others, made fiery partisan speeches of the kind generally guaranteed to turn LBJ on. I felt good about it. I was, in fact, close to elation—until Lyndon Johnson rose to give a sullen, perfunctory performance. He was angry, it turned out, because Mayor Morrison had broken LBJ's "solid South" support before the Democratic National Convention by publicly endorsing John F. Kennedy over the Johnson candidacy. He decided

"I had worked unusually hard to turn out crowds for LBJ's 'Cornpone Special' as he campaigned for vice-president in the south . . . and was furious at his sullen conduct in New Orleans."

New Orleans was the time and place to get even, and he went so far as to refuse to attend the big party the mayor had agreed to sponsor.

I was literally livid. Lyndon Johnson's lukewarm performance turned off the huge crowd and blew a golden opportunity to generate enthusiasm for the Democratic ticket in a state far from safe. His peevish performance and petulant conduct embarrassed me personally with the Louisiana politicians who'd come through for us in grand style, and made me wonder whether my back-breaking work would in the end amount to anything.

"Leader," I said to him, "if there's one thing Southern people can't stand it's bad manners. And you've been guilty of very bad manners tonight. I'm embarrassed for you and I hope you've got the grace to be embarrassed for yourself."

Johnson glared at me and said, "I want to have dinner with my family." He named a good restaurant in New Orleans and asked me to make the reservations.

I said, "Leader, I'll do that for you. But as far as I'm concerned, after the way you've acted tonight, it may be the last thing I ever do for you."

Lyndon Johnson acted as if he hadn't heard. As I turned away he said, "There will be about thirty-seven of us."

Some family! I thought. I did, however, call the restaurant—the Vieux Carré in the French Quarter—and forty-five minutes later Johnson and his huge entourage trooped in to a warm welcome arranged by my good friend, and the owner, Nick Popich. I was sitting at the bar, steaming and drinking scotch. LBJ sent one of his minions to ask me to join his party for dinner. I was so mad I don't recall who his messenger was, but I told him: "I'm not gonna be as rude as Senator Johnson, so I won't tell him to kiss my ass. But you tell him I decline to join him for reasons he'll understand."

I flew back to Washington without further contacting Senator Johnson. A day or so later I was preparing morning coffee at my home when the doorbell rang. I answered to find a stiff and formal LBJ standing there. Before I could open my mouth he said, "Mr. Baker, I don't know what I must do to make peace with you. I need your help and your loyalty and your advice in this campaign, and if you want me to kiss your ass on the left, on the right, or in the middle—well, then, I'll do it." I must admit that I was flabbergasted. It was the only apology I'd heard Lyndon Johnson utter to that time, and I would not hear another until a few months before his death. "Well, leader," I said, "come on in and have some coffee with me."

Johnson's chauffeur, Norman, remained in his limousine while we drank coffee, made small talk about the campaign in general, and avoided direct talk of our New Orleans confrontation. I recall thinking it was the first time we'd ever acted ill at ease with each other, and it saddened me. After a few moments he said, "Mr. Baker, would you like a ride to Capitol Hill?" I accepted, mentally noting that LBJ had not called me Mr. Baker in years—I had long been "Bobby" or "Bakes" to him. Though we made peace, and would join forces in later battles over the next three years, I've always felt that our friendship was never again the same.

I enjoyed drinking with Lyndon Johnson, and though we shared the cup many times I only judged him drunk on four or five occasions. Indeed, he often lectured his employees, associates, and in particular his only brother, Sam Houston Johnson, on the evils of drink. He had been marked, I think, by the fact that his father had a bottle problem and he often said that drinking was a sign of weakness. Sam Houston Johnson has written of how the young Lyndon stood outside saloons in Austin, yelling for his father to come home, until his father would be shamed into leaving. The macho notion that being a two-fisted drinker somehow made one more of a man was not one LBJ subscribed to. "Drinking makes you lose control," he preached. "I don't want anybody around me if they don't know what they're doing. They're no good to me."

Mindful of this attitude, I generally drank sparingly in Senator Johnson's presence. When I accompanied him to receptions or other social functions, I was under orders to head straight for the bar and supervise the pouring of his Cutty Sark and soda. "Make it weak," he emphasized. Where possible I poured the drink myself; otherwise, I surreptiously sampled the LBJ drink to be certain a heavy-handed bartender hadn't sandbagged him. On one occasion, when I slipped up, he became angry. "You trying to make an ass of me?" he demanded.

In more private circumstances, in his office at night or in his house, Johnson was not so particular about the strength of his drinks. Once, when we were celebrating one or another of his legislative victories, we got absolutely belly-crawling, grass-grabbing drunk. Leaving his majority leader's office in the Capitol, I slipped on the marble floor and reflexively clutched at him as I went down; we ended in a sprawled tangle. Johnson had imbibed enough that he took it in good humor, though he did say: "Goddamn, Bobby, help me up before the goddamn Republicans see us."

During LBJ's vice-presidency, he played host to friends one night on the *Sequoia,* the yacht the navy keeps for the pleasure of the president and the secretary of the navy; he had arranged the use of it through John Connally, whom he and Sam Rayburn had persuaded Kennedy to appoint as the navy's civilian boss. LBJ was in fine form that evening on the Potomac, telling political stories and knocking back scotch and sodas without restraint. Senator Robert Kerr began to lecture the vice-president and myself about the evils of drink. "You'd just as well take rat poison," the teetotaling Oklahoman said. "Liquor's nothing but poison. You're killing yourselves." Senator Kerr went on in this vein until LBJ grew nettled. "Look at ol' Bob," he said to me sotto voce—loudly enough for Kerr to hear—"he's preachin' good health to us while he's killin' himself with pie and ice cream." Kerr, who indeed had gluttonous eating habits, reddened a bit and abandoned the lecture.

Johnson had an eye for the ladies, though he was not as compulsive about it as John F. Kennedy. He loved to hear gossip of Kennedy's sexual escapades; I was in a position to keep him posted on numerous occasions. JFK knew that I'd helled around with Senator Smathers in the company of ladies other than our wives, and, in fact, I made it possible for Kennedy himself to meet a couple of lovelies in whom he'd expressed pointed interest. Consequently, when President Kennedy occasionally summoned me to the White House to discuss pending legislation or some political problem, he frequently ended the sessions by amazingly frank recitations of a recent sexual adventure.

"At social functions, I was careful to mix LBJ's drinks or to taste them to be sure the bartender hadn't made them too strong. Once, when I slipped up, the senator thundered, 'Bobby, you tryin' to sandbag me so I'll make a fool of myself?' "

After one such meeting I returned to my Capitol Hill office to be told that Vice-President Johnson, then presiding over Senate debate, had called three times: he urgently needed to see me the moment I arrived from the White House. I rushed to the Senate chamber. As soon as he spotted me, LBJ beckoned me forward. I could feel the eyes of press gallery regulars, senators, and tourists in the visitor's gallery as I approached the presiding podium. Johnson intently leaned forward and whispered, "Is ol' Jack gettin' much pussy?" His eyes sparkled as I related the latest Kennedy tale, though he kept his face as carefully composed as if we might be discussing the arms race with Russia.

(Once during JFK's Senate years, I had occasion to seek him out in the Senate restaurant. He was in the company of a mutual friend and lobbyist, Bill Thompson, and one of the prettiest women I had ever seen. I had no more than approached their table when Thompson said, "Bobby, look at this fine chick. She gives the best head in the United States." I couldn't believe my ears and didn't know whether to squat or go blind. I attempted to splutter out my message to Senator Kennedy and, at the same time, sneak glances at the beautiful, smiling lady who was being so highly advertised. JFK saw my discomfort and laughed:

"Ellen Romesch was a German lady-about-town who sometimes visited the Quorum Club, and I introduced her to Jack Kennedy at his request. . . . Bobby Kennedy couldn't get her out of the States fast enough when the newspapers revealed she'd had an affair with a Russian diplomat, too."
(*Wide Worlds Photos*)

"Relax, Bobby. She's from Paris and she doesn't understand a word of English. But what Bill's saying is absolutely right!")

It was an open secret among insiders that Lyndon Johnson for years carried on affairs with various women; I heard reports that he romanced at least one comely newswoman and the wife of a congressman. Shortly after LBJ was elected vice-president, he told President Kennedy that the congressman in question must be appointed to a federal job in a distant city because of widely circulated reports of LBJ's cavorting with the congressman's wife; this was done. LBJ himself never reported such incidents to me, however: I learned them from the Hill's active grapevine. He was much more close-mouthed about his extramarital activities than was John F. Kennedy. Kennedy seemed to relish sharing the details of his conquests; though he was not without charm or wit in relating the clinical complexities, he came off as something of the boyish braggart. Those who have frequented beer hall or locker room sessions will know what I mean. Lyndon Johnson, prone to scatological references and extraordinarily proud of being well endowed, often joked of sex and endorsed it in general; he did not, however, volunteer his specific escapades. I made certain not to ask. For one thing, I didn't want him asking about mine.

There was a sensational flap during the "Baker scandal" hearings about a pretty German woman, Ellen Romesch, whom I knew. A lot of people knew Ellen. Married to a German army sergeant stationed at an embassy, Ellen was a lady about town who sometimes frequented the Quorum Club. This was a private club in the Carroll Arms Hotel on Capitol Hill, which I had helped to found. Its membership was comprised of senators, congressmen, lobbyists, Hill staffers, and other well-connecteds who wanted to enjoy their drinks, meals, poker games, and shared secrets in private accommodations. All in all, it was about as sinister a place as a People's Drugstore. I'm not saying that nobody ever left the Quorum Club to share a bed with a temporary partner, or that cer-

"Carole Tyler was young, beautiful, and vivacious. What started as a harmless office affair evolved into a romance." (*United Press International*)

tain schemes were not hatched there, but I could make the same statement of Duke Zeibert's, The Rotunda, The Palm, or dozens of other
Washington watering places where the elite meet. When I met my downfall, however, the media made much of a nude painting on the wall and
of scarlet drapes. Mercy!

The fat was in the fire, of course, when the ever-bellicose senator
John J. Williams, an avid reader of Jack Anderson's column, learned
there that I was an official of the Quorum Club and that Ellen Romesch—who'd once had an affair with a Soviet embassy attaché—had
been seen in that club. Suddenly, Ellen Romesch was the greatest threat
to national security since Alger Hiss. Attorney General Robert Kennedy
had her rush-deported to Germany—sending as her escort, oddly
enough, a trusted aide with whom the lady fell in love, causing her to
write a series of embarrassingly intimate letters to him, which now are in
my possession—in order to save the Republic. What the newspapers did
not say, possibly because I've never admitted it before—but which Robert F. Kennedy definitely knew—was that Ellen Romesch had been one
of the women Jack Kennedy had asked me to introduce him to. I accommodated his request.

Most of the playboy politicians of my acquaintance, however, avoided
those entangling alliances generally inherent in office-wife relationships.
"Don't dip your quill in the office ink" long has been a popular vulgarism
on Capitol Hill, though the considerations are more practical than
moral. As Congressman Wayne Hays of Ohio would learn when Liz Ray
went public with her grievances, hell hath no fury like an intimate employee scorned. Disgruntled employees who know not only the secrets of
the files, but the politician's intimate habits and thoughts as well, have
long rated with Communists in their ability to inspire fear among politicians. Because of this potential blackmail power, you'll more likely find
Congressman X sleeping with someone on the payroll of Congressman
Y than with his own employee.

Despite knowing the perils of office-wife relationships, I ultimately
succumbed to one. What started as a harmless affair eventually evolved
into a romance, and I grew to love Carole Tyler. Young and beautiful
and vivacious, at once a former beauty queen and a quick mind with a
flair for politics, she was not difficult to love. Though I knew the guilt of
a longtime family man with a loyal wife and five children, I did nothing
to discourage our romance once it began. I was proud of Carole and the
things we shared, and did little to conceal it. I did not want to flaunt the
affair because of Dorothy, but was indiscreet enough that Capitol Hill
insiders knew of it long before the press sensationalized it and before
Carole was called before a Senate committee looking into my conduct.

Chapter Seven

The Washington Dollar Game

"Bobby, we're broke and we owe $39,000. . . .
See what you can do."

T
HE presumption among politicians, reporters, the man-in-the-street, and those I did time with, was that Lyndon B. Johnson helped me make considerable sums of money, that he somehow feathered my nest. Nothing could be more off-target. LBJ simply was not a man to share. Not once did he offer me so much as an investment opportunity.

Late in my Senate career, when I had overreached financially, I approached the then vice-president to seek help in alleviating my cash-flow problems. "Leader," I said, "my ox is in the ditch. In about thirty days I may have to file for bankruptcy and I'm worried about the political connotations." Johnson shot a guarded look and asked what I was talking about.

"Well," I said, "my partner in the Carousel Motel killed himself. The damned motel's costing three times its original projection. Construction's been held up by disasters including a hurricane that wiped me out, and I've been able to collect only about ten cents on the dollar in damages. If I don't get big money, and get it quick, I'll go under. I may be sued; God knows what all. I'd hate to be an embarrassment to you and I think you ought to know it could get sticky real soon." Lyndon Johnson picked up the telephone. "Bob," he said to Senator Kerr, "*our* boy Bobby's in trouble and he needs *your* help."

Of course, I easily could have called Senator Kerr on my own. He had steered me to profitable investments in the past; he'd loaned me considerable sums or had arranged for various banks to do it. I had not wanted to ride a good horse to death, however, and so I had gone to Lyndon Johnson in hopes of finding relief from a new source. Johnson, however, was quick to pass the buck—or, more accurately, 285,000 of them: that's the amount of credit Senator Kerr arranged for me at an Oklahoma City bank following LBJ's telephone call. The point is, I got nothing directly from Lyndon Johnson. I've yet to meet the man who could boast of having made much profit from LBJ's purse. He guarded it as fiercely as a nightwatchman's dog.

Johnson was supersensitive to criticism that he used his public offices to add to his personal wealth, which was founded on radio and television properties. He avidly promoted the fiction that Lady Bird Johnson was the business genius in the family, and shoved her out front as the owner of record. The truth is that LBJ kept track of every nickle and he had his chief of staff, Walter Jenkins, spend an inordinate amount of time attending the Johnson private enterprises. Each week, LBJ personally examined the revenue reports of his Texas-based salesmen; those who had not lived up to expectations promptly heard about it from Walter Jenkins. Jenkins also approved the program content for the LBJ stations, subject to his boss's inspections. I've heard Johnson raise cain over the smallest matter.

It was no accident that Austin, Texas, was for years the only city of its size with only one television station. Johnson had friends in high places among those who controlled the broadcast industry. George Smathers was his man in the Senate. Bob Bartley, a member of the Federal Communications Commission, just happened to be a nephew to LBJ's patron, Speaker Sam Rayburn. You can bet that others in the regulatory agencies, including those who granted broadcast licenses, were aware of these friendly connections and of Johnson's great power. LBJ demanded, and received, the opportunity to pick and choose programs for his monopoly station from among those offered by all three of the major networks. No other television station in America had such a unique and cozy arrangement.

Once in the Roosevelt Hotel in New York, where we had gone to attend a Bonds for Israel rally, I witnessed Lyndon Johnson twist the arm of a network executive from NBC, in order that LBJ might line his own pockets. Senator Johnson told the network man that he wanted his station paid national advertising rates for the network commercials it carried. "But senator," he was told, "your market isn't big enough down there. The local affiliate is paid according to its share of the audience. Yours just isn't large enough to qualify." "I say it is," Johnson retorted. "I know how you fellows work—you can do anything you want to. Well, *want* to!" The network officials thought it over and decided they wanted to.

That Lyndon Johnson was ever on the lookout for broadcast profits is illustrated by the case involving Don Reynolds, a Silver Spring, Maryland, insurance man, and a pot-and-pan manufacturer, one Albert C. Young.

I had entered into an agreement with Reynolds, a fellow South Caro-linan, to steer insurance customers to him in exchange for a small piece of the business and a commission on any policies he wrote as a result of my efforts. In the late 1950s, Senator Johnson told me of his desperate need to buy $100,000 worth of term life insurance. "I've got this bad heart history," he said, "and if I died suddenly Lady Bird would need a great amount of cash to protect her radio and TV enterprises in a com-munity-property state. The problem is, I can't find an insurance com-pany willing to gamble on my heart."

I told Senator Johnson about my partnership with Don Reynolds, and we agreed to seek the policy through him. Reynolds was delighted at the prospect of doing business with the big man and said that he would refund his sales commission to LBJ. As it turned out there was never a refund.

I put Don Reynolds in touch with Walter Jenkins. The two men later would offer conflicting versions of what happened next, but here's the story as I recall it:

After a first meeting with Walter Jenkins, Reynolds was notified that his services would not be required because another company—represented by LBJ's cousin, Huff Baines—had agreed to write the poli-cies and, additionally, had guaranteed to purchase advertising time on KTBC, the LBJ station in Austin. By the Jenkins version, Reynolds asked to be allowed "to meet the competition"; by the Reynolds version, Jenkins pressured him into buying $1,208 in advertising time out of the $11,000 commission Reynolds would receive for writing two $50,000 policies on Johnson through Manhattan Life. Reynolds, who felt it would make as much sense for a mom-and-pop taco stand in Austin to buy advertising in Silver Spring as it did for him to advertise a Maryland insurance agency in distant Austin, sought relief by "laying off" the Texas advertising—much as a bookie might lay off excessive bets—with Albert C. Young of Mid-Atlantic Steel Company. Under the agreement with Young, Reynolds would share in profits resulting from the sale of kitchenware over the LBJ airwaves. The only profit, however, accrued to Senator Johnson: Young testified that the $1,208 worth of advertising sold only $320 worth of pots and pans. You may be thinking that Sena-tor Johnson spent a great deal of time and effort to clear a very modest profit. Which is precisely my point. He was always on the lookout for the odd nickel or dime.

Lyndon Johnson did have moments of generosity. He sometimes showered gifts upon his employees or associates—including myself—and when they suffered costly health reversals he was there to lend a helping hand. He often promised more than he delivered, however.

"Don Reynolds, the Maryland insurance man, went through me to write a policy on LBJ. Then he kicked back a hi-fi set and $1,208 in unneeded advertising on the vice-president's Texas radio station." (*United Press International*)

One night in the late 1950s, during a Christmas season at the LBJ Ranch, while the senator and I were honoring rural custom by taking a leak beside his car on a lonely Texas road, he grew sentimental under the influence of drink. "Bobby, you're a good and loyal man. Sometimes when I'm rushed and worrying about a thousand things it may appear that I don't appreciate you. But I do, and when I die you'll find it out. I'm gonna take care of you in my will." That's the last I ever heard of it.

Johnson often received credit for generous acts when they had been accomplished by the use of other people's money. He ordered me, in my role as treasurer of the Senate Democratic Campaign Committee, to pay for all airline tickets and $100 Stetson hats he urged upon notables visit-

ing his Texas ranch. Those who received these gifts had no way of knowing they were paid for from the committee's pot, which legally belonged
to all Democratic senators and was not LBJ's to spend on his personal
whims. Johnson several times complained to Keith Linden of Harvey
Aluminum that the ballpoint "LBJ pens" he gave away as souvenirs were
excessively expensive. When Linden failed to take the hint, the senator
bluntly told him, "Keith, now, you aluminum folks have mastered the
mass-production technique and I want you to find a way to produce
those ballpoint pens for me at a reasonable cost." Linden came through,
though possibly at a loss to his company, and Johnson literally gave away
hundreds of thousands of the pens. Of course, they prominently advertised his name and his office. He had no compunctions against using his
corporate airplane for political or self-promoting purposes, and might
have been puzzled had anyone called him to account for it. Like many
public men grown accustomed to the trappings of high office, he accepted without question his right to do as he pleased. And, like many
public men, he reached that point where he no longer could distinguish
between Lyndon Johnson the private citizen and Lyndon Johnson
the political czar. If you play a role long enough, you become the role
itself.

There is a mistaken impression that I was Lyndon Johnson's chief
fundraiser. Not that I didn't raise some funds for him; his primary
money men, however, were John Connally and George R. Brown of
Brown and Root Construction Company. ("Sweet George R. Brown,"
Johnson staffers used to sing in their private recreations, to the tune of
the popular "Sweet Georgia Brown.") These men, and Walter Jenkins,
knew far more about the sources of LBJ's political money than I ever
knew.

Sometimes, however, I was pressed into service. At the conclusion of
the 1960 Democratic National Convention in Los Angeles, LBJ wore a
sad hound dog's look as he said, "Bobby, we're broke and we owe
$39,000 for a hotel bill out here. I don't know where in hell to get it. All I
know is we've gotta have it today. See what you can do." Wonderful!
Here I am exhausted from the fratricidal wars over LBJ's selection as
vice-president on the Kennedy ticket, wanting nothing but a hot bath
and a week of sleep, and I've got to find $39,000 blowing around loose
on the ground.

I went to Bart Lytton, president of Lytton Savings and Loan, with the
sad tale. He required persuading. "I don't have that much available," he
said. "Even if I did I wouldn't want it on record that I'd given it." I assured Lytton that he'd be protected and stressed the benefits of incur-

ring LBJ's goodwill. "On the other hand," I said, "he can be a miserable prick if he feels someone has let him down." Bart groaned, but motioned me into a public men's room nearby.

Bart Lytton and I furtively entered a common stall in the men's room, where he gave me two $10,000 personal checks made out to cash. I delivered them to LBJ, who took one look and said, "Hell, Bobby, this is just a little over half of it!" I said, "Yes, and you can let someone else get the rest of it. Someone who knows more rich folks than I do." Senator Johnson pocketed the checks, though grumbling under his breath, while I thought of the audacity of those who look into the mouths of gift horses. I never checked to determine whether John Connally, or anyone else, raised the balance of the money.

Shortly after the 1960 campaign began, I received a call to go to New York to pick up $25,000 from the head of one of the giant communications corporations. I was handed the cash by a functionary, nervous man who spoke in hushed tones and seemed eager to witness my departure.

Later, after my troubles surfaced, one of ten executives who'd been pressured to "donate" toward the $25,000 kitty—to circumvent the law forbidding corporations from making political contributions—complained to Senator John J. Williams of Delaware. Senator Williams tried to make a big deal of my courier's role. Washington's politicians, attempting to protect LBJ and JFK—and who, perhaps, wanted to protect themselves in similar cases—glossed over the affair and nothing much came of it.

Anyone not blind in both eyes and deaf in one ear can tell you that corporations have routinely circumvented the campaign funding laws. They grant their executives personal "bonuses" which just happen to coincide with the sum total of the money the corporation needs to raise for political purposes; by a strange quirk of fate, these same executives decide to make "personal" political contributions in the exact amounts of their respective bonuses. If you don't believe that's the way it works, ask Maurice Stans.

On one occasion I was asked to transmit $5,000 from Lyndon B. Johnson to a Republican senator, Styles Bridges of New Hampshire. I don't know where the money came from. As was the Washington practice, Johnson handed me the boodle in cash. "Bobby," he said, "Styles Bridges is throwing an 'appreciation dinner' for himself up in New Hampshire sometime next week. Fly up there and drop this in the kitty and be damn sure that Styles knows it came from me. And while you're up there, invent a lot of flowery compliments you've heard me say about Senator Bridges."

Here was a case of LBJ putting his money to good use. Senator Bridges was the ranking Republican on the Senate Preparedness Committee, a unit serving the military-industrial complex which President Eisenhower warned against in his last days in office. In order to secure unanimous reports from that committee, and thus grease the skids for bills later to be acted on by the full Senate, or to assist Defense Department policies, Lyndon Johnson long had flattered him with shameless praise and had bribed him for his goodwill by permitting him to hire as many minority staff members as he wanted for the Preparedness Committee.

Johnson, like my father, knew that "Money talks and bullshit walks." He seemed to sense each man's individual price and the commodity he preferred as coin—whether it might be money, flattery, vote trade-offs, public works projects, or other of the tools of power. I know that to the outsider, reading press reports after my legal problems began, it probably appeared as if LBJ and Bobby Baker linked hands and ran though Washington filling their black bags each day at sundown. That simply wasn't the way it was, however.

Indeed, I've had many nights to wonder whether I might have become as careless as I did had LBJ remained in the Senate. Johnson-the-Leader had so consumed my time and my energies in the business of the Senate, and in his pursuit of political goals, that I had little left over for large mischief. After he became vice-president, however, I was thrown into more frequent and more intimate contact with Senator Kerr. Despite his lack of an official title, insiders knew Kerr as the "King of the Senate." Because LBJ's successor as majority leader, Senator Mike Mansfield of Montana, was not aggressive in his political pursuits, Senator Kerr and I more and more filled the power vaccum. We wheeled and dealed while Senator Mansfield sat alone in a favorite hideaway office, puffing his pipe and reading book after book.

Senator Kerr largely disdained the cajolings and tricks of Lyndon Johnson; no smoke-and-mirrors man, he. His answer to everything was money. If you had enough of it you could do anything you wanted. If you didn't, then you were unlikely to accomplish very much and you simply were not a free man. Like many a good businessman, Bob Kerr knew that it took money to make money. He knew the value of investments and he held that not all investments had to be made in stocks and bonds or commodities or real properties: you could buy people. He would make loans or campaign contributions or gifts to his collegues if it would woo their votes for his favored causes. Many of his favored causes, of course, put money in his own pocket; Senator Kerr could look upon an "investment" in another senator as simply a smart business practice, another form of refurbishing the factory or retooling your machines. Where Senator Johnson at least worried about the appearances of conflict-of-interest actions, Bob Kerr openly defended his pursuit of the almighty dollar whether to friend or to critic. "It happens that my personal interests coincide with those of Oklahoma," he liked to say. "It's a happy union and I don't apologize for it."

Senator Kerr didn't confine himself to Capitol Hill in attempting to buy influential friends. He once astonished Interior Secretary Stewart Udall by saying, "Mr. Secretary, you're from Arizona and you ought to be in the cattle business. I'd be happy to help you get started." Udall said, well, he didn't have the money to start a herd and, besides, he had about all he could handle attending his job as a cabinet member. "That's no problem," Senator Kerr airily said. "I'll sell you the brood stock to begin your own herd and you can have them on credit. Pay when it's handy." Udall declined the offer: he didn't own enough land to run a big herd. "Hell," Kerr said, "let me keep your herd on *my* land. My ranch hands can look after 'em for you and sell off the beef when the time comes. It won't cost you a cent. You can claim your herd when you've got your own land—and I'll make you a loan to buy the land." Udall, who as interior secretary was the keeper of vast oil reserves, knew another potential Teapot Dome when he saw it and so he mumbled his thanks and took his leave. Kerr approached the matter another time or two before giving up on Udall.

Where Lyndon Johnson never suggested even the straightest investment opportunity, Senator Kerr urged me to accumulate and to build the largest possible fortune. "Money is the most powerful substance known to man," he said. "A man who doesn't have money can't operate. Why, if I don't have at least $5,000 on me as pocket change, I'm afraid that taxi drivers won't pick me up." Kerr not only delighted in being rich, he wanted to spend his time with those who were. If you were his friend, he wanted you to earn your membership in his exclusive club by getting ahead. I actually believe that he thought being poor was a disgrace, that poverty was some shameful disease wished only upon the unclean or the inept or the uncaring. He went after the dollar whether in politics or in business or at the poker table—for years he kept those senators or lobbyists foolish enough to challenge him at cards hovering near bankruptcy. He once chortled in delight in saying that he'd won more than $120,000 at gin rummy over the years from Senator Joe McCarthy. Senator McCarthy, in desperation, located the author of an authoritative book on gin rummy and then persuaded him to join his Senate payroll—where his sole duty was to make Joe McCarthy proficient at gin rummy. "Didn't do him a bit of good," Senator Kerr laughed.

Everyone knows that LBJ dominated his friends, his associates, and his family. His urge to put the LBJ brand on everything shows in his wife, his daughters, and his dog sharing his famous initials. He meddled in the hair styles and dress fashions of his secretaries, even dictating shades of lipstick. I found Bob Kerr, however, to be even more dogged in his attempts to shape people as he would like them. He incessantly lectured me against drinking, smoking, or chasing after women.

The Kerr sons and daughter were forbidden to smoke or drink, I knew, but I was startled to hear from one of the senator's daughters-in-law that the prohibition extended even to those who'd married into the family. "You have no life of your own," she said. "We aren't permitted to voice opposition to his policies no matter if they're personal or political." Family members were not permitted to swear in his presence, though Baptist Bob himself could rip off a musical string of oaths inventive enough to shame a navy band. He was—and I hate to say it, because I truly admired and loved that complex man—a petty tyrant in the matter of other people's lives or rights. Crossed in the slightest, he became the most acerbic and sarcastic and pitiless man I've ever seen operate on the Senate floor; had he been a pro-football player he would have been a Jim Taylor or a Larry Czonka or a Marion Motley, preferring to run over you even when it might be easier to run around you. He went so far as to try to make a romantic match of me and his daughter. Nature, however, thwarted him in that case: the daughter, while surely a lovely and gracious woman, had a discouraging advantage over me as pertained to height and weight.

Senator Kerr did, however, influence me in other matters. I wanted to emulate his success, and I envied his quick, bright mind. This man who was born in a log cabin had the finest mind of any I knew in public life, and I do not make exceptions for Lyndon Johnson, Jack Kennedy, or anyone else. I was more than happy to take his business advice, to accept his financial backing, and to play pretty much by his rules. It was exciting and heady. And it was easy to forget that tunnel vision comes easy, or that maybe one shouldn't rush pell-mell through life but should pause to sniff the flowers. It was easy to forget the bad bargain that Daniel Webster struck with the devil, and this forgetfulness eventually would cost me dearly.

Looking back on it, the real glory years—and the truly satisfying years—were those with Lyndon Johnson, and not those dominated by Bob Kerr. Being a viable part of the political processes—making decisions, plotting strategy, counting noses, shaping policy—is what I have missed most of all in the fifteen years since I left the Senate under fire.

While for years a large part of me wanted to be the rich man living in the big white house on the hill, enough remained of the awed young country hustler that not being at the center of large events is painful still. Though I continue to maintain contact with a few senators and other politicians, these are few and perfunctory compared to the past. There is no substitute for being right down there in the trenches, fighting the daily political battles and exulting in the victories. Politics is wearying and often grinding, but those who find politics dull know a different game than I do. The fatigue is a good fatigue, and even defeat may be no worse than bittersweet.

I reveled in the trades and the trickeries of the Lyndon Johnson years, and enjoyed the shows we staged. Often these shows were carefully orchestrated and perhaps even a shade melodramatic, as LBJ's critics have charged, but I see nothing wrong in that. Lyndon Johnson knew that the illusion of power was almost as important as real power itself; that, simply, the more powerful you appeared to be, the more powerful you became. It was one of the reasons for his great success. He was not only a fine actor but a fine director and producer as well. He delighted in striding about the Senate floor, conferring and frowning and giving the impression of great anxiety, while the packed press gallery and the visitors' galleries buzzed and hummed with tensions, even though he knew—and I was one of few people who knew—that he had three decisive votes hidden in some Capitol nook and would produce them at the most effective moment. The Republicans would snort at losing another cliff-hanger, the newspapers would trumpet a new Johnson miracle, and Lyndon Johnson would go off to a fresh Cutty Sark and soda to laugh and laugh.

One of Johnson's great satisfactions was thwarting the passage of the Bricker Amendment by a single vote. The Bricker Amendment, a love child of the marriage between Republican Old Guarders and Dixiecrats, would have taken much control of foreign affairs away from the president and theoretically have vested such control in the Congress. Much sentiment could be found for the Bricker Amendment in 1954, in a country sick of back-to-back wars and especially of the Korean War—or, as the opposition labeled it, "Harry Truman's War." It was "The only war we never won," and so on. With the Republicans in control of Congress, and the bullheaded Senator Knowland cheering for the Bricker Amendment as majority leader, it appeared to be a cinch to pass even though it required approval by two-thirds of all senators present and voting.

"It's the worst bill I can think of," Johnson said. "It ties the president's hands and I'm not just talking about Ike. It will be the bane of every president we elect, and one day a president will be sitting around waiting for the Senate wind tunnel to close down and while the wind's still blowing he'll get a telephone call from the Pentagon saying 'Sorry, Mr. President, but we just lost New York.' We've got to stop the damn thing, and I think we can. We don't want to go putting that idea up on billboards, though."

For weeks Johnson gloomed along with the official wisdom. When Republicans or press pundits predicted as many as sixty-eight to seventy votes for the Bricker Amendment, he shook his head and sighed and gave the impression somebody was about to put his dog to sleep. Behind the scenes, however, he was pulling strings and pitching woo. If he could not convince a Bricker proponent to change his vote, he begged him to find a cause to be absent. "If we can keep enough people away," he said, "they can get sixty votes under the two-thirds rule and we can *still* beat 'em." On the day of the vote, to all outward appearances LBJ was a minority leader about to lead his troops to defeat. "They say they've got the votes," he said to newsmen in apparent surrender. I knew, however, that several Southern Democrats had been persuaded to be absent. I also knew of a special surprise Senator Johnson had prepared for the Bricker proponents.

Senator Harley Kilgore of West Virginia had been seriously ill for weeks in Bethesda Naval Hospital. I knew, because I had arranged the logistics, that he was being rushed by ambulance toward the Senate floor even as the Bricker people confidently cast their votes. Senator Kilgore was whisked to the Democratic cloakroom, wheezing and in pain, and was momentarily made comfortable in the cloakroom until Lyndon Johnson passed the word to bring him in to vote. I have never seen a more stunned Senate than when that old sick man stumbled forward to cast his vote and then, before anyone could recover, was whisked back to the ambulance and to his hospital bed. Kilgore's vote had made the vote 60–31—exactly one less than the Bricker Amendment needed to pass.

Lyndon Johnson preened himself long into the night over that victory. "How's the ADA gonna fault me now?" he repeatdly crowed as he chain-smoked and poured down liquor. "What does Averell Harriman owe me now? How in the hell can the red hots cuss LBJ tonight, huh? Huh? Hell, I saved ol' Ike's chestnuts and even *he* knows it!"

Johnson also stunned the political world when he delivered a unanimous Democratic vote to repeal the Taft-Hartley Act, a move which delighted labor. That he could convince labor-baiting senators such as Harry Byrd of Virginia and James O. Eastland of Mississippi to go along was a miracle just short of walking on water; they had to vote against everything they believed and everything they'd said on the subject.

For weeks, Lyndon Johnson had me scurrying around producing antilabor Southerners and he made his leadership role a personal issue. "All right," he'd say to the Southern recalcitrants—leaning into their faces, standing nose to nose, pressing the flesh, and laying on hands— "you voted me in as your leader, and I'm doing my best to lead you. I haven't pushed you very often. I haven't twisted your arms, no matter what it says in the press, and I haven't cussed and snorted when you voted with the other side. But this time your leader needs you. If I'm gonna do my job you've gotta give me the tools. The Republicans, now, they're gonna be lined up solid on the other side of this issue. They're gonna be carrying water for business. It's my job, and it's your job, to make it clear to the working man that the Democratic party is the only place he has to go. They knew that under Roosevelt, when their bellies were empty. But labor started getting fat and by the time Harry Truman left office and Ike came along, they forgot it. You boys down South, you've always thought you wouldn't have to worry about Republican opponents. Well, look around you. I look around and I see the Republicans shaking bushes all over the South. Well, one day they'll shake the right bush and flush out an opponent for you. You're gonna need some loyal, brass-collar, yellow-dog Democrats who want to be for you because they've got a *reason* to be for you. Vote right on Taft-Hartley and you'll give 'em the reason. My ass is on the line, and your ass is on the line, and the Democratic party's ass is on the line. I'm asking you to pay your dues to the party and to affirm your faith in me." All the time he would be patting and tugging and pulling on the Dixiecrat senator of the moment, crowding him as a good fighter would advance on an addled opponent against the ropes, never pausing to permit the target a moment's respite or rebuttal. When Lyndon Johnson did not want to be told no, he literally refused to let the other fellow get a word in edgewise.

One of his more brilliant performances occurred when the Senate voted to condemn Joe McCarthy, the reckless red-baiting windbag from Wisconsin. Senator Johnson was not out front in that fight, because he chose not to be, but had the nation's newsmen looked a little more carefully behind the scenes they would have discovered Lyndon Johnson's tracks all over the lot.

For years, Johnson had been caught between what my father would have called "a rock and a hard place," liberals urging him to bring Joe McCarthy down and his Texas constituents—many of whom were heavy contributors to LBJ and some of whom were his personal friends—who urged him to champion McCarthy's "great crusade." LBJ made soothing sounds to both sides and said as little as possible in public. Privately, however, he fumed and complained of the trouble McCarthy caused him.

"Senator Joe McCarthy, the reckless red-baiting windbag from Wisconsin, would do anything for a headline." (*United Press International*)

"Joe McCarthy's just a loudmouthed drunk," he told intimates. "Hell, he's the sorriest senator up here. Can't tie his goddamn shoes. But he's riding high now, he's got people scared to death some Communist will strangle 'em in their sleep, and anybody who takes him on before the fevers cool—well, you don't get in a pissin' contest with a polecat."

For months, however, LBJ quietly moved among men whom Mc-Carthy had offended by word or deed, getting his troops ready for the propitious time to strike. Sometimes he sent me to talk with key senators in secret, especially among red-hating Southerners who represented states where McCarthy was judged to be the next thing to God. We concentrated on Senator Stennis of Mississippi, a classic Southern gentleman with unimpeachable credentials, who was full of righteous indignation because of McCarthy's insulting conduct toward his fellow senators. Senator McClellan of Arkansas, the ranking Democrat on the Government Operations Committee chaired by McCarthy, fed details of McCarthy's closed-door antics to us; these were passed along to other senators who might be particularly offended. We consulted with Chief Justice Earl Warren of the Supreme Court and with President Eisenhower's congressional liaison man, General Jerry (Slick) Persons.

After the Army-McCarthy hearings, during which many Americans saw the senator from Wisconsin in full bloom for the first time, watching on television for days on end while McCarthy ranted and raved and giggled and carried on like a crazy man, LBJ felt that the time had come to strike. He sat about attempting to shape the committee which would investigate Joe McCarthy's conduct.

Late one night in his minority leader's office, throwing down drinks, Johnson was despondent and feeling sorry for himself. He was in one of his I've-got-to-do-everything-myself moods, during which he was likely alternately to abuse his staffers and wring his hands. "We can get the votes to censure McCarthy," he said, "but the problem is controlling the committee. We don't want a goddamn circus like that Army-McCarthy thing was. We don't want to lose half our troops while winning the war. I've tried to convince Dick Russell and Walter George to lead the fight from the Democratic side, but they're afraid of sticking their heads in the noose. They say McCarthy's still strong medicine down in Georgia and they've just got no stomach for it. Old Walter George, he's so afraid of the governor down there running against him—Herman Talmadge— that he shakes like a dog shittin' persimmon seeds. Dick Russell don't want to go to the mat because he's afraid he'll get his hands dirty. You know who they're offering me?" he snorted in disgust. "Sam Ervin of North Carolina. The lightweight son-of-a-bitch. Goddamn windbag." Another gulp of the drink. "But I guess I'll have to take him. He's one of the insiders and he's a Southerner and I've got to have one."

Though Johnson as minority leader had no official power to influence the naming of Republican chairman of the investigating committee, he got the man he wanted: Ralph Flanders of Vermont, known for his flinty integrity. He accomplished this by talks with President Eisenhower, Chief Justice Warren, and Senator Margaret Chase Smith of Maine, all of whom brought behind-the-door pressures on Bill Knowland and other leading Senate Republicans. "I also recommended they put Karl Mundt of South Dakota on the committee," Johnson said with a diabolical grin. "He's so goddamned dumb he won't know what's going on, and he's so ineffective he can't make anything happen, but it will look good to have a staunch pro-McCarthy man sitting in judgment of him." In this, too, LBJ got his way—and he proved right.

Johnson persuaded the members not to include in its bill of proceedings a charge that Senator McCarthy had abused General Zwicker, whom McCarthy had told—during the Army-McCarthy hearings—that he was "unfit to wear the uniform." "Zwicker gave a poor performance in the Army-McCarthy hearings," LBJ argued. "Some people question his popularity and he may not be overburdened with brains. He might provide the excuse for ten or more Democrats to vote against censure, if Zwicker becomes one of the issues. We've got enough votes to hang Joe McCarthy right now. What's the profit in cluttering the charge up with an issue that could cost us votes?"

Everyone knows, of course, that the Senate did handily condemn Joe McCarthy and he was never a factor again. His reign of terror and intimidation was over.

I had mixed feelings about the McCarthy censure, though I had worked hard to bring it about. I didn't approve of Joe McCarthy's rough-and-tumble methods and to this day I remain unconvinced that he ever caught or discovered a single Communist in a government he claimed to be honeycombed with them. He was, in my view, a demagogue looking for a handy issue and stumbled onto the Communists-in-government issue at a time when the country was ripe with fear. Yet, I had a morbid fascination with the man—perhaps as one might view a snake from a safe distance—and I had some left-handed admiration in a purely technical sense for the way he'd managed to con and slash his way to power. He had, to use an old South Carolina expression, managed for a while to make chicken salad out of chicken shit. A political technician had to feel some kinship for the man, despite what he was. For months after McCarthy's censure, as he hobbled about on crutches and drank himself to death, I felt twinges of guilt each time I caught a glimpse of him. Perhaps something in me knew—subliminally, subconsciously—that one day I, too, would sit on the hot seat while a Senate committee went about the business of shattering my future.

Chapter Eight

Trades, Alliances, and Accommodations

"Bobby, I'll do anything to kill that bill."
"Yeah? How much money can you spend?"

T HERE are more ways than one," my mother used to say, "to
skin a cat." The expression always puzzled me until I grew
up and learned how perfectly the old adage applies to the passage of legislation in Congress.

Comparatively few of the thousands of bills introduced during each
two-year term make it through the legislative jungle to become law. As
many as 40,000 bills may be introduced. Some of these contain hare-
brained schemes not to be taken seriously; others may be introduced at
the request of some constituent or constituent group and then virtually
abandoned by their sponsors of record once the home folks have been
satisfied. Still others—such as Medicare, equal opportunity bills, or bills
establishing benefits for the self-employed—may languish for years as
ideas whose time has not yet come. Perhaps a hundred or so bills each
term become major public laws applicable to meaningful numbers of
people. Another few hundred may pass but affect only the private relief
of one individual or apply only to small groups—a local water district, an
employee credit union—or establish a national historic site in a small
area. Unlike bills affecting the lives of us all, these fail to attract the attention of the media or of the masses. Often, indeed, the public at large
is unaware of legislation that will in time hit large numbers of people in
their pocketbooks. Special-interest groups—home builders, bankers,
farmers, even morticians—may quietly slip through bills raising interest
rates or obtaining subsidies.

I used to grin, perhaps a bit cynically, when I chanced upon one of
the more popular documents congressmen send to their constituents in
order to advertise themselves. Each Senate or House member is supplied

with a variety of publications printed at public expense—infant-care booklets, pamphlets on the growing of house plants, agriculture year-books, and so on—to be mailed at public expense to their constituents. (There was even one called "Twenty-Eight Ways to Cook Rabbit," which Democrats, remembering the Hoover Depression, thoroughly enjoyed until President Eisenhower quietly had it deep-sixed.)

The booklet which caused me wry amusement was entitled "How a Bill Becomes a Law." It traced the sixteen steps from introduction through assignment to the appropriate committee for hearings, and on until the president signs it into law. Not that it wasn't accurate in the strict civics class sense: it just failed to tell the whole truth. What is left out was how the winnowing processes work: the trade-offs and the private agreements or understandings between politicians. Often the merits or demerits of a bill have little or nothing to do with whether it becomes law. If certain people in power reach a private trade or accommodation, then it likely will become law. If not, then it may not.

John F. Kennedy might not have gotten his nuclear arms limitation treaty with Russia had it not been for the alleged indiscretions of an Eisenhower White House aide whom we shall call Joe Jones. Here is the story, as told by my old friend the late Senator Everett Dirksen of Illinois to my personal physician, Dr. Joe Bailey, and to me:

Attorney General Robert Kennedy and other Democrats took office loaded for bear. One of their long memories was that President Eisenhower's attorney general, Herbert Brownell, had sent Matthew Conally and T. Lamar Caudle of the Truman administration to prison for alleged irregularities in public office. The Kennedy crowd was determined to find some similar punishable instances of official malfeasance among Ike's old confidants. President Eisenhower, in retirement, got wind of this—specifically that a federal grand jury in Philadelphia was on the verge of indicting his former aide, "Mr. Jones," whose wife was particularly close to Mamie Eisenhower. Mrs. Eisenhower reported her fear that Jones might commit suicide, and asked Ike to intervene with President Kennedy.

Ike called Senator Dirksen and said, "Ev, I'm embarrassed to ask you this favor, but I understand a grand jury has voted, or is about to vote, to indict Joe Jones for income tax evasion and he's simply in a terrible state. You and I know, Ev, that if the government is determined to find ir-regularities in anyone's tax returns then irregularities may be found al-most every time."

"Mr. President," Dirksen said, "what can I do?"

"I need your good offices," Ike said. "I don't really know John Kennedy. I've met with him only twice in my life. Ev, I was president for eight years and I think I have the respect of the American people and I want to retain it. I believe the day will come when President Kennedy will need the public assistance of a former president whose name has prestige and who's beyond partisan arrows. I'd like you to ask President Kennedy, as a personal favor to me, to put the Jones indictment in the deep freeze. You have the authority to advise him he'll have a blank check in my bank if he will grant me this favor."

According to Dirksen, he called the White House and met at 5:30 P.M. that same day with President Kennedy. After they'd had a drink he said, "Mr. President, I would like for you to surrender your title for a few minutes and join me for a stroll in the Rose Garden to discuss a very personal and private matter. It simply must be two friends—Jack and Ev—talking on a personal basis."

The two men went into the Rose Garden where Senator Dirksen relayed Ike's message. JFK said he had no knowledge of the matter, but volunteered to return to the Oval Office and telephone the attorney general, his brother Bobby. RFK affirmed that the Jones indictment was to be announced at a press conference in Philadelphia the next day. "Cancel it and do it now," Senator Dirksen quoted President Kennedy as saying. "Don't sign the indictment. Place it in deep freeze." Robert Kennedy is said to have responded, "This will destroy us politically, to grant a special favor to a tax evader." Evidently they had a hot exchange which culminated in JFK's saying, "I'm president. If you can't comply with my request then your resignation will be accepted."

Within a few weeks, the Kennedy administration had been beaten decisively in Congress on a number of issues. The nuclear arms limitation treaty was before the Senate and needed to be ratified by a two-thirds majority. J. Edgar Hoover and other conservatives were leaking information that the Russians would destroy us in time should the treaty be ratified. My head count showed that we could get a simple majority—but would fall short of the necessary two-thirds. After Senator Dirksen made an eloquent speech against the treaty, I telephoned President Kennedy and told him all was lost. "Maybe not," he said.

Those cryptic words later caused me to check with Senator Dirksen to see what had transpired. It was then he told me of the Jones story and concluded, "President Kennedy called me to the White House and said, 'Ev, I must write a check on you and Ike. This atomic treaty is important to me and to the country and, I think, to all mankind. It's imperative that it be approved. Ike said I had coin in his bank, and you say I have coin in yours.'

"I told the President," Senator Dirksen said, "that yes, we owed him one. He then said, 'Ev, I want you to reverse yourself and come out for the treaty. I also want Ike's public endorsement of the treaty before the Senate votes. We'll call it square on that other matter."

Dirksen said, "Mr. President, you're a hell of a horse trader. But I'll honor my commitment, and I'm sure that General Eisenhower will." Both men shortly came out for the bill, and that's how JFK got his nuclear arms limitation treaty.

Once President Kennedy called me to the White House to discuss why his investment credit tax bill had stalled in the Senate. As it provided a tax break for businessmen and investors, JFK was puzzled by Bob Kerr's failure to act on it as chairman of the Senate Finance Committee. "Hell," he told me, "that goddamn bill ought to make Bob Kerr dance for joy. Wilbur Mills is going along in the House, but Kerr's dragging his feet. Why?" I asked the president's permission to use his telephone and contacted Senator Kerr. The senator said, "Tell him to get his dumb fuckin' brother to quit opposing my friend Ross Bohannon for a federal judgeship in Oklahoma!" "Is that all?" I asked. "Hell, ain't it enough?" Kerr responded. The president grinned, picked up the telephone, and—attempting to imitate a Southern drawl—quoted Senator Kerr to "his dumb fuckin' brother." Ross Bohannon soon was confirmed as a federal judge, and Kennedy soon got action on his investment credit bill.

The "how laws are made" pamphlet doesn't say so, but legislators sometimes trade their votes for committee assignments they covet. Olin Johnston of South Carolina was an atypical Southerner in that he had an almost one hundred percent voting record for labor; despite his mushmouth pronouncements against civil rights—which he dared not *not* do at the time—he was a very liberal senator. Once, after he'd spoken against a civil rights bill and stood at the rear of the Senate chamber, taking in the background of cream and dark-red marble, gold silk damask walls, and the rich gleam of mahogany desks, he listened a while to the states-rights and white supremacy spewings of his South Carolina colleague, Strom Thurmond, and then turned to say, "Listen to ol' Strom. He really *believes* all that shit."

Because of this maverick attitude, Olin Johnston was not in favor with the mossback conservatives of the Senate, and he was considered too independent—or unreliable—by Senators Lyndon Johnson and Bob Kerr. He tried, in vain, to land a place on the Democratic Steering Committee but wasn't trusted because he might harm the cause of oil. One day he came lumbering up to me in the cloakroom, pulled me aside, and said, as he chomped on a wad of chewing tobacco, "Bubby, I ache in my bones to git on that Steering Committee but your friends Lyndon and

Bob Kerr won't hear to it. Whut I got to do?" I said, "Well, senator, they're a little concerned about how you'd be on oil." He nodded, masticated his tobacco, lumbered over to a spitoon—a big man with ill-fitting clothing always spotted by tobacco juice—and, after making his splashy deposit, shuffled back to me in his flat-foot gait. "Awright, then," he said. "You go tell Lyndon and Bob I'll vote for their natural gas bill and anything else oil wants, short of hanging all the poor folks. Hell, if it'll do any good, I'll comb my hair with crude oil." Lyndon Johnson whooped with glee when I told him the story—complete with my version of Olin Johnston's accent, walk, and tobacco-chewing techniques—and the trade was made. The minority leader loved making a good swap. "Nothing tickled my daddy more," he'd say, "than trading a bad mule for a good mule." The son enjoyed the technique as much as the father.

Another senator who knew how to trade for what he wanted was Senator James O. Eastland of Mississippi. "Massa Jim," as his detractors call him, is still going strong in his seventy-fourth year and, as always, is a mover and shaker in the inner circles. Senator Eastland's proximity to power—and his real friendships with the Kennedys and other national leaders—has always puzzled outsiders who know only his image as a fat, cigar-chomping, mushmouth who looks like—and often is credited with acting the part of—a political neanderthal. He's right out of the pages of Robert Penn Warren's *All the King's Men,* a wealthy plantation owner who is undisturbed by press criticisms of the hundreds of thousands of dollars he accepts in farm subsidies each year. "I qualify under the law" is the only explanation or defense he offers. ADA liberals love to froth at Jim Eastland's anti-civil rights, pro-law and order, and anti-red stances. His longtime press secreaty, Ralph Hutto, used to joke, on the level, "My job is to get Jim Eastland's name in the Mississippi newspapers—and keep it out everywhere else."

Yet, I found Jim Eastland to possess one of the quicker, more brilliant minds in the Senate. It's a tribute to his political genius that he's managed to satisfy the most reactionary element of his Mississippi constituency and, at the same time, remain a working power and influence among his Senate colleagues. No dumb man could do that.

Senator Eastland was the politician's politician. You could make deals with him. Publically, he might rant and rave, as when James Meredith racially integrated the University of Mississippi in 1961, but behind the scenes he worked closely with President Kennedy and Attorney General Robert Kennedy to defang Mississippi's governor, Ross Barnett, who did not have a very bad dose of the smarts, and who the Washington Establishment feared might make a terrible situation even worse. Senator

Eastland got along equally well with Lyndon Johnson; he reached his ze-
nith during the Nixon years when the so-called Southern strategy was in
vogue. Yet, he took Senator Edward Kennedy under his wing when the
youngest of the Kennedy brothers arrived in the Senate and told him,
"Boy, your brothers never made it here because they used the Senate to
run for president. You may want to run for president someday yourself,
but you'll be happier here and make more friends if you'll do your
homework. Don't try to avoid the ditch-digging. It's part of the job."
Senator Eastland also gets along with his colleagues by allowing his committee members—as chairman of the Judiciary Committee and ranking
Democrat on Agriculture—many patronage plums and large staffs;
though few know it, he always has been one of the top fund raisers for
the Democratic Senatorial Campaign Committee through tapping his af-
fluent oil and agri-biz contacts.

Senator Eastland not only is a pragmatist, he's a man of his word. I
learned this when the Alaskan statehood bill came up for action on the
Senate floor.

Lyndon B. Johnson had fled to Texas so he would not be involved in
the statehood proceedings—Texans, coveting their distinction as citizens
of the nation's largest state, did not want to relinquish the title; their hostile opposition to Alaskan statehood was almost comically unreal. Privately, however, LBJ favored the bill. "I'm leaving you and Mike Mansfield in charge," he told me, "and I want you to hold those senators here
until they vote. The Dixiecrats are gonna be filibustering, but I want you
to break it up. When I get back, I want us to have forty-nine states."

I persuaded Senator Mansfield, who only reluctantly consented, that
Lyndon Johnson's order should be taken quite literally. We would, indeed, "hold those senators here" by having continuous sessions throughout the filibuster. We'd end one legislative session at 11:59 P.M., and then
immediately begin a new legislative day two minutes later at 12:01 A.M.
The theory was to give the filibustering senators no rest. They'd have to
remain in or near the Senate chamber the clock around, in order to be
certain they'd not lose the floor to the proponents of Alaskan statehood,
who'd been advised to use all the parliamentary tricks and guiles at their
disposal. In this way we'd break the spirit of the filibuster gang and,
eventually, the filibuster itself. LBJ would get his vote.

We put the plan in effect to great cries of anguish from senators who
did not cotton to grabbing naps on hard, narrow cots and taking whore's
baths at their office sinks rather than lolling in the bathtub. Jim Eastland
came to me in furious temper. "Bobby," he said, "this is a disgrace. This
is no way to treat United States senators. You're likely to kill a bunch of
old men here and you ought to be ashamed of yourself."

I said, "Senator Eastland, I don't enjoy it either. But I'm following the majority leader's orders. Your people are trying to talk this bill to death, and I'm instructed not to let that happen."

Eastland said, "Bobby, this can't go on. If a senator's heart fails him because he's fatigued, you'll be marked for life. You'll never have a decent night's sleep."

I knew the senator was trying to psych me out, so I said, "Well, senator, *I* can't stop the filibuster. But there are those who can. It seems to me that if a senator died and I'd had the *power* to stop the filibuster, but had refused to use it, maybe *then* I'd have blood on my hands."

Senator Eastland knew I'd lobbed the ball back into his court, and he came as near grinning as I ever saw him. After a moment he said, "Alright, I hear you. But we've got to make a substantial record for our home folks, so I can't call it off immediately. But I'll make a deal with you. If you'll see to it that the Senate adjourns early tomorrow morning—Friday—until 10 A.M. on Monday, I'll give you my word that the unlimited debate won't run past Tuesday."

I said, "Senator, you've got a deal. And your decision is gonna make a lot of people happy, including me. I'd like a little rest and recreation myself."

We shook hands on it. True to his word—and despite some angry rhetoric in opposition from Strom Thurmond—Senator Eastland turned the filibuster off on Tuesday. That's how we got a vote on Alaskan statehood and, of course, the bill easily passed.

Senator Bob Kerr knew more ways to skin the legislative cat than most. Of course, he had more resources than most. Not only was he gifted in his understandings of power, he had all the components to make power work. If need be, he could threaten and bluster while employing the Senate's fastest and most acerbic tongue. He also was a master of silver-tongued oratory and could charm a snake when required. His largest advantage, however, was knowing what money could do. When he wanted to pass a bill favorable to the oil industry or to banking, or to gain public works projects for Oklahoma, he did not hesitate to dip into his personal fortune to buy votes. Or, as with Medicare or national health insurance proposals—which he hated—he would spend money to bottle a bill up in committee or otherwise deal it a fatal blow.

The Oklahoma senator handled these transactions personally, though often I knew when he had his eye on another senator's integrity because he'd ask me for information concerning that senator's financial situation or general approachability. Naturally, when Kerr made a buy he and the other party to the transaction called it a "loan"; senators, after

"Senator James Eastland said, 'Bobby, this can't go on. If a senator's heart fails him because he's fatigued, you'll be marked for life.' I knew the crafty old Mississippi pragmatist was trying to psych me out." (*Wide World Photos*)

all, have their dignity to keep. He once wryly said, "A certain kind of business has to be done behind the door. If I didn't handle these deals personally, or if I failed to dress them up with pretty little speeches, most of these fellows would be spooked."

Senator Kerr once told me he'd arranged for several friends and relatives of a congressman highly placed on the tax-writing House Ways and Means Committee, to buy into proven, producing oil wells at bargain prices; he said he did the same for a powerful senator on the Senate Finance Committee.

If Senator Kerr knew the benefits of taking care of others, he also took pleasure in feathering his own nest. During the Eisenhower years, Senator Kerr arranged—through Admiral Strauss, chairman of the Atomic Energy Commission—for the conglomerate in which he was a partner, Kerr-McGee, to sell all the uranium it could produce to the government.

As chairman of the Senate Space Committee, Senator Kerr worked through our mutual friend Fred Black—top lobbyist for North American Aviation—to create plants in Oklahoma which would hire 20,000 of Kerr's constituents should North American become the Apollo missile prime contractor. Kerr then pressured James Webb, director of the National Aeronautic and Space Administration—and, conveniently, an executive on loan to the government from the senator's own Kerr-McGee company—to give North American Aviation favorable treatment on the Apollo contract. Webb certainly did nothing to stand in the way, and North American got it. Earlier. North American Aviation officials had met with Kerr to say that yes, they could provide 20,000 jobs in Oklahoma in exchange for the Apollo contract. But one of them added, "However, we've got a problem, senator. Some of the equipment will be so large it can't be moved except by water. And Oklahoma is landlocked." Senator Kerr said, "Tell me how wide and deep you want the ditch and the government will dig it." At, of course, the expense of the nation's taxpayers.

I discovered in 1962 that just as Senator Kerr bought some senators, he was not above putting himself up for sale should the price be right. President Kennedy had sent to the Senate a tax bill that would have taxed savings and loan associations at the rate the commercial banks were taxed on their profits; this would have amounted to about five percent increase in taxes for these institutions—forty-three million dollars. Predictably, the savings and loan boys reacted as if they'd found a dead mouse in their soup kettle. Despite all the savings and loan people could do—and their members from all across the nation descended on Washington like a swarm of locusts in a lettuce field, buttonholing their senators and representatives in an effort to stop the tax bill—it went forward. The Senate Finance Committee favorably reported out the tax bill on July 10, 1962; it passed the full Senate on September 6 of that year. Since the House had passed a slightly different version, it became necessary for a conference committee, comprised of members of both legislative bodies, to iron out the differences and present a bill acceptable to both bodies.

At this point I was approached by Glenn Troop, chief lobbyist for the United States Saving and Loan League, who was an old friend, and he was having conniptions. "Bobby, that fucking bill will ruin us," he said. "We figure it will cost us a minimum of $43 million *annually*. We just can't live with it. My ass is on the line. Help me."

"What can I do?" I asked.

"Give us some help with Senator Kerr," he said. "He's on the conference committee and he can kill or amend that bill."

I said, "Are you crazy? He's one of the sponsors of that bill. He's a commercial banker and he's not favorably disposed toward your people." We were eating lunch in the Quorum Club, and I paused over my steak to permit Troop to respond. He said, "Bobby, we'll do anything to kill that bill. *Anything!*"

"Well," I said, "I'll have to go to Senator Kerr carrying a lot of ammunition. I can't just say, 'The poor savings and loan boys have stepped in deep shit and I'd appreciate your helping 'em out.' Frankly, I doubt there's much that can be done. All your arguments have been presented in committee and on the floor in both houses and you got your ass beat."

Troop urged me to have lunch with several of his clients, top guns of the nation's larger savings and loan companies. He set it up at the Statler-Hilton. Among those who attended were Kenneth Childs, representing the Home Savings & Loan Association, which had twenty-three branches and more than $2 billion in assets; Howard Ahmanson, principal owner of the Home Savings & Loan Association; Stuart Davis, chairman of the board of Great Western Financial Coproration; Charles Wellman, president of First Charter Finance Corporation; and Mark Taper, chairman of the same company; Glenn Troop also was present. I did not feel they made a strong case, and so—a few days later, after having told them to come to me with more compelling arguments—I hosted a luncheon for the same executives in my Capitol Hill office. Again, they failed to overwhelm me with information. Ultimately, however—at Glenn Troop's urging, and because he was my good friend—I approached Senator Kerr and began to lay out their case.

Senator Kerr astonished me by cutting me off in midsentence. "My friend," he said, "I have no sympathy for those bastards. I'm a commercial banker and I feel strongly that they should pay equal taxes. But if you trust the people you're dealing with, tell them it will cost them $400,000 if I'm successful in their behalf."

I simply couldn't believe it, couldn't find any words to say. While I knew that Kerr worshipped money, I couldn't believe he'd reverse himself on a bill important to commercial bankers, himself incuded. Yet, he was telling me that for $400,000 he'd sell out his banker buddies.

"This won't be an easy job," Kerr grumbled. "Jack Kennedy and Wilbur Mills are allied together for the bill. I'll be fighting the entire power apparatus. And I'll need my money in cash."

When I found my voice I said, "Senator, can you stop or amend the bill at this late date?"

He said, shortly, "If I didn't think I could I wouldn't make the proposition."

When I reported this conversation to Glenn Troop, the lobbyist dropped his mouth open and said, *"Jesus shit!"* Then he said, "Let me talk to my people and get back to you. I'm not at all sure we can raise that much money."

I secretly felt relieved, and half hoped he couldn't raise it. I'd started feeling uneasy about my role in the scheme. Not that I permitted myself to think it through and say to myself, *Baker, you're breaking the law. Don't do it. Don't get involved in a conspiracy.* No, I pushed those thoughts away. But I did feel vaguely uneasy and had bad karma. Even though I'd seen a lot, and had closed my eyes to a lot, this one felt different. How many times since have I wished I'd listened to those nervous ripples within myself!

Within hours, however, Troop called me back and said, "Tell your man he's got a deal."

I recall that we were walking in the grassy park separating the Capitol Building from the Supreme Court Building across the way, tame squirrels and fat pigeons scurrying about under the trees, when I told the senator that the deal was on. "How well do you know this fellow Glenn Troop and how much do you trust him?" he asked.

I said, "Senator, I'd trust him with my life, my wife, and my pocketbook. We're close personal friends. We take vacations together. We socialize together."

"Does he drink?" he asked.

"Yeah," I said, "but just about everybody does except you and Billy Graham."

The senator did not think it funny. He said, "Goddammit, Bobby, I mean does he have a drinking problem? Does he get loose-lipped when he's drinking or can he keep his damn mouth shut?"

"I'd make book he won't talk. He couldn't keep his job if he gossiped about what he knows."

"If you trust him," Senator Kerr said, "then make the arrangements. Handle it personally. I don't want those bastards coming to see me every thirty minutes, either. Tell them to keep their distance."

"Well," I said, "I know that Troop and maybe one or two of his bigshot clients will want to visit with you. You can't expect 'em to buy a pig in a poke."

"Just one of 'em can see me," he said. "And tell them not to bring money and not to mention money. *You* handle that part of it."

On September 24, 1962, Glenn Troop and I arranged for Kenneth Childs—largest of the savings and loan moguls—to meet with Senator Kerr in a large, stately anteroom just off the Senate floor. Mr. Childs would later testify that they talked only of mundane and inconsequential matters.

Though I did not know it at the time, Glenn Troop would later attest that he had met in California on September 27—only two days after Senator Kerr had delivered an acceptable bill—at the home of Howard Ahmanson, with the host, plus Kenneth Childes, Mark Taper, and another savings and loan official named John Marten. On returning to Washington from Los Angeles, Troop rushed to my office, carefully closed the door, and said, "Bobby, I'm embarrassed. My people say they

"I said, 'Dammit, Troop, Bob Kerr is gonna piss all over me. He'll hold me responsible.'" Far left, lobbyist and friend Glenn Troop of the savings and loan interests.

can't come up with more than $200,000 in hidden cash without robbing their own companies, and they aren't about to do that."

I said, "Glenn, you son-of-a-bitch, I told Bob Kerr your people would stay hitched and I told him that on the basis of your word to me."

"I'm helpless," Troop said. "I work for those people and I follow their orders. And they just can't come up with $400,000. We're not trying to be cute or embarrass you; it just can't be done. Here's what we *can* do: $100,000 now, or as soon as we can get the cash together. Plus another $100,000 in 1964, and that's it."

I said, "Dammit, Troop, Bob Kerr is gonna piss all over me! He'll hold *me* responsible!" Troop tugged at his fingers and looked miserable, mumbling apologies.

Senator Kerr exploded on hearing the bad news. "I told you those bastards were no fucking good!" he shouted as he pounded his desk. "Those pricks have always tried to do everything on the cheap and they always will. They'll be sorry for this, those cocksuckers! I'm gonna fuck 'em at every turn from now on." When he'd exhausted his store of invective and had calmed himself a bit he said, "Alright. If that's it, then that's it. But they're gonna regret it. Get me my money."

On October 21, I received a telephone call from Stuart Davis of Great Western Financial Corporation. He said he was just in from California and "I've made the arrangements you discussed with Mr. Troop."

I asked him to meet me at the Carlton Hotel, not far from the White House; I had a key to a suite kept there by Fred Black (the North American Aviation lobbyist from whom Senator Kerr consistently profitted at cards), where Black, myself, and other Washington politicos sometimes repaired for private recreations. When we had settled back with drinks, Davis handed me two white enevelopes. "It's not all there," he said. "We need a little more time." I counted the money. One envelope contained $33,100; the other contained $17,000. Davis said I could expect the balance of the first $100,000 within a few days.

The next morning, as I have testified, I visited Senator Kerr in his Washington apartment, at 1500 Massachusetts Avenue, and delivered the partial payment. He was most unhappy. "Those bastards are trying to welch on the deal," he complained. After having coffee, I walked the few blocks with him to the National Savings and Trust Company, about a block from the White House, where the senator deposited the $50,100 in his lockbox. On October 31, John Marten of Great Western Finance met me in the Black suite at the Carlton Hotel and handed me another white envelope. I counted it and found $16,200. "You're $33,700 short," I said. Marten explained that each of several companies had been assigned a certain amount of money to raise, and that the balance would "be coming soon" from another source. Senator Kerr was in Oklahoma campaigning; when he returned on November 5, I again visited his apartment and turned over the cash. He said, "Goddammit, Bobby, this has gone far enough. Tell those pricks to quit dribbling this in." Again, I walked with him to the bank where he once more placed the cash in his lockbox.

I went to Glenn Troop and told him that Kerr wanted the balance of the $100,000 and he wanted it damn quickly. Troop has sworn that he telephoned Charles Wellman of First Charter Finance Corporation, in Los Angeles, and told him I would fly to California on November 9, and "You should be prepared to fully assist him." This meant he should have the money ready. I flew to L.A. where Wellman met me, and took me to see Mark Taper in his office. After we'd exchanged brief pleasantries, Mr. Taper handed me an envelope and said he thought I'd find everything in order. I put the money in my briefcase without counting it. Mr. Wellman drove me back to the airport and I caught a plane for Washington within minutes. En route, I counted the money in the airplane's restroom and found $33,300. "The bastards" had come up $400 short. "I'm not a damn bit surprised," Senator Kerr said when I told him of the shortage. That was the last money Senator Kerr would collect from "the bastards": he would die on January 1, 1963, a year before the next $100,000 payment was due. And I would go to jail over that money.

Chapter Nine

Fear and Loathing
in Los Angeles

*Senator Kerr slammed me in the face with his open
palm. It sounded like a dynamite cap exploding.*

QUESTIONS about my fall usually come at a late hour, after my
inquisitors have lost their social inhibitions, though I've had
sober strangers accost me with the same hard questions in the glare of
day. I wish I had a neat, packaged answer capable of satisfying both my
inquisitors and myself. There are too many maddening "ifs," too many
dark ironies, too many decisions made in haste and repented at leisure,
to permit a clear picture of a very personal puzzle composed of many
complicated parts. My reactions are necessarily subjective.

To be "objective" about events that have radically changed and consumed one's life requires more of a saint than I ever expect to be. I have
no doubt that fifteen years of legal troubles, investigations, public hearings, bad publicity, official harassments, mental anguish, costly attorney's fees, and a prison stretch of more than sixteen months have combined to age me prematurely and shorten my life expectancy—to say
nothing of having destroyed my life's work. Sorry, but I can't be entirely
"objective" about that.

I do not mean to claim that Bobby Baker was an angel. When I attempt to summarize my mistakes, and they were many, I think of a
phrase once used to describe me in better days. Senator Joe O'Mahoney
of Wyoming, offering generous remarks about my work as executive
director of the platform committee at the 1956 Democratic National
Convention in Chicago, warmly described me as "a child of the Senate."
In quite another context, I agree with him. In other words, I too un-
thinkingly reflected the careless attitudes and the self-serving values of
the Senate at a time when the rules of personal conduct were fast and
loose. I fell victim to the arrogance of power.

Like my bosses and sponsors in the Senate, I was ambitious and eager to feather my personal nest. As they opened Washington "law offices" through which they funneled fees for personal services, even though rarely visiting those offices or actually practicing law, so did I. As they presumed their high stations to entitle them to accept gratuities or hospitalities from patrons who had special axes to grind, so did I. As they took advantage of privileged information to get in on the ground floor of attractive investments, so did I. As they used their powerful positions to gain loans or credit that otherwise might not have been granted, so did I. It was a monkey-see monkey-do situation, and I did not stop to consider where it might be leading.

It's easy, now, to say that Bobby Baker—or anyone else—should have known better; that there is no free lunch, that the piper must always be paid for his tune. I agree. But that's in retrospect: after the fact, post-prison, post-Watergate. But when you are young and hungry, and you see presidents, vice-presidents, senators, and cabinet members living the good life free of the normal restraints—riding high and mighty and receiving public adulation despite their private sins or errors, and when those same powerful men are blowing smoke up your ass and inviting you to join the feast—well, you are likely to sit down at the table and not worry about the eventual tab or think that you are the likely one to pay it.

Perhaps more than most I understand how the Cubans who broke into the Watergate complex, or the former CIA men who directed them, did so without pausing to reflect on their improprieties. This does not mean that they were not guilty of bad judgment or even of crimes, but my own experiences tend to make me both sympathize and empathize with them. They knew of "black bag jobs"—burglaries—by the FBI, and worse from the CIA, and they knew these unlawful activities had been officially condoned in the highest places. I can even understand how those involved in the Watergate cover-up rationalized their actions, by telling themselves they were protecting their causes as much as themselves, before suddenly finding themselves mired in deeper legal bogs than they'd suspected—though, as you will come to know, I harbor no special love for certain members of the Watergate gang. They pressured me to deliver derogatory information on leading Democrats, under the threat of sending me back to jail when I had been out of prison but a matter of weeks, and the idea of again being locked up simply petrified me. I walked away from that unsavory experience thinking: *Nothing's changed. The strong still walk on the weak and erring politicians in power will use any tactic or leverage to cover their own asses.*

I often saw and heard my presumed Senate betters when they were not at their best. "Good" senators as well as "bad" senators lavishly junketed around the world at taxpayers' expense, spending foreign-deposited tax-counterpart funds for personal items and to entertain

"I was executive director of the platform committee at the 1956 Democratic National Convention in Chicago." Here, on the left, I kneel to listen to Senator Stuart Symington of Missouri. Others, seated left to right: House Majority Leader John McCormack, Speaker Sam Rayburn, Congressman Clarence Cannon.

themselves and their ladies, while claiming to be investigating this or that legislative problem. Almost all senators abused their franking privileges by mailing out self-serving promotional materials at the expense of the taxpayers rather than themselves. Because they were afraid to vote themselves legitimate pay increases to keep up with inflation, out of fear of retributions by the electorate, they quietly and frequently boosted their office allowances, stationery allowances, telephone and telegraph allowances, travel allowances, and numberless other perks. They put relatives on their payrolls or had cozy brother-in-law arrangements with other senators: you hire my son and I'll hire your daughter. They accepted generous "honorariums" to speak to special-interest groups for whom they carried legislative water, and never thought of their fees as a form of bribery. They took cash "contributions" in nonelection years, or when they had no opposition or only token opposition, and stuck the money in special banks in the Capitol Building where no tax agent or FBI man or anyone else might pry unless the full House or Senate passed a simple resolution authorizing it—and no such authorization has been given in all history.

In my day, though the practice has been discontinued, every congressman or senator elected would immediately be offered a commission as an officer in whatever branch of military service he had been in, no matter if he'd been no more than a PFC in his prior incarnation. (Senator Barry Goldwater of Arizona became the highest ranking armchair warrior on the Hill, an air force general.) Each branch of the military had its special Capitol Hill reserve unit; its white-collar soldiers accepted drill pay and credit toward retirement pensions for meeting once a week to drink coffee, plan their next junket, and listen to Pentagon officials scare them into voting more money for their particular branch of service. Thus when Pentagon rivalries flared, each service extended the battle to the legislative halls by leaning on its Capitol Hill partisans, no matter that such infighting produced duplicate programs and other costly or wasteful practices.

One of the more spirited fights I recall from my Hill days pitted General Dynamics and the U.S. Navy against Boeing Aircraft and the army, in a competition for the contract to develop the controversial TFX fighter plane. Vice-President Lyndon Johnson, Speaker Sam Rayburn, Congressman Jim Wright of Fort Worth (now House majority leader), in whose home district General Dynamics was located, and Secretary of the Navy John Connally, also a Texan, championed the General Dynamics–navy team; Senators Scoop Jackson and Warren Magnuson of Washington, the home of Boeing, carried water for that company and for the army. The Washingtonians proved no match for the powerful Texans, who persuaded Defense Secretary Robert McNamara and President Kennedy to come down on the side of General Dynamics. The makings of a first-rate scandal were there: boondoggling cost factors, suspect sworn testimony as to tests and performance, and multiple malfunctions in the development of the aircraft. Senator John McClellan of Arkansas conducted well-publicized hearings, but little was accomplished or mended. Lyndon Johnson was among those who brought quiet pressure on Senator McClellan to permit the TFX hearings to peter out without unduly embarrassing the mighty.

Getting elected to the House or Senate gave a man a good leg up on getting about half rich. Should a representative or senator land on the Banking Committee in his respective body, he was certain to be offered opportunities as a stockholder or director in numerous financial institutions; most availed themselves of the opportunity. Members of the Housing Subcommittee might be offered cut-rate homes if they would let word get out they'd bought into a given housing development. The examples of *quid pro quo* are endless.

Sometimes the balm desired by certain senators proved comical. Old Senator Olin Johnston, of my native state, was a costume jewelry freak. He loved to present gaudy baubles and trinkets to almost every woman he met; one can only hope the tastes of such ladies were as abominable as his. A friend of mine once advised a lobbyist, "If you want to get close to Olin Johnston, take him a gunnysack full of costume jewelry, pour it out on his desk, and let nature take its course." The lobbyist did so. He later reported, "Senator Johnston's eyes glittered and he ran his hands through those cheap-ass trinkets like a miser fondling gold. It was the best investment I ever made."

Bob Kerr also got some weird satisfaction out of a situation involving Claude Wilde, lobbyist for Gulf Oil, who once told him that I had a bad reputation and was a crook. "What's ol' Claude got on you?" he teased. I was flabbergasted. "Senator," I said, "I've never had a nickel's worth of dealings with that man. I don't know him except to say 'hello' to. Have I ever lied to you, or misled you?" Senator Kerr grinned and the grin turned into a chuckle. He said, "Well, maybe you and Claude ought to get to know each other a little better. He's got $5,000 that Gulf Oil wants to deliver to Senator Joe Hickey [of Wyoming] and I want you to go with him to make the delivery." I did so, refraining from asking questions, while wondering what perverse strain of misguided humor had caused Senator Kerr to make that peculiar arrangement. I can only conclude, since Bob Kerr always had likened me to a son, that he somehow wanted to inflict some measure of humiliation on the lobbyist or extract some unspecified revenge by pairing him with a man he'd badmouthed. Mr. Wilde seemed most uncomfortable as we walked together to the Old Senate Office Building, where he surrendered the cash to Senator Hickey in my presence. To tell you the truth, I rather enjoyed his discomfort. (Claude Wilde later would be one of numerous lobbyists fined for making illegal corporate contributions in the 1972 campaign.)

Senator Hugh Scott, the Pennsylvania Republican, made many pious and partisan speeches against me during Senate hearings into my business activities. This irked me in the extreme, as it later came out that the Gulf lobbyist, Claude Wilde, had for years paid Senator Scott $10,000 cash dollars per year as legal fees. Though Senator Ed Brooke of Massachusetts demanded an investigation, the Senate Ethics Committee voted him down, five to one. Senator Scott, after these and other embarrassing disclosures, opted to retire from the Senate in 1976.

That same Senate Ethics Committee, however, employed a double standard when it came to Senate staffers. Where it refused to investigate Senator Scott, it recommended the dismissal of an administrative assis-

"Senator Hugh Scott, the
Pennsylvania Republican,
made many pious and par-
tisan speeches against me.
. . . He accused me of running an abortion ring and
inquired whether I knew
gamblers and white-slav-
ers I'd never heard of."
(*United Press International*)

tant to Senator Daniel Inouye of Hawaii because he, too, had accepted
cash funds from Claude Wilde. This reminded me of the attitude of
senators years earlier, when the hearings into my conduct were getting
underway. Asked about rumors that some senators reportedly had been
involved in business dealings with me, Chairman Everett Jordan of
North Carolina snapped, "We're not in the business of investigating
senators." Only Senate employees, lobbyists, and nonsenators were
grilled about their associations with me—and many of the lobbyists were
only gingerly and perfunctorily questioned before being excused.

It was near-comical during the Senate hearings into the "Baker scandals" to hear Bedford Wynne, a wealthy Texan, attempt to give a pass-
able answer when asked why he had sought me out when one of his
many companies became interested in getting a government contract to
operate experimental saline water plants:

MR. McLENDON (committee counsel): "Mr. Wynne, I don't want to be critical, but
of the thousands of people that live in the District of Columbia, why would you
pick Bobby Baker?"

MR. WYNNE: "There are thousands of people who live here, yes. It just happens that I knew him better than most, and he is a friend of mine, as I told you, and had been for a number of years."

It would not have done for Bedford Wynne to have made an affirmation of the obvious: that I was highly placed, that while I had a reputation as a Mr. Fixit I often acted as the functionary of powerful senators or accomplished my purposes through them, and that he might have fared less well had he sought out a taxi driver, hot-dog vendor, slum lord, or any other of the "thousands" of people living in the District of Columbia. Bedford was a tough and experienced businessman who knew how to play the Washington game; he knew that the senators did not really want him to explore Capitol Hill's operations—especially should the tracks lead into senatorial offices which might be their own. So he offered them a namby-pamby answer and kept a straight face while the senators solemnly nodded and accepted it. The Senate, indeed, always takes care of its own. What I temporarily forgot was that I was not one of its own, merely "a child of the Senate"—or maybe just a stepchild.

I was the man to whom people came when they wanted to cut a big deal, and I was the man who went to my powerful superiors to relay the offers. I recall when a man who'd been in Princeton with John F. Kennedy (JFK spent a semester there before transferring to Harvard) approached me with a flat $1 million offer if he might be named ambassador to England, France, Italy, Germany, or Spain. This was during the 1960 campaign; I arranged to see Jack Kennedy at his apartment in the Waldorf Towers in New York. After exchanging pleasantries with Mrs. Jackie Kennedy, I told the Democratic nominee that I needed to confer with him. He led me into the kitchen unit of the Waldorf apartment, and peeled an orange while I named the New York socialite who'd made the offer and related what he required for his money.

Senator Kennedy, talking low so as to save his voice for the campaign stump—and possibly so that his wife might not hear—said, "Bobby, you were right in coming straight to me rather than to go through intermediaries. But first, Bobby, that guy's simply a prick. Second, we could all go to jail should this go any further; it's illegal as hell to sell ambassadorships. As much as we need the money there's no way we can do it. That prick would be the first one to tell." The senator did not lecture me on the impropriety of having approached him with an illegal offer; nor did he pick up the telephone to alert the Justice Department. He treated it as an offer he found expedient and prudent to refuse, and there was no moralizing about it.

President Kennedy also used me to carry a message to Lyndon Johnson. One day a few months before I fell from grace—it must have been in the spring of 1963—I was about to leave the president's Oval Office when he asked me to resume my seat. He lit a cigar, crossed his legs, and reared back in his famous rocking chair.

"Bobby," he said, "I really feel sorry for Lyndon. I know he's unhappy in the vice-presidency. It's a horseshit job, the worst fucking job I can imagine. The duties are so limited under the Constitution, and the president must make the day-to-day decisions and set policy—he simply can't delegate much of substance to the vice-president. Lyndon's done a terrific job in everything I've asked him to do, but there's not all that much to occupy him."

The president puffed on his cigar and then continued, "Lyndon's an activist if ever one was born, and he's simply a miserable son-of-a-bitch in that office. I watch him in our cabinet meetings, and solicit his opinions, but he's so cautious that he won't say much or make major contributions. I *know* he's suppressing his instincts out of a sense of loyalty to me, but it would help if he'd speak up. I really want to know what's on his mind, and I'm sure he'd feel better if he did."

I said, "Mr. President, I agree. It's in Lyndon Johnson's nature to speak up. But, begging your pardon, I think he's afraid to. I think he feels that some of your cabinet members and the 'palace guard' are looking to cut his throat and dump him from the ticket in 1964."

President Kennedy made an impatient gesture. "Shit, I've read all that crap in the papers," he said. "It distresses me and I've told my people I'll kick ass if I hear them spreading that horseshit around. What I want you to do is tell Lyndon how much I truly appreciate him as vice-president. Convey to him I know he's got a tough role and that I'm sympathetic. Get it across that he's a valuable man to me and that he has nothing to fear"—and here the president flashed a grin and imitated the cadence of Franklin Roosevelt—"but fear itself."

I said that I would pass on the message, and hesitated in the hope that the president would ask me what he might be doing, or not doing, that made Lyndon Johnson so unhappy. I wanted to tell him that LBJ felt offended because he thought the Kennedys excluded and snubbed him socially, except for formal state dinners at the White House; that the vice-president yearned for nothing so much as to relax with Jack Kennedy over a few drinks in the family quarters, kick off his shoes, and talk politics in the informal way he'd always done as Senate majority leader. I was reluctant to volunteer this information, however, because it seemed such a personal matter and I didn't want to give the impression that LBJ had been grousing and whining behind the president's back—even though he had been. The president did not solicit my comments, however, and soon stood as a signal that our meeting was at an end.

I added a little sugar and butter to JFK's praise of his vice-president when transmitting it to Johnson, and stressed the president's hope that LBJ might be more forceful in cabinet meetings. He did not seem impressed; indeed, during this entire vice-presidency, LBJ had a glum hang-dog air about him. He was almost impossible to cheer up. "If I speak one word of disagreement with the cabinet and White House staff looking on," he said, "then they'll put it out to Joe Kraft and Sander Vanocur and everybody that I'm a damned traitor. You don't know how they treat me over there. Oh, sure, Jack Kennedy's as thoughtful and considerate of me at those meetings as he can be. But I know his snot-nosed brother's after my ass, and all those high-falutin's Harvards, and if I give 'em enough rope they'll hang me with it. So I'm gonna do what Jack Kennedy asks me to, when he asks me to, because he's my president. But I'm not gonna stick my head in the noose at cabinet meetings. All Jack Kennedy's gotta do, if he really wants my opinion, is pick up the telephone." And then, sure enough, he began to complain anew of being socially snubbed at the White House and claimed that Lady Bird was hurt by the Kennedys' inattention more than he was. For all his talents and strengths, Lyndon Johnson often was a professional crybaby. Should he be denied his slightest whim, then there was a worldwide conspiracy against him: he was the only guy, to hear him tell it, who was four-square for mother and for God and against communism. Everybody else was either confused or mistaken.

On an earlier occasion, when I was leaving the Oval Office after a conference with the president, JFK said to me in a hearty and jovial manner, "Bobby, how about this damned Texas tycoon, what's his name? Billy Sol Estes? Is he a pal of yours?" I sensed that the president was on a fishing expedition, attempting to find out what I might know of any connections between his vice-president and the Texas wheeler-dealer who'd just been charged with any number of crimes including swindles involving federal agencies, lending institutions, and many individuals ranging from oil moguls to dirt farmers. Matching his mood, I said—and truthfully—"Mr. President, I thought I knew every thief who'd ever crossed the Potomac with his hand out. But we got lucky on the Estes thing. He's in the political camp of Senator Ralph Yarborough of Texas, and you know, sir, that Lyndon and Ralph have always gotten along like cats and dogs. So I'm proud to say I've never had any association with Billy Sol. He was never an LBJ man." Kennedy grinned, looking visibly relieved, and said, "Yeah, that's what Lyndon tells me. I guess you can't lose 'em all."

Though I transported messages, money, and offers of mischief between powerful men, and tried to do it affably, there were times when my temper snapped or someone else's did. I suppose the Democratic National Convention at Los Angeles, in 1960, set a record for tensions, frustrations, and personal snits where I was concerned.

Lyndon Johnson, having denied for four years that he was a candidate for president, hit Los Angeles a newly declared candidate and began to fight with bare knuckles. As one accustomed to the rough and tumble of politics, after which foes might sit down together over a drink, I thought nothing about Senator Johnson's roundhouse swings at Jack Kennedy, who was the obvious leader among a half-dozen Democratic aspirants. Consequently, when I saw Robert F. Kennedy standing in line to eat breakfast in the Biltmore Hotel, I invited him to join me and my wife Dorothy. He readily accepted. After we'd ordered breakfast and engaged in the normal banter between political adversaries, I said something to the effect that I thought Teddy Kennedy had been a little rough in saying in Texas that Lyndon Johnson had not recovered from his heart condition. "He's made an amazing recovery," I said, "and everybody knows it." Perhaps I shouldn't have said it, and I would not have said it had I know the reaction it would provoke.

Bobby Kennedy immediately grew so red in the face I thought he might have a stroke. "You've got your nerve," he snapped. "Lyndon Johnson has compared my father to the Nazis and John Connally and India Edwards lied in saying my brother is dying of Addison's disease. You Johnson people are running a stinking damned campaign, and you're gonna get yours when the time comes!" He was leaning forward, clenching his fists, thrusting his face into mine. I was shocked. Realizing that people were watching us, I tried to calm Kennedy. He continued to berate me in harsh terms, saying something to the effect that Johnson's people were no damned good, that they were crooks and a disgrace to decent Democrats. Suddenly he jumped up, slammed three one-dollar bills down on the table, glared at me, and stomped off. After he'd departed I began doing a slow burn: all I'd done was extend a warm invitation to breakfast, make one mild criticism of his younger brother, and in return has suffered a sudden torrent of abuse.

Frankly, I didn't think I'd been any rougher on Bobby than he'd been on me earlier in the year. I'd gone to see the Washington première of *Guys and Dolls,* starring Frank Sinatra. Bobby Kennedy had been standing in the theater lobby, dressed in blue jeans in contrast to the suits and ties of everyone else, and he stopped me to say he had some show business friends he wanted me to meet. I stuck out my hand to accommodate him, and was astonished when Kennedy said, "This is Little Lyndon Johnson and you should ask him why Big Lyndon won't risk running in the primaries against my brother." I was both flabbergasted and irritated that he'd not introduced me by my name, and had made such a crack; when I tried to turn the remark away with a lame joke, Bobby Kennedy persisted: "They're supposed to make 'em tough in Texas, but Big Lyndon doesn't look so tough to me." The put-down left me in a foul mood—as, later, did the stormy scene in Los Angeles at my breakfast table.

My mood worsened after the roll call at the convention a few nights later—on Wednesday, July 13—which Johnson lost to Kennedy 806 to 409; Senator Stuart Symington of Missouri finished with 86 votes, Adlai Stevenson got 79½ as his swan song, and all other candidates totaled 140½ votes.

The results came as no real surprise to me, though I was disappointed that LBJ had received about 45 to 50 fewer votes than I thought he would, and about 100 less than I'd hoped for in my wildest flights of fancy. It was my opinion that Senator Johnson had badly botched his preconvention campaign. For more than a year he'd played it coy, pretending not to be involved in the delegate search being conducted by Walter Jenkins, John Connally, and other loyalists. He claimed no connection with the Citizens for Johnson campaign, based in Washington's scruffy old Ambassador Hotel, though it was manned and operated by his close personal and political friends. I think it was Lyndon Johnson's deep fear of defeat that caused him not only to dodge many primary contests but also led him to declare himself a noncandidate even while holding behind-the-door meetings to hear reports from the dozens of advance men who fanned out across the country to woo delegates for him.

I thought Senator Johnson to be making a mistake. Had he selectively entered primaries in the Southwest, the West, the South, and the Midwest, I think he might have won a number of them. Frustrated, I once called on Speaker Rayburn to urge him to prevail upon his old friend to declare himself a candidate and make a first-rate fight for the nomination. The old man's natural and perpetual scowl deepened. He said, "Bobby, I've already done everything but hold a gun to Lyndon's head. We've had more trouble between us about this damn campaign than anything within my memory. Lyndon's using his friends to raise money and court delegates and he's making them as well as himself look silly by declaring himself a noncandidate. He ought to shit or get off the pot."

LBJ did not declare himself until a few days before the Los Angeles convention. When I learned of his tardy plan I said, "Leader, it may be a little late. Kennedy's won all those primaries and he and the other candidates are gonna say you refused to subject yourself to the judgment of the electorate and now you're trying to steal the prize." He swelled up

"Mr. Rayburn said, 'I've already done everything but hold a gun to Lyndon's head. We've had more trouble about this damn campaign than anything within my memory." From left: LBJ, Congressman John McCormack, Speaker Sam Rayburn, Senator Mike Mansfield.

like a toad and said, "Jack Kennedy and other senators can go gallivantin' around the country kissin' asses and shakin' hands when they want to. But if I'd done it, the Senate business wouldn't have gotten done and the press would have crucified me for running out on my job." I said, "Well, leader, you've said a thousand times you were not a candidate, you were not interested in the job, and now you're likely to look a little foolish changing your tune at the last minute." This really set him off. For five minutes he waved his arms and shouted that he had been sincere in his proclamations, that he was only entering the presidential sweepstakes even now because Sam Rayburn, John Connally, Price Daniel, and others of his friends had driven him crazy on the subject. Then he said, "And now that all you bastards got me to stick my neck out, all I hear is this 'can't win' bullshit. *I've* been consistent all along. It's *you* peckerwoods that keep wringin' your hands and changin' your minds." I bit my lip to hide my irritation at this revisionist history.

For the fact was that Senator Johnson had convinced himself that his and Sam Rayburn's cronies in Congress would deliver their state delegations to him, out of a combination of affection and fear. He believed that because he and Rayburn controlled the flow of congressional business they could call in due bills and twist arms. There were two reasons LBJ made this miscalculation: in a one-party state, such as Texas then was, he and Rayburn could snap their fingers and get what they wanted; he thought it that simple a matter in states where political power was more diffused and diverse. Second, he had not yet recognized that all power no longer flowed from Washington, as it had in the New Deal days, but increasingly was vested in governors and state politicians. LBJ knew few of these.

Johnson also believed that Jack Kennedy never could be nominated. "He's winnin' those beauty contests," he said of the primaries, "but when it gets down to the nut-cuttin' he won't have the old bulls with him." It was his contention that Kennedy, Symington, Stevenson, and others would cut each other up and that the convention—guided by the congressional captains of the various states—then would turn to him as the compromise candidate.

Lyndon Johnson had taken a stubbornly myopic view of his "non-campaign." His attitude was "I'm not running but I'm gonna win." He had been short-fused and distrustful of those who'd told him he had less than a good chance to obtain the Democratic nomination. Once, hearing oral reports from advance men who'd stumped several states, he cut off with a curt "Next!" the poor advance man who'd been in the process of relating how and why Jack Kennedy had Wyoming locked up. LBJ told Walter Jenkins the man was "a defeatist," and soon he no longer was advancing for Johnson. Consequently, fewer and fewer people who had Johnson's ear told him the truth as they saw it. I think he was truly shocked by his first-ballot loss and especially by Kennedy's almost two to one margin of victory.

Humiliated, after the balloting Johnson was like a petulant child in his suite at the Los Angeles Biltmore. He barked at aides, cursed, slammed down telephones. For several days, since arriving in Los Angeles, he'd been receiving bad tidings: three votes had slipped away in Delaware, Pennsylvania was proving disappointingly solid for Kennedy, there was little or nothing for LBJ in Michigan, he now could count on no more than six of Wyoming's fifteen votes. Johnson acted as if he hadn't heard such reports, bounding from delegation to delegation to address the delegates, attacking Jack Kennedy and in particular "the Founding Father," Joe Kennedy; in his own words he was energetically "kissin' asses and shakin' hands."

I had found it my duty to bring more bad news to LBJ. Senator Eugene McCarthy had looked me up to say, "Bobby, I know I told you I'd go with Lyndon. But Adlai Stevenson's asked me to place him in nomination and Mrs. Roosevelt's pressuring me to do it. I think Adlai's foolish for thinking he can win a third nomination, but I owe him my support if he's determined to try. I hope that you'll release me and there'll be no hard feelings on Lyndon's part." I told Senator McCarthy that I was certain LBJ would understand; we shook hands, and Senator McCarthy went on to make the most electrifying nominating speech I've ever heard.

Lyndon Johnson had not been pleased, however. He muttered of a double cross. All these factors had contributed to the foul mood which claimed LBJ that night in the Biltmore.

With Irv Hoff, a politico from the state of Washington, John Connally, and others, I had arranged a party for loyal LBJ campaign workers; some of them had knocked themselves out for a year, traveling the nation to seek delegates or working at Citizens for Johnson campaign headquarters in Washington. I now reminded LBJ of the party. He said, "Well, you can forget that. I'm not goin' to any goddamn party. You don't celebrate when you lose."

I knew that LBJ had ample reason to be weary, irritated, and disappointed. So I spoke in a conciliatory tone. "Leader, a lot of people have worked very hard for you under difficult circumstances. You're not a loser to them. They still love you and believe in you and they'll want to be with you tonight. Your appearance will be the only reward they can expect for their efforts."

Johnson muttered that he had other things on his mind. "I can appreciate that, Leader. But you can't be rude to your friends. They've been disappointed once tonight and you can't disappoint them again. You *did* promise to attend and those people are expecting you." Senator Johnson raised his voice and waved his arms: "You can talk 'til you turn blue, but I'm not goin' to any goddamn party. And I *didn't* promise to attend. First I've heard of the damn thing. That's it and that's final."

It was typical of Lyndon Johnson, when in a snit, to back out of something to which he had agreed when in a better mood. I stalked out of the Biltmore suite in a huff, mumbling about sore losers who go off to hide and pout like little children. I did not know it at the time, but LBJ had learned that the Knight newspapers on the West Coast would be out with

"In his own words, at the 1960 Democratic National Convention, Lyndon Johnson was energetically 'kissin' asses and shakin' hands.' "

a midnight edition saying that John F. Kennedy was considering three men for the vice-presidential spot—and that LBJ was not among them. Johnson felt then, and forever after, that Bobby Kennedy had planted the story in an effort to embarrass him.

The party for the Johnson workers was more of a wake than not. Many loyalists and old friends were openly crying or had tears in their eyes: because of the loss, because of sheer fatigue and frustration. For a while, half hoping that LBJ might change his mind, I kept it to myself that he would not make an appearance. At a given hour, however, it became necessary to invent lame excuses explaining his absence: the senator wasn't feeling well, he was being consulted by Democratic leaders, etc. The announcement only deepened the gloom and brought fresh tears. I might have cried myself had it helped; instead, my therapy was to get independently and calculatedly drunk. Dorothy and I did not get to bed until a very late hour.

The next morning, Thursday, July 14, I was awakened at 7 A.M. by a pounding on the door which equalled that in my head. When I opened the door Bill Moyers blurted, "The boss wants to see you right away." I said, "Well, he'll just have to wait. I haven't got my nap out and I've got a hangover that may be a world's record." Moyers was adamant: LBJ wanted me immediately. "He got his ass beat," I said grumpily "Tell him if he doesn't believe it to read this morning's *Los Angeles Times*. There's not a damn thing I can do about it now. I'll see him later." I shut the door and returned to bed. It seemed that my aching head had no more than touched the pillow before there again was a loud knocking on my door. Moyers was back, and in an agitated state. "Come on," he barked. "It's urgent. The boss can't wait." I grumbled that I'd be along after a shower and a shave. "There's no time for that," Moyers said. "Pull a robe over your pajamas and come on." I dressed hurriedly, feeling like a man who'd awakened in hell with his back broken.

My room was four doors down the Biltmore corridor from Senator Johnson's corner-bedroom suite. I recall thinking, as I stumbled along behind Bill Moyers, of what a contrast the empty hall was compared to the knots and clumps of shoving, sweating newsmen and cameramen who'd been posted there for days, flashing lights into the eyes of all who entered or emerged from LBJ's suite and peppering them with shouted questions. Now the empty hall was a reminder of how quickly people desert a loser.

Lyndon Johnson, still looking glum, beckoned me into his corner bedroom; Lady Bird, a robe over her nightgown, reclined on one of the twin beds. She greeted me with a tired smile and I recall thinking how wan and disspirited she looked. "John Connally's on the way over here," he said. "When he gets here we'll talk about a telephone call I just got from Jack Kennedy." I held back impatient questions, knowing what curiosity had done to the cat; fortunately, Connally almost immediately walked in. As always, he was impeccable in dress and brisk in manner. Unlike the rest of us he didn't look as if he were about to bleed to death from the eyes or had a headache.

"Jack Kennedy's on the way here," Johnson said. "I tried to tell him I'd come to his place, but he said he wasn't anywhere I could reach him handily and he insisted on comin' here." We eyed each other. It was obvious Jack Kennedy wasn't coming over to talk baseball. LBJ then said, "I'd like to hear your thoughts on what I should say if he asks me to run with him." Johnson turned directly to me: "Bobby, you know Jack Kennedy better than we do. What do you think?"

I thought immediately of what Sam Rayburn had advised Adlai Stevenson in 1956. It ran to the effect that Stevenson should choose as his running mate the most able man among the availables, and that it should be someone Stevenson would trust as his successor or to look after his family.

I suggested to Senator Johnson that should Kennedy ask him to join

the ticket he should inquire whether Kennedy sincerely considered him
(1) the most able of the availables, (2) worthy of succeeding him, and (3)
whether he enjoyed the full measure of Kennedy's trust. "And if he says
yes, then you've no choice but to accept. It will be your duty."

Lady Bird, who privately feared that increased political pressures
might endanger her husband's heart, interrupted to express what may
have been her secret hope: "Oh, I'm sure Senator Kennedy's coming to
consult Lyndon. But I doubt if he's coming to ask Lyndon to run." Mrs.
Rose Kennedy—she said—had raised her children to be gracious and
well mannered; she concluded from this that Senator Kennedy would be
paying a courtesy call as a mark of respect to his vanquished opponent.
"No," John Connally said firmly. "I don't think he'd come here without
wanting to do serious business. It's logical that he'll ask Lyndon to run.
We've got to proceed on that assumption."

I said, "Mr. Leader, it's no disgrace to hold the second highest office
in the land and be one heartbeat away from the presidency. If you reject
Jack Kennedy, you'll be rejecting the Democratic party as well. It could
make Kennedy angry and bitter and it could make good Democrats in
the Senate angry. If you force Kennedy to turn to Senator Scoop Jackson or Governor Orville Freeman or someone even more liberal, they'll
be out to gut-shoot you. In time, you could be unseated as majority
leader." John Connally said, "Yes, and you're the only man who can
carry the South for Kennedy. He'll never beat Nixon in Texas unless
you're on the ticket."

"You've already milked everything you can out of being Senate majority leader," I said. "Likely it won't be as powerful a position with a
Democrat in the White House." While Ike was president, Lyndon Johnson and Sam Rayburn had virtually dictated the Democratic program
and had rebuffed the efforts of Paul Butler, Democratic national chairman, to intrude on their domain. When Butler publicly announced
plans to form a liberal committee to shape the Democratic legislative
program, Rayburn and Johnson had made it clear they would be their
own men, thank you, and had ridden roughshod over Butler. "A strong
Democratic president," I said to LBJ, "will send his own programs up
from the White House. The majority leader might be no more than a
figurehead or a cheerleader. I don't think you have a thing in the world
to lose by running with Kennedy."

Johnson had remained passive. Then he said, "Well, I'll probably
have some trouble with some of my Texas friends if I decide to run.
Somebody mentioned the possibility last night to Sam Rayburn and he
dismissed the idea. I don't know. I'll have to talk to Mr. Rayburn and some
other people first."

Moments later Senator Kennedy was ushered into the suite. He'd apparently been able, at that early hour, to shake off pursuit by the press. We met in the living room, congratulated him, and then the two senators went into the bedroom and closed the door. Time passed slowly while Connally, Mrs. Johnson, and I chit-chatted. I think another LBJ aide or two came and went. Probably Kennedy was with Johnson no more than five or six minutes, however. When he left, with quick nods and a smile, LBJ asked us back into the bedroom.

"He asked me to run," Johnson said. LBJ reported that Kennedy said he had talked to his father, to *Washington Post* publisher Phil Graham, and to columnist Joe Alsop, and " 'They agreed with me that no one would add more to the ticket.' " I recall thinking it odd that JFK had mentioned no political sources, only his father and a couple of newsmen. Lyndon Johnson said, "I told him I'd have to consult with Speaker Rayburn, with my wife, and with others whose judgment I respect."

Senator Johnson's intuition that he might have trouble with his Texas friends proved correct. Speaker Rayburn quoted another Texan, former Vice-President John Nance Garner: "The office ain't worth a pitcher of warm spit." Governor Price Daniel sneered at a Kennedy-Johnson ticket as "One that would have all its strength in its hind legs." Several Texas congressmen, spoiled by LBJ's special attentions to their pet legislative schemes, begged him not to leave his powerful Senate post. These and other disenchanteds spread word of the Kennedy-Johnson flirtation; soon Senator Bob Kerr came barrelling into LBJ's hotel suite.

Kerr literally was livid. There were angry red splotches on his face. He glared at me, at LBJ, and at Lady Bird. "Get me my .38," he yelled. "I'm gonna kill every damn one of you. I can't believe that my three best friends would betray me." Senator Kerr did not seem to be joking. As I attempted to calm him he kept shouting that we'd combined to ruin the Senate, ruin ourselves, and ruin him personally. Lyndon Johnson, no slouch as a tantrum tosser himself, had little stomach for dealing with fits thrown by others; he motioned me to take Senator Kerr into the bathroom and mumbled something about explaining things to him.

Senator Kerr was a huge man—six feet four inches, and about 250 pounds—and as I turned to face him in the bathroom he slammed me in the face with his open palm. It sounded like a dynamite cap exploding in my head. I literally saw stars. My ears rang. Tears were streaming down Kerr's face as he shouted, "Bobby, you betrayed me! You betrayed me! I can't believe it!"

I couldn't believe the senator had just about knocked my head off either. No man ever hit me harder. As soon as I could talk I said, "I'm en-

titled to a hearing. If you'll calm down I'll give you my reasoning." Kerr
was attempting to regain control, and now seemed shocked at having hit
me.

I said, "Senator Kerr, everyone's underestimated Jack Kennedy from
the first. They said he couldn't win because he was Catholic, but he won
the primaries. They said he'd be stopped in West Virginia, but he wasn't.
They said he'd be deadlocked at the convention, but that didn't happen.
I think he's got a chance to beat Dick Nixon, but only if the ticket's right.
If we've got a prayer of carrying the South and the Southwest, Lyndon
Johnson must be on that ticket."

"But we need Lyndon in the Senate!" Kerr cried.

"Senator," I said, "if Lyndon Johnson doesn't prove to be a party loy-
alist now, what's his future? The ADA liberals and the Walter Reuthers
and the Soapy Williamses hate his guts, just like they hate yours, and
they're looking for any excuse to hurt him. One of the charges they
make against him is that he's not a fully committed Democrat. Where
does that leave him if he turns down his party's call?

"I know Jack Kennedy better than any of you. I think he'd be hurt
and angry if Lyndon Johnson turned him down. Frankly, I think he'd
cut off Senator Johnson's political pecker. And look at it this way: even if
a Kennedy-Johnson ticket loses, LBJ gets better known nationally, he'll
have more of a call on the nomination in 1964, and the ticket's loss will
be blamed on Kennedy's religion."

"But either way, Bobby, we lose him in the Senate."

"If he's elected vice-president," I said, "he'll be an excellent conduit
between the White House and the Hill. He'll still be around to consult." I
knew that LBJ had arranged a Texas law permitting him to run for
reelection to the Senate at the same time he sought any national office;
he later, indeed, would be reelected senator from Texas *and* vice-
president on the same day and on the same ballot. I recalled this cozy
situation to Senator Kerr and finished, "So what in the world's he got to
lose? I think it's a tremendous opportunity. It's a lot of pluses and I don't
see the minuses."

Senator Kerr put a burly arm around me and said, "Son, you are
right and I was wrong. I'm sorry I mistreated you." We shook hands.
Senator Kerr whirled, marched out into the bedroom, and in turn hugged Lady Bird and Lyndon. "I'm sorry I lost my head," he apologized. "I
love you dearly and if you decide to accept Kennedy's offer I'll be with
you all the way."

John Connally, Phil Graham, and others had been working on
Speaker Rayburn and he, too, came around. Teased by Johnson for having changed his mind he said, "I'm a damn sight smarter than I was last

night." But Sam Rayburn also told LBJ, "I don't think you ought to have to fight for the nomination. If Kennedy wants you, let him draft you. Let him pave the way and do the sweating."

By now rumors of the Kennedy-Johnson negotiations had reached the press. Once more the hall was crowded with reporters screaming for information and photographing anything that moved. Reporters, waving newspapers predicting in large headlines that Senator Symington would be JFK's choice, demanded to know what was going on. "I'm as confused as you are," I retorted and kept moving on my various missions. I kept trying to reach Walter Jenkins and others scattered hither and yon in the Johnson camp, to learn what they were picking up of a rumored liberal rebellion against LBJ, but the telephone situation was impossible. The Biltmore's communications system simply was not up to the traffic generated by a national political party at horse-trading time.

In midafternoon, Senator Johnson shooed everyone out of his bedroom except Lady Bird and Phil Graham. Graham later wrote that LBJ told them Bobby Kennedy then was meeting with Sam Rayburn and John Connally in a nearby room to make a firm offer of the vice-presidency. This understandably puzzled Johnson, who'd assumed that Jack Kennedy's offer at the morning conference was as firm as could be. As it turned out, Bobby Kennedy first asked whether Lyndon Johnson might be interested in becoming Democratic national chairman. Testy old Speaker Rayburn answered with a single word: "Shit!" Bobby Kennedy then said he would like to offer the vice-presidency to LBJ in person. Mr. Rayburn entered the Johnson bedroom to inform the senator of this.

"I've never argued with you, Mr. Sam," Lady Bird Johnson said, "but I don't think Lyndon should talk to him." Phil Graham agreed. He said to the senator, echoing what LBJ and Sam Rayburn earlier had agreed to, "You don't want it, you won't negotiate for it, you'll take it only if Jack drafts you, and you won't discuss it with anyone else." Graham then went to another hotel room to telephone Jack Kennedy and affirm that Johnson position. Meanwhile, Bobby Kennedy and John Connally waited tensely in a third room.

Once Phil Graham got through to Jack Kennedy he was told that things were in a general mess, that many liberals were angry at the prospect of Johnson's being on the ticket, and that "no one has anything against Symington." I'm glad I didn't know of this waffling on JFK's part; my heart might not have stood it. Graham made a pro-Johnson spiel; JFK promised a decision "within three minutes." Graham gave him another ten minutes for good measure, then wasted another ten in the telephone system's delays. When he got through, Jack Kennedy said.

"It's all set. Tell Lyndon I want him and I'll have David Lawrence [of Pennsylvania] nominate him."

Meanwhile, however, Lyndon Johnson and the rest of us sat wondering what in hell might be going on: Bobby Kennedy, rebuffed in his attempt to see LBJ, had told Sam Rayburn that his brother would momentarily telephone Lyndon Johnson directly to offer the vice-presidency: all this, now, as if the early-morning meeting with JFK in Lyndon's bedroom had not happened. (In retrospect, it appears that Jack Kennedy did not tell his people he'd called on Lyndon and thus added to the confusion; it also appears that JFK several times waffled during the day under the fire of red-hot liberals. Either that, or he had not made as firm an offer at the morning meeting as LBJ had said he did.)

About a half hour had passed since Bobby Kennedy said his brother would call, and there'd been no call. (We didn't know it at the time, but JFK assumed that his conversation with Phil Graham made such a call unnecessary. But Graham had not yet returned to report their conversation to us.) Johnson was fretful and testy; attempts to call other sources were frustrated by the communications system slowdown. In the midst of this supreme confusion about fifteen members of the Hawaiian delegation, dressed in loud aloha shirts, shoved into Lyndon Johnson's suite and added to the general hubbub. No one knew why they were there. Johnson kept yelling "Thank you boys for all your help" to them. They ignored this hearty dismissal.

Johnson, having conniptions, ordered Bill Moyers to find Phil Graham and find out what was going on, "for Christ sakes." Moyers shortly returned literally dragging Graham along; a half dozen of us pushed into the big corner bedroom. LBJ—as Graham later wrote—"seemed about to jump out of his skin." He began to shout that Bobby Kennedy had just come in and told Sam Rayburn there was too much opposition to his candidacy and that LBJ should withdraw for the good of the party. John Connally had snarled, "Who's the candidate, you or your brother?" Stunned, Graham said, "That can't be right. Jack Kennedy just told me it's all set and David Lawrence has agreed to nominate you." "Phil," Rayburn barked, "call Jack Kennedy and straighten out this mess."

While Graham was on the phone, I had a fleeting thought of how the press had written of the "smooth Kennedy machine" as it seemingly had purred its way to victory in primaries across the nation: *Hell, they're as confused as we are.* This thought reminded me of what Will Rogers had once said: "I don't belong to any organized political party. I'm a Democrat."

When Graham got through to JFK and told him of Bobby Kennedy's puzzling actions, Jack Kennedy coolly said that his brother had been out of touch and didn't know what was happening; he had just issued his statement naming Lyndon Johnson, and LBJ should now issue his own statement agreeing to run. Graham handed the telephone to Johnson, who spoke a few terse words of agreement to whatever Kennedy was saying and then rose to go out into the hall and face the TV cameras. At this point, Phil Graham would write that both Lyndon Johnson and Lady Bird had the appearance of having "just survived an airplane crash." I, too, felt as if I'd been put through the wringer and I think everybody in the room did. Though Lyndon Johnson transformed himself to give a relaxed and enthusiastic impression on camera, he became glum again as soon as his performance was over and he spoke of Robert Kennedy in terms of "that little shitass" and worse.

It had been a hell of a day, I thought in my hotel room late that night. Dead tired, I said to Dorothy: "I don't know, but I think that any little ol' boy from Pickens who in one week has a fight with Bobby Kennedy, Lyndon Johnson, and Bob Kerr may be overmatching himself."

Chapter Ten

Riding High

*"You've got more powerful contacts than any young
man in America. You want to throw that away?"*

AFTER the Kennedy-Johnson team defeated the Nixon-Lodge
entry in November of 1960, I began to have serious
thoughts of leaving the government. For one thing, I was exhausted.
Lyndon Johnson, in his fierce desire to carry the South for John F. Kennedy, had worked me to the bone. I felt that if I never saw another plate
of grits, never heard another Southern drawl, never sat on another podium listening to the same old campaign promises and platitudes, never
refereed another dispute over who sat at the head table, or never had to
attend to another outsized ego, it would be too soon. We had, indeed,
carried the South for JFK and without the South he would not have
become president. I should have felt a great sense of elation and satisfaction. Instead, I was weary and restless and downcast. It's always easier to
consider walking off a job, even one you have loved, when you are at a
low physical ebb.

But there were other reasons I considered resigning. Just as I felt
that LBJ had pretty well milked the Senate majority leadership for everything he could get out of it, I felt the same applied to me as secretary
to the Senate majority. With the Democratic program being shaped
from the White House, rather than concocted on Capitol Hill, and with
Lyndon Johnson soon to be gone from the Hill scene for all effective
purposes, I assumed that my own role would diminish. Frankly, I had
grown accustomed to being a wheeler-dealer power who operated
among select Senate insiders; it did not excite my soul to contemplate
going through the motions in what might prove, under new leadership,
to be little more than a caretaker's job.

I knew, too, that I had made powerful enemies on the Hill. I had,
after all, been an instrument in carrying out LBJ's policies—some of
which were sometimes high-handed—and natural resentments had ac-
crued. Senator Quinten Burdick of North Dakota had accused me of

blocking his appointment to the Senate Judiciary Committee in favor of Senator Ed Long of Missouri; others who did not always get what they wanted from the leadership—whether campaign funds, hearings on their pet bills, or coveted assignments—often took out their frustrations on me. I knew that malcontents and partisans who held old grudges against LBJ might be tempted to excise me once they had little or nothing to fear from Lyndon Johnson.

Dorothy had given birth to our fourth child, a little girl we named Lynda, and I had begun to think on the high cost of raising and educating children. More money was to be made outside of government; I felt an increasing urge to begin to accumulate and build for the future as rapidly as possible. I had a special dream of building and operating a motel-nightclub in Ocean City, Maryland, a seashore resort town less than a three-hour drive from Washington. Ocean City was growing by leaps; within a few years its oceanfront property values would zoom out of sight. Given the general prosperity of the period, and the trend toward increasing leisure time for most Americnas, I calculated that a first-class resort complex could not help but be a profitable venture.

In late November, or perhaps in early December, I told Lyndon Johnson I was giving serious thought to leaving Capitol Hill for private business. Johnson was sitting in his ornate Senate majority leader's office, the one known behind his back as the "Taj Mahal," with his feet propped up on a desk big enough to straddle a dray horse. He was a lame-duck leader now, and his long face showed it. He appeared listless and dissipirited.

"I wouldn't blame you," he said when I told him my tentative plans. "I'm sure Mike Mansfield can use you, but he may prefer to have his own man. Mike's a good man but unless somebody's spurrin' him on he'll just let things drift. He needs somebody who knows the ropes, but maybe you've been tainted by associating with me." This latter comment told me for certain that LBJ was feeling sorry for himself.

After more desultory talk we agreed that it might be better for me to step aside. Walking down the Capitol corridors to my office, I knew that I would miss the Senate and perhaps sometimes moon over it sentimentally as over some lost old flame. I knew that operating even a successful resort complex would not afford half the thrills of politics. I would be giving up the opportunity to rub shoulders with the mighty, to sit at their right hands, to assist them in their dreams and schemes. These were important considerations. To leave the Senate, I suddenly understood, would almost be like running away from home. It literally had been the place where I grew up.

When I told Senator Kerr of my decision to quit, he exploded. "Are you crazy?" he said. "You've got more powerful contacts than any other young man in America. Do you want to throw that away? There's nothing in the world that says you can't make money in a public job. You've got the same right to borrow, invest, and make a profit as any other citizen. I don't want to hear anymore about such nonsense."

I went to Senator Mansfield to tell him of my inclination to resign. He had not yet been formally designated as the new majority leader, but it was a foregone conclusion. "I hope you won't do that," Mansfield said. "You know the operation here better than anyone I might train for the job. I'd certainly hate to lose you and I'll consider it a personal favor if you'll reconsider." He made a low-key sales pitch, the only kind of which he was capable, and was altogether warm and complimentary. I left his office in some confusion about what to do.

Within a couple of days Jack Kennedy telephoned. There had been newspaper speculation that he might choose me to become his White House liaison man to Congress; when he first began to talk of the importance of good relations with the Hill and of getting off on the right foot there, I thought he might be leading up to offering me that job. But ultimately he said, "Lyndon tells me you're thinking of leaving your post. I think that would be a mistake. I know Senator Mansfield wants you to stay and certainly I can use your expertise up there. You can help by showing my liaison people the paths and pitfalls of the Hill and by keeping me apprised of congressional tempers." He continued in this flattering manner. Then he said, "You know, Bobby, you're a pro. You gave me good advice in 1956 when you told me to barnstorm for Adlai Stevenson rather than sitting on my ass on the beach. None of my people had told me that and I've never forgotten that you did. Campaigning for Stevenson helped me make contact with many Democrats who helped me later. It was an invaluable experience." Perhaps it was mere political softsoap on JFK's part, but I've got to confess that I liked what I heard. By the time we concluded our conversation, I think I'd made my decision to remain on the job. What a load of grief I might have been spared had I decided otherwise!

Less than a month before he would take office as vice-president, Lyndon Johnson telephoned and asked me to come to the Taj Mahal. There was a bouyancy about him that lately had been missing. He waved me to a chair and prowled the room. "Bobby," he said, "I've been thinking about where I can do Jack Kennedy the most good. And it's right here on this Hill, the place I know best. Jack, you know, was an indifferent senator; he never learned how things operate around here and he still doesn't know. All those Bostons and Harvards don't know anymore about Capitol Hill than an old maid does about fuckin'." Johnson's eyes twinkled as he said, "I'm gonna keep this office"—he waved his hand in an arc—"and help Mike Mansfield and Bob Kerr and Hubert Humphrey pass the Kennedy program. It's gonna be just the way it was! You can keep on helpin' me like you've always done."

I was a bit discomfited. LBJ seemed excessivley manic. He stood near me and lowered his voice. "Just between me and you and the gatepost, Bobby, I'm workin' it out with Mike and Hubert to attend meetings of the Senate Democratic Caucus. Maybe even preside over 'em. That way I can keep my hand in. I can help Jack Kennedy's program, and be his eyes and ears. Whatta you think of that?"

To tell the truth, I was both astonished and horrified. If anyone knew the United States Senate, its proud members and its proud traditions, it was Lyndon B. Johnson. Surely he knew that the prerogatives of membership were jealousoy guarded, that no member of the executive branch—even a Lyndon Johnson—would be welcomed in from the cold. Indeed, it seemed apparent that senators who long had chaffed under LBJ's iron rule would have conniptions at the very idea of his continuing to exercise control over their affairs. In 1959, and again in 1960, liberal Democrats led by Albert Gore of Tennessee, William Proxmire of Wisconsin, and Ralph Yarborough of Texas had attacked LBJ's procedures, his conduct of the caucus, the makeup of his hand picked steering committee, and so on. Johnson and the Senate Establishment had easily turned back their challenges, true. But this would be a new ball game with new rules, and I originally couldn't believe that LBJ believed he might have his way in the circumstances. *Probably,* I thought, *he's just full of himself and talking to hear his head rattle.* Yet, as he continued to expound on his new scheme, I realized he was serious.

I saw a disaster in the making but had a hard time saying so. When Lyndon Johnson was in a manic mood, conversation with him turned into a soliloquy; in a ninety-minute conversation he might dominate eighty-eight of those minutes and then drum his fingers impatiently while the other fellow claimed his alloted two minutes. Still, I tried diplomatically to interpose reservations about LBJ's hot idea and to indicate that some senators might not be enchanted by it. Blinded by his plans, his ego, and his past Senate successes, however, he overrode them and chattered on. "Do a little pulse-taking for me," he instructed. "Let me know what you hear."

What I heard in my soundings was not comforting. Senators aware of my longtime close association with LBJ were prudent and reserved in their responses. One could sense an underlying resentment, however, and at best a great apathy for LBJ's self-aggrandizing notion. LBJ did not seem to take my reports seriously and proceeded with his plan: at the Democratic caucus on January 3, 1961—seventeen days before LBJ would become vice-president and no longer a member of the Senate— Mike Mansfield would formally be elected to succeed him as majority leader. Mansfield, in turn, would move that Lyndon Johnson be invited to attend all future meetings of the caucus—and, more incredibly, to preside over those meetings. Then old cronies and allies in many former wars would rally 'round the LBJ flag and whoop the motion through.

I was nervous when we entered the Democratic caucus on January 3; if LBJ was, he didn't show it. Flowery speeches were made complimenting him on his great tenure as majority leader, he responded in kind, and then after more of the expected flatteries Mike Mansfield formally was elected. At this point the scenario LBJ had written came apart at the seams.

There was a moment of utter silence after Mansfield's motion and then, one by one, senators began to climb to their feet and speak their objections. "We might as well ask Jack Kennedy to come back up to the Senate and take *his* turn presiding," Albert Gore fumed. Joe Clark of Pennsylvania rose to sputter and snap out his objections. I sneaked a look at LBJ; his face had reddened. When I next looked at him, he had gone completely ashen. What had shocked him was that three longtime friends and supporters, all Senate insiders—Willis Robertson of Virginia, Olin Johnston of South Carolina, and, unbelievably, Clinton Anderson of New Mexico—had also spoken their objections. These three based their objections on the constitutional separation of powers, and were careful to praise Lyndon Johnson for his past contributions, but there was no getting around that they were inviting him out of their Senate inner circle. Mansfield, embarrassed, threatened to resign from the leadership post he'd been elected to just moments earlier, should the caucus not uphold his motion. Johnson sat tight-lipped and white-faced, saying not a word, as the rebellion deepened. Under Mansfield's threat to resign, the caucus did uphold his motion, forty-six to seventeen, but everyone in the room knew that Johnson had been rebuffed and that he would be a divisive force at any future caucuses. (Johnson got the message; he never attended another.)

LBJ stalked out of the caucus as quickly as he could. I shortly joined him in his office. He was white with fury. "Those bastards sandbagged me," he said. "They'd plotted to humiliate me, all those goddamn redhots and troublemakers. If they didn't want me all they had to do was say so privately to me or to Mike Mansfield. Hell, we didn't pull any big surprise on 'em! But no, they had to humiliate me in public." He was particularly embittered over the opposition voiced by Clint Anderson, an old crony with whom he'd long shared political jokes and a love of the blooded cattle they each raised, and he never fully forgave him.

I had a couple of drinks with my former leader and said all the soothing things I could think of, but he was bitter to the bone and could not be consoled. I left his office feeling very sad and older than my years; an era was coming to an end; the king was dead. I knew that Lyndon Johnson had just met the first of many disappointments likely to visit him as vice-president. Perhaps I should have discouraged Senator Mansfield from having made the fatal motion, but I had not done so for two reasons. First, I had not yet formed a close working relationship with the new majority leader and so my advice might have seemed cheekily presumptuous. Second, it would have amounted to an act of personal disloyalty to Lyndon Johnson. In short, my heart remained more with my old king than with my new.

There can be no doubt that Lyndon Johnson deeply despised Bobby Kennedy, and vice versa. They simply had terrible chemistry between them. But for LBJ, however, Kennedy might never have been confirmed as his brother's attorney general. This is something I know for sure. I saw it happen.

Many senators had serious reservations about Bobby Kennedy's confirmation. Lyndon Johnson agreed. He saw it as his duty, however, to assist President Kennedy where he could and he knew that opposition to Bobby's confirmation would grow unless it could be nipped in the bud. "I don't like the little son-of-a-bitch and I never will," Johnson gloomed as we shared a drink in his office after work. "But I think any president has the right to choose his own people, even if they happen to be kin to him. I've got a brother. Sam Houston. He drinks too much, but before the booze got 'im he performed many valuable services for me. And one of my regrets is opposing Admiral Lewis Strauss as Ike's secretary of commerce. You remember that."

Not only did I remember it, I had encouraged Senator Johnson to oppose Strauss. My opposition to Strauss primarily reflected the influence of Senator Clint Anderson, chairman of the Joint Atomic Energy Committee, and one of my close friends in the Senate. Senator Anderson so despised the rather pompous and stiff-backed admiral that he had warned President Eisenhower against naming him to a second six-year term as chairman of the Atomic Energy Commission. Anderson's dislike for Strauss had carried over. He opposed even his confirmation as secretary of commerce. Clint Anderson asked me to help persuade Lyndon Johnson to block confirmation. I began to tell the majority leader that there was much opposition in the Senate.

"There can be no doubt that Lyndon Johnson deeply despised Bobby Kennedy, and vice versa. . . . But for LBJ, however, Kennedy might never have been confirmed as attorney general." (*United Press International*)

When Lyndon Johnson sent me out to take a head count on Strauss, I'm afraid that I overstepped my bounds. I said something to the effect that "we" are against the confirmation of Admiral Strauss and, naturally, some senators took this to mean the Democratic leadership. Actually, I don't think at that point LBJ cared much one way or another. But as I came back with reports of senators who were in opposition to Strauss (though some of them may have been influenced by my representations)—Jack Kennedy, Richard Neuberger of Oregon, Alan Bible of Nevada, Allen Frear of Delaware, Herman Talmadge of Georgia—and as Clint Anderson and I worked on LBJ, he took up the attack. When Senator Tom Dodd of Connecticut insisted on speaking for Strauss, Lyndon Johnson scheduled the speech for a late hour, when most senators would be out for dinner; Dodd thus spoke to an almost empty chamber. The Senate ultimately refused to confirm Strauss, 49–46. Actually, except for being arrogant by nature, there was little wrong with Admiral Strauss. He had simply incurred the wrath of a powerful Senate insider in Clint Anderson, and he paid the price. It was not one of the Senate's finest hours. Nor one of mine.

Now Lyndon Johnson was saying, "Unless there's overwhelming evidence for cause against a president's nominee, the Senate ought to confirm him. Otherwise, you can tie a president's hands and take away the tools he needs. It's a different matter if some ol' boy hasn't got sense enough to pour piss out of a boot, but I don't think you can say that about Bobby Kennedy. He may be a snot-nose, but he's bright."

"I don't know Bobby Kennedy well," I said, "but I've got no reason to doubt his competency."

"Well," Lyndon Johnson said, "Dick Russell is absolutely shittin' a squealin' worm. He thinks it's a disgrace for a kid who's never practiced law to be appointed as the highest lawyer in the land. Personally, I agree with him. Russell and a lot of others fear that the Justice Department might become too politicized with the president's brother heading it. They might have a point. But I don't think Jack Kennedy's gonna let a little fart like Bobby lead him around by the nose. If I learned anything in the last year it's that Jack Kennedy's a lot tougher, and maybe a lot smarter, than I thought he was."

As I mixed our second round of drinks Johnson said, "Jack's asked me to tone down the Dixiecrats and I need you to help me. We've got to make a real crusade out of this because it's the first thing he's asked me to do, and it's very personal with him. You know, he wasn't any too hot about appointing Bobby, but old Joe Kennedy just insisted on it." Johnson sampled his drink and then said, sarcastically, "Well, since the old bastard bought the office I guess he's got a right to get his money's worth." Though LBJ grew to like Jack Kennedy sincerely, and to admire him in many ways, his bitterness at having lost to him—and at having lost his Senate power—occasionally spilled over.

"I want you to lead all our Southern friends in here by their ying-yangs," Johnson said, "and let me work on 'em. We've got to smooth Dick Russell's feathers, and kiss ol' Jim Eastland's ass, and mute Strom Thurmond's brayin'. I'm gonna put it on the line and tell 'em it's a matter of my personal survival."

Which is exactly what he did. "Now, look," he'd say, standing nose-to-nose with recalcitrant senators, kneading their lapels. "Jack Kennedy's put this thing square on my head. It's the first job he's given me, the first test he's put me to, and if I have to go back and say 'Mr. President, I'm sorry, but I can't persuade my friends to confirm your brother,' why shit, I'm ruined before I get started. You think he's gonna trust me with any- thing else, huh? Now, there's gonna come a time when *you*"—and here LBJ might poke his target in the chest—"come to me and ask me to get the administration to build you a dam or appoint you a judge or some- thin'. And if I don't have any influence with my president because *you* wouldn't help me confirm his brother, where's that gonna leave us? Huh? You think Jack Kennedy's likely to break his back tryin' to help us? Huh?"

With some senators, LBJ made Bobby Kennedy's youth and lack of experience appear to be assets: "Now, I don't think anybody's gonna shove Jack Kennedy around. I thought *I* could"—a wry grin—"and I bear the scars of battle because of it. You think he's gonna let his little brother take him over? Why, don't you know Bobby Kennedy won't get to go to the bathroom unless Jack Kennedy feels like takin' a pee? But if Bobby's rejected and some tough old lawyer who wants to impress the president gets the job, we could have ten times more trouble out of him than we'd have with a baby brother!"

To oil-state senators he would confide, "During the campaign Jack Kennedy told me, 'Lyndon, my father's made a big fortune, and I be- lieve that of the ten million dollars in my trust fund about a million is in- vested in oil. I can assure you that I'm not going to preside over the de- struction of my own fortune and you can tell your oil friends this. As long as I'm president, nothing is going to happen to the oil depletion al- lowance.' " Then he would say, "Jack Kennedy's gonna take care of you. Now how about helpin' me to take care of him?"

Lyndon Johnson particularly leaned on Dick Russell with his argu- ment that if he failed to achieve the confirmation of Bobby Kennedy he would be ruined "before I get started." It was this reasoning, I'm certain, which caused Senator Russell to grumpily agree not to make a fight. As Johnson saw Senator Russell waver, he applied the clincher: "He's gonna be confirmed. It can be by a big margin and everybody can feel good, or it can be close and embarrass everybody. Now, what good will it do me if Dick Russell—*the best friend I've got in the whole world*—gets up and snorts and fusses and embarrasses me and the president and the president's brother and his mama and daddy?"

Johnson worked tirelessly with Senator Mansfield, Senator East- land—the old firebrand who chaired the Judiciary Committee—and others to obtain a voice vote rather than a roll-call vote. This served both the administration and those opposed to the Kennedy confirmation: the Kennedys would not be embarrassed by a given number of senators going on record against the confirmation; those who were opposed would not have to suffer the painful experience and the political risk of incurring First Family wrath.

Dick Russell went along with this strategy. But when the presiding officer of the Senate intoned "all opposed so signify by saying nay," the aging Georgian, his eyes as sharp and fierce as those of a diving chicken-hawk, bellowed out a thunderous "Nay" that probably could have been heard on the far side of Stone Mountain. Even so, the "Ayes" safely had it.

Working for Mike Mansfield, compared to working for Lyndon Johnson, was like lolling on the beach as opposed to picking cotton. I truly liked Senator Mansfield. He was a decent, gentle, kind man, and keenly intelligent. Sometimes, however, I missed the fiery performances and gusto provided by Lyndon Johnson: the juices and the sap and the ginger that make a man eager to get up each morning and approach the day in the spirit of high adventure—if for no other reason than that he fears he might miss something.

Except for two or three hours each day, Mansfield disappeared to private haunts, there to read books and meditate. Nothing wrong with that. American politicians might be a better breed if more of them did it. I was not, however, accustomed to that. If Senator Mansfield's working habits made life easier for me—fewer immediate pressures and emotional earthquakes—conversely, they sometimes made things more difficult. Senator Mansfield often might not be available when consultations or decisions were required. Or he might suck his pipe and procrastinate rather than make decisions which would assist the flow of Senate business.

In a way, I had more power under Mansfield than I'd had working for LBJ. I had never been bashful about filling a power vacuum and so in that category I had no complaints. But the job was somehow less fun. There was less sense of immediacy and crisis or give and take. With Lyndon Johnson I always knew where I stood; with Mansfield, there was more of mystery in it and, consequently, more uncertainty.

Senator Mansfield was not all-consumed with politics. He was not fascinated by the shifts and changes of the political winds and he took few senatorial pulse readings. Certainly he did not know every nook and cranny as Lyndon Johnson had. He failed to develop a close rapport with the White House. Relations between the White House and Capitol Hill, consequently, ranged from the ineffectual to the disastrous.

John F. Kennedy's man for congressional liaison was Larry O'Brien, later postmaster general under Lyndon Johnson, and national Democratic chairman when he became the target of the Watergate burglars.

"Working for Mike Mansfield, compared to working for LBJ, was like lolling on the beach as opposed to picking cotton." (*United Press International*)

An affable soul, O'Brien may have been out of his element as a congressional liaison man. He knew little of the processes; he was not well known on the Hill, where personal relationships go a long way in controlling the ebb and flow.

O'Brien came to me when he'd not long been in the job to seek support for enactment of the Medicare bill. I was very much for this legislation, feeling it would improve the lot of the aged and the indigent, and promised to help him with senators as much as was within my power. Shortly thereafter my good friend Bob Kerr, who had committed himself to the American Medical Association to fight Medicare, asked for my nose count showing how senators stood on the bill. I consulted with Mike Mansfield to see if this were proper. Senator Mansfield said, "Give it to him, Bobby. He's a member of the Senate and he's entitled to it."

Senator Jennings Randolph of West Virginia told me he was undecided about Medicare. I included this information in the report I gave to Senator Kerr. Senator Carl Hayden of Arizona, president pro tem of the Senate and generally an administration supporter, was in a tough spot. He was coming up for reelection the following year. Medicare had been a hot issue in Barry Goldwater's reelection campaign in 1958, and a big majority of Arizona's voters had shown themselves opposed to it.

Senator Hayden asked me if we had the votes to pass the bill. I said, "I still don't know how Senator Randolph will vote. If he votes with us it will be a tie, and when the vice-president breaks the tie we'll win. If he doesn't vote with us, we'll lose. It's that close."

The old senator said, "I'd like for you to release me from my commitment to vote for the bill if you see you are going to lose. There's no profit in my stirring up my Arizona folks for nothing." I suggested that he stake himself out in the cloakroom and wait for word from me.

As the roll call on the vote proceeded, Senator Randolph voted against the bill. I knew then that we would lose. So I went to Senator Hayden and told him he was released from his commitment to vote for Medicare. He, too, voted against the bill and, of course, it failed.

Larry O'Brien had no appreciation for such complexities, for the necessary and practical courtesies of the Hill such as I had extended to Senator Hayden and that Senator Mansfield had extended to Senator Kerr; in short, he had no more idea than a small child of what had gone on—though it was precisely his job to know. O'Brien also needed a scapegoat to save his own ass, since he'd led the White House and his friends in the press to believe that Medicare would pass. Consequently, he leaked stories to newsmen that I had misled him in giving the results of my nose count, in the case of Hayden, and that I had double-crossed the administration by letting Senator Kerr know that Senator Randolph had been undecided. He also told President Kennedy that I had "gone to bed with Bob Kerr" and had "betrayed" the administration. I knew that credibility might be given to O'Brien's charges because of my close friendship with Senator Kerr.

I went to Vice-President Johnson, explained what had happened, and ended by saying, "You know that's the way things work up here." Johnson said, "You know it, and I know it, but they don't know it at the White House. The trouble with Jack Kennedy's operation is that he's got the minnows in Congress but not the whales. Those kids come up from the White House and start yelling 'frog' at everybody and expect 'em to jump. They don't have any idea of how to get along and they don't even know where the power is."

Though I sent word to President Kennedy as to exactly what had happened, and received word that he was satisfied with my explanation, the true story was never told in the press. When my big troubles arrived, the tale of my so-called betrayal of the Medicare bill was repeated and repeated and repeated.

I had no respect for Larry O'Brien thereafter. I'm human enough

that I let my feelings further harm the administration's already weak intelligence operations, I'm now sorry to say. Thereafter, if Larry O'Brien
wanted information as to the temper of the Senate or what might be
going on behind closed doors, he had to seek me out. I volunteered
nothing to him. If there was something I thought it imperative the White
House know, I transmitted the message through other sources. I think
one of the reasons President Kennedy called me to the White House for
numerous meetings was because he knew of my distaste for Larry
O'Brien. He was much better at picking my brain anyway.

"Larry O'Brien had no appreciation for the complexities of Capitol Hill. . . . I had no respect for
him." (*United Press International*)

I never understood why Jack Kennedy didn't make better use of
Lyndon Johnson on Capitol Hill. JFK was far from a dummy; he knew
his congressional relations were often in tatters and he dispaired when
his programs bogged down. "When I was a congressman," he once said,
"I never realized how important Congress was. But I do now." Yet, he
seemed strangely reluctant to call on Lyndon Johnson and he thus for-
feited his vice-president's main strength. Perhaps he feared that LBJ
had made so many enemies on Capitol Hill that he might do the administration's causes more harm than good. LBJ could come through
when called on, however, as he proved in the matter of Bobby Kennedy's
confirmation and in other isolated instances.

Vexations with the Hill may explain Jack Kennedy's spontaneous
remark when he came into his Oval Office one day for a meeting with
key Hill leaders, and found Barry Goldwater sitting in his favorite rocking chair. Senator Goldwater hastily started to rise from the rocker.

"Keep your seat, Barry," President Kennedy said. "And you can have
this fucking job, too, if you want it."

If President Kennedy only occasionally grew disenchanted with his office, his vice-president lived in a near-constant state of discontent. I worried about his attitude and his health. It was in Lyndon Johnson's nature to scream and cuss when displeased; it seemed unnatural to discover him brooding and bottling up his emotions day after day.

I knew that Lyndon Johnson sorely missed running the Senate. It was doubly frustrating for him to sit as the presiding officer of the Senate—a constitutional duty of the vice-president—and yet have no power at all in its operations. So near and yet so far. Johnson yearned for personal items of gossip about senators; for reports on who might be doing what to whom. Almost until the time I resigned from my Senate job in October of 1963—only forty-six days before John F. Kennedy's assassination—I made it a point to try to call on Lyndon Johnson every day he was in Washington and keep him posted on the political stories, happenings, and rumors I'd picked up. It may sound strange that a citizen walked around feeling sorry for the vice-president of the United States, but I certainly did. I don't care how rich you are, or how important others may think you are, you're going to be miserable if you're unhappy in your work. And Lyndon Johnson was.

Almost every day he had some new complaint. Some were serious, some were niggling, some were funny. I well recall the morning he said of Chester Bowles, a rather pompous and self-centered man who then was an ambassador, "He's losing us friends all over the world with his goddamned halitosis. I got a whiff of it the other day and if it had been Khrushchev instead of me, there'd likely be a war on now." He was offended when White House staffers called him "Lyndon" rather than the more respectful, and more proper "Mr. Vice-President." Often he complained that he was rotting on the vine, doing nothing while his original power base in Texas withered away. His complaints against Bobby Kennedy were frequent and may have bordered on the paranoic: Bobby Kennedy and Ralph Yarborough were combining to reduce him to a cut-dog impotency in Texas and to drive him from the national ticket. For a while he even toyed with the idea of resigning from the vice-presidency and returning to Texas to run against Senator Yarborough in 1964.

"Leader," I said—I called him that throughout his life, no matter his office—"why in the world would you want to do that? You'd come back as a junior senator and you'd be every bit as unhappy as you are now."

"No," he said flatly. "You don't really have any idea how unhappy I am now."

Johnson never found his role as vice-president. It is an office difficult enough to define for any man; its only function, when you get down to the licklog, is to provide a standby successor in the event of the president's death. Perhaps knowing, even subliminally, that you are on a perpetual death watch, is what accounts for much unhappiness in that office. Lyndon Johnson seemed to have ambivalent feelings about how he should conduct himself as vice-president. On the one hand he was careful to observe protocol and show his loyalty by always addressing Jack Kennedy as "Mr. President" even in private conversations, in never walking faster than JFK and keeping slightly to his rear, in doing anything the president asked him to but never volunteering more out of a fear that he might be considered pushy or improperly ambitious. On the other hand, he went to great lengths to illustrate that he wasn't left out in the cold, that he was valued and consulted.

He became strangely upset when President Kennedy publicly said that LBJ had taken part in every major decision in the administration "with the exception, of course, of the Bay of Pigs." The president obviously was attempting to fairly absolve LBJ of any blame for that fiasco. Johnson, however, couldn't stand the idea of people knowing that he'd not been consulted when the administration faced its first large crisis, not matter how disastrously it had turned out. For days he attempted to convince newsmen and associates that he had, too, been in on the Bay of Pigs planning.

For all his pretensions, and despite President Kennedy's rhetoric, LBJ was not consulted about other major matters. Kennedy neither sought his advice, nor gave him warning, when he abruptly attacked U.S. Steel for having raised steel prices by $6 per ton and thus creating new inflation. He did not invite Johnson to participate in major decisions made during the Cuban missile crisis. Even more puzzling, when violence broke out at the University of Mississippi over the racial integration of the school by James Meredith, Lyndon Johnson—who perhaps could talk to small-town Southerners better than any other public man in America—was not consulted. LBJ just might have been able to persuade Mississippi officials and leaders that they were bringing more heat and trouble down on the head of the beleaguered South by failing to take firm steps to prevent violence and by failing to show stronger, more responsible leadership. I can see him now, grasping hands and poking chests and grabbing lapels, saying to the Southern politicians something like "We got a chance to show the way. We got a chance to get the racial monkey off the South's back. We got a chance to show the Yankees that we're good and decent and civilized down here, not a bunch of barefoot, tobacco-chewin' crazies." LBJ was not called in, however; when a reporter took note in print that he'd been isolated on his ranch in Texas during the Mississippi outburst, Johnson telephoned him to pretend that he'd been in close touch with Washington all the way, that he'd been relied on and listened to.

The vice-president came to feel that he had been "double-crossed" in

"Privately, the vice-president fretted that President Kennedy didn't invite him to his White House quarters and otherwise snubbed him socially. Lyndon Johnson wanted nothing so much as to kick off his shoes and talk politics with JFK." (*United Press International*)

the matter of Texas patronage; typically, he blamed it on Bobby Kennedy rather than on the president. In truth, nobody double-crossed him. His Texas rival, Senator Yarborough, simply refused to knuckle under to the White House or LBJ and won the fight. What happened was this:

John F. Kennedy, hoping to keep LBJ happy if possible, told him shortly after the 1960 election, "Lyndon, you may be number two in the country but I'll see to it you remain number one in Texas." He then said that LBJ would have a veto over any appointments in the Lone Star State and, in effect, that Johnson would have a virtual monopoly on Texas patronage. This was not smart of Kennedy. It excluded Senator Yarborough—the senior senator from Texas, once LBJ vacated—and took away his traditional patronage prerogatives. This made the fiery Texas liberal hopping mad. He felt that Kennedy, whom he'd enthusiastically supported for president, had sold him out to his rival.

Sixteen of the Johnson men required confirmation in 1961. Nothing happened. Not a nomination was acted on. Senator Yarborough had exercised his right, and an old Senate tradition, in going to the proper chairmen and labeling each of LBJ's nominees as "personally obnoxious" to him. This is a device by which senators traditionally have stopped confirmation of home-state nominees of whom they disapprove. It is *always* honored; no president or vice-president or any other outsider can persuade the Senate not to honor that rule.

It became necessary for the administration to approach Senator Yarborough hat in hand. "Give me half the appointments in Texas," Ralph Yarborough said. "Have Lyndon withdraw eight of his nominees and I'll clear the other eight. And it's got to be fifty-fifty from this day forward." It was.

Had Lyndon Johnson been in Senator Yarborough's shoes, he would have reacted the same way. It was an old, if effective, ploy known to every senator and certainly LBJ never was one to forfeit a right or overlook any weapon in a power struggle. Somehow, though, he got it in his head that Bobby Kennedy had conspired with Yarborough to thwart him, that he had been "double-crossed." He just couldn't be rational where Bobby Kennedy was concerned.

There's no doubt that Bobby Kennedy, and not a few White House staffers, had their stingers out for LBJ. Some were willing to embarrass him when they could. They called him "Uncle Cornpone" behind his back and asked each other "Whatever happened to Lyndon Johnson?" Johnson heard and read of such things, and he was deeply hurt. Though he was careful to go through the White House staff to make appointments with the president, rather than call him direct as he might have done, he sometimes had to wait for days to receive a decision. (He remembered this treatment; as president, Johnson once told a staff aide who'd kept Vice-President Hubert Humphrey waiting, "If you ever do that again I'll kick your ass.") Robert Kennedy once severely criticized the work of the President's Committee on Equal Employment Opportunity in an open meeting, talking to its members as if they were retarded children or labor goons, while the chairman of that group sat as if his face had been carved from stone. The chairman was, of course, Lyndon B. Johnson.

I thought one of Johnson's finest hours in the vice-presidency came when he gave dignified, personal treatment to Bashir Ahmed, a Pakistani camel driver, who visited the United States as his personal guest. Johnson was in the campaign-trail habit of loosely asking people to visit him in Washington. In Pakistan he made such a remark to Bashir Ahmed, a poor and illiterate fellow, who in his unsophisticated way thought he'd been singled out and soon began to tell everyone he was going to America to see his friend the vice-president. When the stories surfaced in the world press, there was a snickering that LBJ had painted himself into a corner; some charged that he'd made himself, and the United States, appear to be foolish or cynical.

Johnson seized the day, however. He arranged for the State Department to pay for the visit of the penniless camel driver. He met him at the airport in New York, took him to the White House to meet the president, flew him to his Texas ranch, and generally acted as the perfect host. There's no doubt he scored a propaganda victory for the United States; what began as a bad joke ended as a warm, human story played big in the news media around the world. Later, Johnson would say with some satisfaction, "They thought they had me by the nuts about my camel driver. I knew there was a lot of joking and laughing at me and I decided to make it backfire on 'em. Some newsmen and some of the Harvards thought they'd play it as a joke, but I called editors and Jack Kennedy and Dean Rusk and told 'em it would be a disservice to the country, and to my camel driver, if he was treated as less than welcome. I was determined nobody was gonna make a jackass outta that poor man, or of me."

The difficult vice-presidential years might have been made more bearable had not Johnson's mentor and great friend, Speaker Sam Rayburn, died in November of 1961. LBJ was not merely speaking pretty words for the record when he said, "The Capitol will be a lonely place

" 'They thought they had me by the nuts about my camel driver,' Lyndon Johnson said, 'and I decided to make it backfire on 'em. I was determined nobody was gonna make a jackass outta that poor man, or of me.' " (*Wide World Photos*)

without him." He was crushed by the loss at a time when he felt very much adrift and sorely needed an anchor.

The Rayburn-Johnson relationship went back to LBJ's youth. As a young man, Sam Rayburn served in the Texas legislature with LBJ's father, Sam Ealy Johnson; the young Lyndon often visited among legislators at the State Capitol in Austin. He renewed the acquaintance when he came to Washington in 1931, as secretary to a Texas congressman; Rayburn took Johnson under his wing when LBJ was elected to the House in 1937 following the sudden death of a sitting member. There are those who presume the relationship to have been one way, but that's not correct. Sure, Rayburn—older and originally with more power—played the mentor's role for years. LBJ became more than a junior partner in time, however. Indeed, in the early 1940s, Lyndon Johnson—who'd captured Franklin D. Roosevelt's fancy as a young congressman—intervened with President Roosevelt to smooth things over after FDR had become incensed at Rayburn because of his opposition to a third-term president. It's even conceivable that Sam Rayburn might not have become speaker had Roosevelt chosen to oppose him.

The Rayburn-Johnson relationship was not always smooth. Rayburn, the father figure, sometimes experienced the frustrations and irritations a parent feels toward an erring child. Though himself crusty and testy when provoked, Sam Rayburn was a gentleman of the old school who was always careful to grant each man his own dignity. I doubt whether he ever knowingly hurt anyone's feelings, though he ill suffered bores and jackasses. LBJ, on the other hand, could be cutting and cruel even to his most loyal minions or colleagues. Rayburn often lectured Johnson against this shortcoming.

Now and again LBJ took me to meetings of Sam Rayburn's "Board of Education" in a hideaway room deep in the bowels of the Capitol. It was small, private, unmarked, and unstaffed. Here, after the official working day, Rayburn invited a few intimates to relax over drinks and let down their political hair. It was, in effect, an after-hours private club for the men who called the tunes in Congress. In addition to Rayburn and Johnson, a typical session might include House Majority Leader John McCormack, a committee chairman or two, perhaps the Republican leader—Joe Martin or Charley Halleck—and a trusted newspaper friend such as William S. White or Bascom Timmons.

In such company a young Senate employee spoke only when spoken to. It was reward enough just to be there. Only the trusted were invited because the conversation was frank, open, and without guile. I listened in fascination as these powerful men talked of issues and personalities, of the Congress and the presidency. They were living examples of the

"Sam Rayburn and Lyndon Johnson truly loved each other . . . [but] in 1960 Rayburn told me, 'I wish LBJ would shit or get off the pot. He's got to know what his goals are.' " (*United Press International*)

necessity of having in government men with just plain good common sense. As far as I was concerned, they made the term "Board of Education" a fitting designation for the meetings in Speaker Rayburn's hideaway office with its scarred old furniture that might have come from a junkheap.

Despite occasional squabbles, "Mr. Sam" and LBJ truly loved each other. When, at age forty-seven, Lyndon Johnson suffered a massive and near-fatal heart attack, Speaker Rayburn was disconsolate and near tears. Despite his advancing years and a hectic schedule, he called on LBJ at the hospital as soon as it was permissible, and he telephoned him often.

I was taking a rare holiday that weekend. Dorothy and I had rented a cabin on the beach at Ocean City, Maryland. It had no telephone, which suited me fine, as I was exhausted from six months of hard work. It was one of the few times I had not left word at the Capitol as to where I could

be reached. I therefore had no way of knowing that LBJ, after holding a
news conference in Washington on Saturday morning—during which
he'd responded in anger and disdain to a couple of irritating questions—
had suffered a heart attack shortly after arriving for a weekend visit at
the Virginia farm of George R. Brown, the Brown and Root mogul.
Johnson originally thought he had a severe case of heartburn, first
drinking a Coke and then taking a pinch of baking soda to overcome it.
But when another of Brown's weekend guests, Senator Clinton Anderson, took one look at the sweating, pain-ridden LBJ he said, "Lyndon, I
think you're having a coronary." Anderson, himself a heart attack veteran, knew the signs.

It was not until Sunday morning I learned from the newspapers that
Johnson had been rushed by ambulance to Bethesda Naval Hospital on
the outskirts of Washington. I telephoned Walter Jenkins, and the news
was bad. "He thinks the end is near," Jenkins said, "and he's been asking
for you." Of course, I immediatey abandoned my holiday and rushed
back to Washington. LBJ had gone into shock soon after arriving at the
hospital and was under an oxygen tent. No matter how badly he thought
he needed to see me, he could have no visitors.

For about ten days I stayed at the hospital almost around the clock,
leaving only to grab a few random hours of sleep and to take showers.
Though there was little I could do, access to LBJ being held to a minimum, I felt it my duty to be there. In time, however, I was persuaded
that I might better look after my leader's affairs by staying at the Capitol.
Actually, we didn't do much more than conduct a holding action in LBJ's
absence.

One morning Mrs. Johnson telephoned to say that the senator
wanted to see me. I found a quiet and sober man who talked of how close
he'd come to death, of how he would be forced to curtail his activities,
and of how he might no longer prove able to act as Senate majority
leader. "I had a close call," he said, "and I may be forced to resign from
the Senate. If I did, would you resign and go home with me to run a
radio station? I'd like to buy the station in Brownsville, near the Mexican
border. It's also near the water. You and Dorothy and the kids could
have a fine life in the sun. That part of Texas is even further South than
Miami." I said, "Leader, we'll talk about that when you're feeling better.
You're my leader, and I'll follow where you lead. But your decision can
wait."

Within a few days, of course, Lyndon Johnson had changed his out-
look; I think his talk of resigning was little more than mental gymnastics
in a low moment. You'd have had to cut off all LBJ's limbs and perform
a frontal lobotomy before he would have quit politics. Soon he was de-

manding that I bring him all the news and gossip. How was Earl Clements doing running the Senate in his absence? What was happening on the legislative calendar? Who was absent from roll calls? Who'd been drunk recently? Tell Senator Kerr this. Tell Speaker Rayburn that. Bring me a copy of this committee report or that *Congressional Record*. Johnson seemed pleased when I told him that not much was happening in the Senate, that it was conducting a mere holding action until he could return to work.

I was rushing down the seventeenth-floor corridor of the Bethesda Naval Hospital toward Lyndon Johnson's room, overburdened with paperwork he had demanded, when I met Speaker Rayburn. His old face split into a rare grin. "I'm happy to see you taking him all that work," he said. "It would kill him if he relaxed. I know he's getting better because he fussed at me." Daily after that, he came by the hospital to play Dominoes with the Senator.

Lyndon Johnson, in turn, had occasion to worry about his beloved friend's health. In early 1961 he said, "Bobby, I'm worried sick about Mr. Sam. The poor old fellow can't see anymore and he's losing weight. He's got no appetite and he has a lot of pain. He insists on blaming it on what he calls 'lumbago' but I'm scared to death the old man has cancer. I've been trying to get him to go to the Mayo Clinic for a checkup but he insists it's just another bout with lumbago."

Rayburn returned to Texas before the 1961 session of Congress ended, pretending that a little rest would make him whole again, but those close to him knew he was going home to die. Shortly after he'd left Capitol Hill, I had drinks one night with Senator Johnson and a couple of Rayburn's longtime staffers, D. B. Hardaman and John Holton. There were many affectionate stories told of the old man, and a few tears glistened. "He's been so tired and so unlike himself," Hardaman said. "Crabby, worried, unable to function because he's got no strength." We knew we were holding a wake for a grand old man.

I attended Speaker Rayburn's funeral in Bonham, Texas. President Kennedy was there along with two former presidents—Harry Truman and Dwight Eisenhower—and, of course, a future president: Lyndon Johnson. "You'll never know how much I miss him," LBJ often said of the speaker in subsequent years. On his first night as president, back from Dallas and the bloody scene there, he looked at a picture of Rayburn and said, "Mr. Sam, how I wish you were here."

I visited Mr. Rayburn's home during that sad trip. I was amazed to see how old-shoe and unpretentious it was. To all appearances, it wasn't the home of a big shot or one of the most powerful men in America. It was simply a neat, well-ordered white frame house that might have been the home of any small merchant or farmer who'd attended his business well. It might well have belonged to any of his rural neighbors. Perhaps I might have been better off, in the long run, had I thought more deeply on how that simple house reflected what was good in Sam Rayburn's character and symbolized the best of our better public men.

Chapter Eleven

Becoming a Paper Millionaire

*"The way you're buying that stock you sure must
know something. Can you get some for me?"*

L IFE had never seemed rosier than it did in 1961. In a way I had
more power under Mike Mansfield than under Lyndon
Johnson. Senator Mansfield both delegated and abdicated, two traits
foreign to Johnson. Because Mansfield was frequently closeted with his
private Muse, and thus relatively inaccessible, more and more people
came directly to me for favors or to obtain decisions. As time went on
and nobody objected, particularly Senator Mansfield, I increasingly
made unilateral decisions.

There was more traffic to my office, too; Democrats controlled not
only Congress but also the White House. Lobbyists and their clients
came in search of vital appointments with administration sources: looking for favorable executive rulings on regulatory matters, crying their
wares, seeking contracts, seeking jobs, seeking legislation to benefit their
firms. The Kennedy-Johnson administration contained a number of my
old cronies, associates, or acquaintances in decision-making posts. I
could open more doors than just those on Capitol Hill.

Losing Lyndon Johnson as my patron saint had not proved as profes-
sionally traumatic as expected. Senator Kerr was increasingly living up
to his nickname as the "King of the Senate" and was replacing in influence the aging Dick Russell. Hubert Humprhey was coming on fast in
the inner circle; he frequently consulted me. Even some senators whom
LBJ, with his gift for hyperbole, had dubbed "the bomb throwers"
seemed more friendly than when I'd been tagged "Lyndon's Man"; my
friendships grew with such mavericks as Wayne Morse of Oregon, Paul
Douglas of Illinois, Eugene McCarthy of Minnesota.

Yet, somehow, my job was simply not as dramatic, demanding, or as
much fun as when Lyndon Johnson ran the show. Where once I had occupied many evenings in his company, talking politics or plotting action,
I began to become more of what LBJ might have called "a party-going

"As time went on and nobody objected, particularly Senator Mansfield, I increasingly made unilateral decisions." In foreground: Republican Leader Ev Dirksen of Illinois, Democratic Leader Mike Mansfield of Montana." (*Robert Phillips*)

playboy." I also began to expend more time in my private business pursuits. I don't think I neglected my duties, though certainly I felt freer to absent myself occasionally or to diversify my energies than during the hectic Johnson years. The Senate's pace had slowed. Where once I worked sixteen to eighteen hours a day, I now could do the job in ten or less.

By 1961 my net worth, on paper anyhow, was about $300,000. My best investment had been with Mortgage Guaranty Insurance Company of Milwaukee—known in financial circles as "MAGIC"—in which I had invested $28,750 in 1959. How did I come to invest? Through my friend Glenn Troop, I had met Henry Bubb, the chairman of the board of MGTC.

Mr. Bubb told me of the amazing growth his company was enjoying. Though in 1957 the founder and president—Max H. Karl—had had difficulty raising $250,000, to get it off the ground, it had grown by leaps. MAGIC was founded to insure low-down-payment mortgages against foreclosures, in competition with the Federal Housing Administration, which had a virtual monopoly in the field. Mr. Karl became convinced that he could woo away FHA business because people were sick of the red tape and routine delays of the bureaucracy, and because FHA ceilings on mortgage interest rates were below the yield from conventional mortgages. He offered insurance at half the cost of FHA, and speedy service. Henry Bubb told me that his company was on the verge of a sensational growth explosion: MAGIC had recently attracted to its board a number of powerful savings and loan executives with access to big money, and it appeared that a very favorable tax ruling was in prospect. A friend said, "Bobby, you should invest even if you must borrow money against your salary."

I borrowed the money. When I bought into MAGIC, its stock went for $3 per share; I was permitted to buy some stock for as low as $1.56 per share (President Max Karl later would tell investigators, "I was impressed with the title he bore. I felt MGIC should have prominent stockholders, and I thought Mr. Baker knew a lot of people"). Within a year my stock would be worth $22 per share and by 1964 would be worth $51 a per share; it later went to $98. I eventually would own 16,567 shares; in 1962, my holdings in MAGIC were valued at approximately $495,000.

I also recommended the company to friends. John Yingling, then a lawyer on the Senate Banking Committee staff, made about $30,000 on my recommendation. Alfred and Geraldine Novak, who would become my partners in the Carousel Motel venture, cleared about $38,000. Cliff Jones, former lieutenant-governor of Nevada, and several of his Las Vegas casino associates, also cleaned up.

"Where once I had occupied many evenings . . . talking politics or plotting legislative action, I began to become more of what LBJ might have called 'a party-
going playboy.' " Here, with actress Dorothy Malone.

One of the big reasons MAGIC proved so profitable so quickly was
because the Treasury Department, in 1960, exempted half of its pre-
mium payments from income taxes for fifteen years. This was the ruling
Henry Bubb had told me he anticipated in 1959, and though I had no
hand or influence in that ruling, I knew it would benefit the company
and its investors. MAGIC had brought pressures on Treasury by an old
ploy: having a bill introduced in Congress containing the special tax
treatment it desired, then encouraging its congressional sponsors and
supporters to insist on a favorable executive ruling. In those days, the

federal agencies were responsive to congressional pressures and, often, quite easily caved in. The congressional sponsor of the tax bill to benefit MAGIC was Representative John W. Byrnes, a Republican power from Wisconsin. Later it would be revealed that Congressman Byrnes had invested $2,300 in the company, at preferential rates, and within a short time his money had increased tenfold. When this news went public, Congressman Byrnes took the floor of the House to say that he'd done no wrong, invoke his good reputation, cry, and promise to donate the controversial profits to charity. His colleagues gave him a standing ovation.

"Congressman John Byrnes of Wisconsin had invested in MGIC. When this news went public, he took the House floor to invoke his good reputation, cry, and promise to donate the controversial profits to charity." (*United Press International*)

Word got around that I had heavily invested in MAGIC and was recommending it to others. One day in 1961 former Senator Allan Frear, of Delaware, came into my office.* He had been appointed by President Kennedy, following his 1960 defeat for reelection, to be a member of the Securities and Exchange Commission. The SEC is the regulatory agency charged with policing the offering, sale, and issue of stocks and bonds.

"Bobby," Allan Frear said, "the way you're buying that MAGIC stock you sure must know something."

Yes, I said, I had gotten in on the ground floor—but it was no longer a secret that MAGIC enjoyed a very liberal tax write-off situation and would for the next fifteen years. It had new money to expand and diver-

*See pages 236–239 for Mr. Frear's contrary recollections.

sify, would soon be in the business of insuring mortgages on mobile homes, and had no way to go but up. "The company can't help but make money," I said, "unless we have the damnedest depression in history. Nothing on the horizon suggests that."

Mr. Frear said, "Well, I'd love to have some of it. Do you think you could get me a thousand shares?"

"I think we can work it out," I said. We discussed the details. Frear

"I telephoned [former Senator Allan] Frear and told him I had something for him . . . I gave them to him in a plain white envelope." (*United Press International*)

said he would return with the cash, and did—$27,500 worth. I gave $13,775 to one of my employees, Dick Darling, instructing him to buy stock in his name. In turn, he would sign the stock over in blank—that is, he would not designate its recipient. A neighbor, John Lane, similarly agreed to accommodate me. He refused to accept cash, however, because of periodic audits of his law firm, and he didn't want to have a huge wad of cash to explain. I then deposited the remaining $13,725 to my own account—writing "Frear" on the deposit slip—and issued my personal check in the amount of the deposit. John Lane endorsed this check over to Bache and Company, a stockbrokerage firm; he delivered to me, signed over in blank, the stock meant for Allan Frear.

I telephoned Frear at the Securities and Exchange Commission, told him I had something for him, and soon he appeared to claim the stock certificates. I gave them to him in a white envelope. Later, during investigations into my activities, Frear claimed never to have had any business dealings or financial transactions with me. Only recently a document has come to light quite strongly indicating to the contrary.

The document is an office memo written by a lawyer named Abe Krash, who then worked for the more famous Abe Fortas. I originally hired Abe Fortas to represent me when the "Baker scandals" broke. I was in his law office when word flashed that John F. Kennedy had been assassinated in Dallas. Abe Fortas was a longtime friend and confidant of Lyndon Johnson, and had been since New Deal days; President Johnson later would name him to the Supreme Court, from which he would resign after his own financial entanglements came under fire. All that was in the future on November 22, 1963, however. As soon as I heard of JFK's assassination, I said, "Mr. Fortas, I know Lyndon Johnson will be calling on you for many services and your advice. If you represent me it might be embarrassing to the new president, and it might put you in a conflict-of-interest situation. I release you as my attorney, and I'll have a confirming letter on your desk by tomorrow."

But nine days earlier, on November 14, Mr. Krash wrote a memo, labeled "HIGHLY CONFIDENTIAL" to the files.

It said in part:

I wish to record the following concerning a conference in our office this morning at which Senator Frear, Abe Fortas, and myself were present. The meeting was arranged last week by Mr. Baker. Senator Frear arrived in our office at around 9:30 A.M. and he left shortly after 11 A.M.

Mr. Fortas opened the conference by explaining that we had been shown Baker's check stubs by the accountant in New York and that one of these stubs, dated October 24, 1961, indicated that Baker had purchased MGIC shares as Senator Frear's nominee. Mr. Fortas also briefly described the history of MGIC's three registration statements before the S.E.C.

Senator Frear told us the following: He was defeated for reelection to the Senate in 1960. On the day following the election, he received a telephone call from Senator Kerr who expressed his disappointment at the outcome and who urged Senator Frear to get started now on campaigning for reelection in 1964. Frear said he regarded himself as a good friend of Senator Kerr's. He explained that he had worked with Senator Kerr in connection with the DuPont tax bill.

Commencing sometime in 1961, Senator Kerr from time to time gave Senator Frear envelopes containing money. Senator Kerr told Senator Frear to hold the envelopes in safekeeping. It was Frear's impression that the money was being transmitted to him for possible use in connection with a 1964 campaign and that he was holding the money in escrow in behalf of Senator Kerr.

Sometime in October, 1961 (Frear is not certain of the date), Frear received a

"I was in the law office of Abe
Fortas when word was flashed
that John F. Kennedy had
been assassinated. . . . 'Mr.
Fortas, if you represent me it
might be embarrassing to the
new president.'" (*United
Press International*)

telephone call from Kerr who told Frear that Bobby Baker needed some money
and that Frear should take $27,500 of the money which Kerr had entrusted to
Frear and deliver this amount to Baker. Kerr told Frear that if the amount
previously transmitted to him was less than $27,500 he should let Kerr know.
Frear checked the envelopes and found there was about $300 in excess of
$27,500. He removed the excess amount and delivered an envelope containing
$27,500 in cash to a person employed in Baker's office. He told this person to
give the envelope to Baker.

Frear says he does not know the source of the money. He doubts that it origi-
nated with the DuPonts.

Sometime shortly before Kerr's death on January 1, 1963, Baker saw Frear
and told Frear that he had something for Frear which he had held for a long
time and wanted to deliver to Frear. Baker gave Frear an envelope. Frear placed
this envelope, together with the two or three hundred dollar excess cash, in a
safe deposit box held in his wife's name in a bank in Dover, Delaware. The
envelope is presently in that box. Frear states that there is a handwritten note at-

tached to the envelope which states, he believes, "Check with Senator Kerr or Bobby Baker." This note is in Frear's own handwriting.

Frear says he does not know what is in the envelope. He states that Baker did not tell him that an MGIC stock certificate or certificates were in that envelope.

With respect to MGIC, Frear states that Bobby Baker telephoned Frear when he was a Commissioner to urge him that action be taken with respect to the MGIC registration. Frear said that he received many calls from Baker as well as from many senators and congressmen and the Attorney General. When the MGIC registration came before the Commission in October, 1961, Frear said that he did not vote on the matter. He states that he did not disqualify himself, but he is certain that he did not vote.

After the registration statement was approved, Frear states that Baker approached him and asked whether he was interested in MGIC stock. Baker told him that he felt it was a good proposition. Frear said that he told Baker that since he was an S.E.C. Commissioner he could not buy such shares. . . . He states that he did not join Baker in buying Mortgage Guaranty stock.

Frear stated that he had not been associated with Baker in any business transaction. . . .

Well . . . *"Frear says he does not know what was contained in the envelope."* Didn't look in it? Just *assumed* that I'd paid back $27,500 to the penny without counting it? Had no curiosity about it?

"He states that Baker did not tell him that an MGIC stock certificate or certificates were in that envelope. . . . Frear said that he told Baker that since he was an S.E.C. Commissioner he could not buy such shares. . . . He states that he did not join Baker in buying Mortgage Guaranty Stock." Then why would Bobby Baker have gone around the horn to have two friends buy the stock in the blind? Why would I then surrender the signed-over, blank stock certificates to Allan Frear? Certainly, with the certificates safely in Mrs. Frear's lockbox, I could not have somehow conspired to convert them to my own use. If I didn't buy the stocks on Allan Frear's authorization, then on whose? Is it logical that I would buy $27,500 worth of stock for a man who had specifically told me he wanted no such stock? And, had I owed Frear money as he claimed, what tortured logic would lead me to pay him back in blank stock certificates? *To a member of the S.E.C.?* Come on, now!

The *real* significance of the Fortas interoffice memo, and its political implications, we shall save for a point where it more dramatically illustrates my story.

In 1961 it appeared that my longtime dream of a luxury motel-nightclub in Ocean City would at last come true. I had no way of knowing the dream would turn into a nightmare involving death, a killer storm, near bankruptcy, civil suits, and accusations of fraud. Everything that could go wrong did.

Borrowing money on my MGIC stock and other holdings, I bought two blocks of beachfront property at 118th Street and Ocean Drive in Ocean City. Within a short time I formed a partnership with two friends, Alfred and Geraldine Novak, whom Dorothy and I had been seeing socially for a couple of years, to build the motel-nightclub. We decided to call it the Carousel—an apt choice, since it kept me on the merry-go-round for so many years. Al Novak, an accountant who'd once been with the General Accounting Office, had made money building small housing developments in Maryland; he was a good detail man, while I was not. Geraldine Novak worked for the Senate Small Business Committee; she impressed me as being bright and level-headed.

Construction on the Carousel began on October 1, 1961; I foolishly believed we'd be open for business within a matter of weeks or months. But there were constant delays—bad weather, the contractor failing to always provide a full complement of workers, delays in deliveries, and down-turning business conditions combined to thwart us. By March of 1962 we had the cinderblock laid. We were now ready to brick the structure, then go on to the finish work, the furnishings, and soon hear the cash register sing. Then, abruptly, we ran out of money. Al Novak had most of his assets tied up in forty to fifty small houses he'd built in Maryland; he originally had presumed to sell them, turn a profit, and plow the receipts back into the Carousel. But he simply couldn't sell the houses. The tight money market made it difficult for middle-income people to swing the necessary loans. Novak became so despondent that he several times threatened suicide. "Oh, shit, Al," I once responded, "why don't we just shoot each other and get out of our misery together?" It was a flippant remark tinged with sarcasm; I was attempting to get him out of his morbid mood and, frankly, I didn't take him seriously. Ultimately, however, he so persisted in the theme that I had a physician friend talk to him and prescribe tranquilizers. I sold some MGIC stock and thus increased my share of the Carousel partnership from one-third to one-half. I also took pains to invite Al Novak to social events in an effort to cheer him.

In late February or early March I saw Al Novak at the wedding of the daughter of my friend Tommy Webb, the ex-FBI agent who then worked for the Murchison interests. I said, "Al, it's not any damned disgrace to go broke, but we're not going broke. We've got contacts and resources and we've just got to redouble our efforts." It didn't seem to help. The following Saturday, on March 3, 1962, Novak's wife discovered him dead in his garage, with the car motor running and the door open only a fraction of an inch. (Months later, to show you that when it rains it pours, the *Washington Daily News* ran a big, black three-tiered headline: SENATORS TO PROBE / MYSTERY DEATH OF / BOB BAKER PART-

NER.) On finding her husband dead, Geraldine Novak went to pieces. I took over the funeral arrangements, reassured and comforted her as much as possible, took over the records of our building project in an effort to make some sense of the confusion, and generally tried to hold the pieces together. I had to have big money and have it quickly.

The day after Al Novak's death Ocean City suffered the biggest hurricane within the recorded memory of the U.S. Weather Bureau. For four days, Sunday through Wednesday, the Eastern Seaboard was lashed by all of nature's fury. Damage ran past the $1 billion mark; our motel was left in ruins. Damage to the beach and to the building was estimated, I think conservatively, at $60,000. I believe the true figure to have been nearer $100,000. At any rate, the place was a shambles. Sand drifts fourteen feet deep covered much of our site. Wind and water had chewed great gaping random canyons across the property. We had no storm insurance. Our situation was desperate.

We applied for a Small Business Administration disaster relief loan. The SBA ultimately said it could permit a loan of $54,400. This was much less than was needed; if real damages approached the $100,000 mark, the delay in final completion had to cost much more. Meanwhile, bills for work now negated by the killer storm continued to press us.

Then the Small Business Administration dropped another speck in the churn: it could not permit even the $54,400 loan unless we provided a financial statement showing our ability to otherwise survive and repay the loan. It was another case of what people often experience when attempting to borrow money: "If you can't prove you don't need it, then you can't have it." I canvassed a number of personal friends but had little luck. Joseph Rahall, a friend from Beckley, West Virginia, was the only one who came through—and even he could only supply $10,000 of the $50,000 I asked for.

The Carousel was proving a bottomless pit. Desperate, I took a shortcut. It was not illegal in the strict sense. I won't claim, however, that I didn't hit on a sharp business practice or use my connections. I approached friends at the American National Bank of Silver Springs, Maryland, to say that I needed a $100,000 loan for fifteen days. I would not draw on the account. The money would repose in the account untouched and then revert to the bank. I got the loan. I also got a deposit slip for $100,000 and *that's* what I wanted. The Small Business Administration then permitted our disaster relief loan to go through, on the basis of the deposit slip, no questions asked. Later, when this transaction was brought out to the embarrassment of the SBA, the agency tightened its regulations to prevent similar incidents.

The wolf was not gone from my door, however. By early July I could hardly answer the telephone because of dunning creditors demanding payment: lumberyards, contractors, subcontractors, equipment houses, plumbers, banks. Geraldine Novak badgered me constantly to pay this or that pressing account. "I'll get the money," I told her, "don't worry." Since I was worrying enough for two, I tried to put a good face on things for her. We were due to open the motel in late June but everyone from liquor wholesale houses to furniture stores were holding up deliveries until their accounts were attended. I went to Lyndon Johnson with my troubles. "I told you long ago," he said, "that you'd get your ass in a crack trying to be a tycoon." He shortly telephoned Bob Kerr to say "Our boy Bobby needs your help."

I told my sad tale to Senator Kerr, concluding, "I must have an immediate credit line of $300,000 or I'll be forced to abandon the Carousel project and go into bankruptcy."

"That's a ton of money, Bobby."

"But not a dime more than I need to survive, senator. I had to pay out $187,000 to keep going just before the March storm, and I borrowed $145,000 of that from the American Security and Trust Company here. Now that note's due, and since the storm I've been flat on my ass."

Senator Kerr picked up the telephone and called Grady Harris, president of the Fidelity National Bank and Trust Company in Oklahoma City. The upshot was that the bank, in which Senator Kerr owned a great deal of stock, agreed to extend a $250,000 line of credit. "Bobby," Senator Kerr said, "I'll also make you a personal loan of $50,000. Will that see you through?" I thanked the senator profusely; it was all I could do not to kiss his feet. The senator said, "Would you like a $10,000 advance on that loan now?" I nodded. Senator Kerr first locked the door connecting his private office with his staff's quarters, then opened his office safe and counted out the cash.

The $250,000 credit line was gone before you could say Jack Robinson. Immediately, $145,000 was drawn to repay my loan to American Security and Trust. I withdrew $55,000 to settle with creditors, assure the delivery of vital goods to the Carousel, and finance the lavish grand opening I'd long planned. If the Carousel was to catch on as the hideway fun spot for Washington's "advise and consent" set, we needed to make a splash in the news media.

Sure enough, with the assistance of Washington public relations man Warren Adlee, the press went ga-ga over our opening on Sunday, July 22, 1962. Vice-President Johnson and Lady Bird tooled down to Ocean City in his official limousine. I rented a fleet of limousines to transport other celebrity guests, including Senators Maurine Neuberger of Oregon, Howard Cannon of Nevada, Dennis Chavez of New Mexico,

Gale McGee of Wyoming, and George Smathers of Florida; and Congressmen Bob (Fats) Everett of Tennessee, Daniel K. Inouye of Hawaii, Mike Kirwan of Ohio, and Bill Ayres of the same state. Former Senator Earl Clements was in attendance, as was actress Ilona Massey, songwriter Hank Fort, hostess Perle Mesta, and many reporters and columnists.

Seven buses transported 200 friends including congressional staffers, lobbyists, and not a few comely young women. Each bus was equipped with a bar dispensing champagne and brunch; the goodies were served by employees of The Place Where Louie Dwells, a restaurant not far from Capitol Hill. My guests were fed a buffet dinner and free drinks; they could swim in the ocean or in the Carousel's heated pool. Some played badminton or touch football on the beach. My two cocktail lounges—the Fog Cutter and the Sinkalaglas, the latter named for Captain Blood's ship—reverberated with laughter and music. Ten hostesses in tight-fitting black outfits and sheer hose were kept busy toting drinks. Guests inspected the downstairs nightclub in the three-story Carousel, and some partied in a number of the forty-five private guest rooms.

Throughout the day people slapped my back and congratulated me. The presumption was that I soon would grow filthy rich. "Bobby, ol' pal," said Congressman Fats Everett, "you fair got you a bird nest on the ground here." *If they only knew,* I thought. My head was barely above water and I floundered in a financial morass. Few among my guests knew of the troubles that plagued me, or the worries running through my head. For all my smiling front, I felt like a man no more than one hour ahead of the posse.

By October, I had to withdraw another $25,000 from the Oklahoma City bank for daily operating money; before the end of the year I took the remaining $20,000 to settle the mounds of new bills. In the interim, Senator Kerr had delivered on the remainder of his personal loan. In Washington, he gave me $25,000 from his Senate safe. In late November, when I stayed overnight at his Black Angus Motel in Oklahoma en route to the Albuquerque funeral of Senator Dennis Chavez, he supplied the final $15,000 of the loan. All this money, too, went down the Carousel maw.

Increasingly, after Lyndon Johnson left the Senate, I began to accept fees through my law firm partner, Ernest Tucker, or split fees with another lawyer-lobbyist and old friend, Wayne Bromley; Bromley had been a Senate page with me, a law school classmate, and I'd once gotten him a job in the Senate library. Bromley was by the 1960s a vice-president—chief lobbyist, really—for the National Coal Policy Council.

"I rented a fleet of limousines to transport Washington's biggies, such as Perle Mesta and Nevada's Senator Howard Cannon, to the grand opening of my Carousel Motel. My guests did not know that the Carousel was a bottomless pit, and had me on the edge of bankruptcy." (*Wide World Photos*)

He often operated out of my office almost as if it might be his own. I used Wayne Bromley as a conduit in accepting some fees. When retained by various firms to make deals for them or put them in touch with the right people, I sometimes had them pay Bromley rather then myself. This was not so that I might evade taxes, as later was charged, but was a subterfuge to keep my activities private. Bromley would cash the checks and hand over the money.

A couple of times in the late 1950s, and again in 1960, Lyndon Johnson had counseled me against outside activities. I think the first time was after I'd bought into Mecklenberg Enterprises, along with then Governor Luther Hodges of North Carolina and others, to construct a Howard Johnson Motel Lodge in Charlotte. Nor was he pleased at news that I'd been speculating in Florida land. I'm sure LBJ had my own good at heart, though I'm equally certain he may have been motivated by wanting to use all my energies on his projects and by a fear that I might get in a situation that would reflect badly on him.

"I don't want you moonlightin' or sundownin'," he said. "You've got a full-time job in the Senate. Don't try to practice law after hours." When he heard of another business deal I had in the hatching stage he said, "Bakes, goddammit, you've got enough to keep you busy. Don't go mixin' your public and private lives. A young man like you will have plenty of time to get rich later." After this admonition, I began to use Wayne Bromley as a conduit. Johnson had not approved, either, when I'd gone into partnership to build the Carousel; by then, however, he no longer was Senate majority leader and had no responsibility for me.

Payments of $500 per month came from U.S. Freight Company. I'd been hired when Stanley Sommer, a Washington public relations man, told me that Morris Forgash, president of U.S. Freight, was interested in acquisitions and investments; he would pay me for putting him in touch with opportunities involving the right people. I also recall putting Mr. Forgash in touch with former Senator Allan Frear to settle some difficulty with the SEC (though I never learned the outcome) and I kept him posted on the content, status, and prospects of the freight forwarders bill.

Cliff Jones channeled $10,000 through Wayne Bromley in exchange for my efforts to get his Las Vegas group the casino concessions in the Dominican Republic and Puerto Rico. Though I made the necessary introductions and set up meetings with officials in those latitudes, nothing came of it.

Keith Linden, counsel for Harvey Aluminum, met me on the street one day and said, "Bobby, I could certainly use somebody with your know-how on the Hill. We've got a lot of business in Washington and there's nobody who knows the ropes like you do." A few days later I called Linden and we agreed that I would be paid $1,000 per month for general unspecified services. These checks were forwarded to Wayne Bromley for ten months and were discontinued after investigations were launched into my activities. I was helpful to the Harvey company in concluding a bauxite deal in Africa. Looking back, it's amazing how little one was called on to do for some firms paying generous fees. Perhaps they just wanted to assure themselves of an agent in high places should they need him.

I also split a $5,000 fee with Bromley from the Redwood National Bank in San Rafael, California, for assisting in speeding up the granting of that bank's federal charter. I made two telephone calls to earn my fee: one to express interest in prompt action on the charter, and another to inform the client it had been granted. Since the investors were reputable men of impeccable financial credentials, their charter would surely have been granted anyway. In short, they wasted their $5,000. Businessmen long have believed it's better to be safe than sorry when dealing in Washington, however. This works to the advantage of some lawyer-lobbyists who do little more than write memos to their clients telling them how very hard they are working in their behalf.

In 1961 I began receiving a commission from the Haitian-American Meat and Provision Company, commonly known as Hamco, as recompense for helping to arrange a permit—through the Democratic leader of Puerto Rico, José Bonitez—for that company to export meat from Haiti to Puerto Rico and the United States. I was to receive one cent per pound for all meat so imported, up to a maximum of $30,000 per year. Nothing like that potential was reached; I averaged about $6,000 per year on the deal. Hamco, incidentally, was controlled by the Murchison interests of Texas.

I continued to invest in all stocks that looked good when given the opportunity. In April of 1961, Bob Thompson of the Murchison interests recommended investing in a conglomerate known as Investors Diversified Services. "Bob," I said, "I'd love to. But I'm pretty well extended financially. I just don't have anything to invest." Thompson said, "Well, you've accommodated me and the Murchisons many times. I'll put up your half of the money as a loan." We bought $111,000 worth of stock. In October, about the time we started construction of the Carousel, I sold my shares for a profit of $13,082—and had not risked a cent of my own money.

Shortly thereafter I entered into another, more profitable, investment. The opportunity came about through Senator Kerr and Fred Black. Fred was a superlobbyist who drew a $300,000 salary from North

American Aviation. He was paid another $75,000 or so per year by Melpar, Inc., a subsidiary of North American. His other income sources, and I'm not sure what they were, brought him an income of about a half-million dollars per year in the late 1950s and early 1960s—and you can imagine what they would translate to in terms of present values. But a half-million per year just wasn't enough money for Fred Black. He was a playboy of the first order; if he couldn't go first class, then he wouldn't take the trip.

He kept a hotel suite at the Sheraton-Carlton in Washington where he and his friends—and I was among them—repaired to conduct business, drink, play cards, or entertain ladies. Though we did not then know it, that suite was bugged by the FBI. They must have heard some interesting doings. Black also owned a huge home which shared a backyard fence with Vice-President Lyndon Johnson, after Johnson bought Perle Mesta's house in the exclusive Spring Valley section of Northwest Washington.

Black thought nothing of betting $5,000 on a horse race. He lost thousands at cards to Senator Kerr. What he didn't lose at the racetrack or to Senator Kerr he lost to Las Vegas casinos. He had a quick eye and a grand way with shapely ladies. He loved booze. In short, Fred Black thought little more about tomorrow than did a fattening hog; though he always filed his income tax returns in timely fashion, he rarely had the money to pay his taxes when due.

Senator Kerr and Fred Black originally proposed to go into the vending machine business together. There was big money to be made, Kerr said, by gaining a near monopoly on soft drink, candy, and cigarette machines to be installed at sites where companies were performing defense-related work that depended on government contracts. I've heard that Clark Clifford, the Washington lawyer-lobbyist who's been close to every Democratic administration beginning with Harry Truman's, talked Senator Kerr out of investing in the scheme because it clearly would constitute a conflict of interest on Kerr's part.

Senator Kerr then told Fred Black, "I want to help Bobby Baker. I'll get you the financing if you guys want to go into the vending machine business. There's a fortune to be made." True to his word, Senator Kerr obtained a $400,000 loan for us from the Fidelity National Bank and Trust Company of Oklahoma City, in which he owned stock. We spent the money for vending machines, installing them—among other places—at North American Aviation and at several subsidiary sites. Within a couple of years the Serv-U Corporation we founded—along with my law partner, Ernest Tucker; a Las Vegas hotel-casino man, Eddie Levinson; and a Miami investor and gambler, Benjamin B. Siegel-

baum—was grossing $3 million annually. I owned 28½ percent of the
Ser-U Corporation in those days—none now.

But if money flew in on quick wings, it almost immediately flew off
again. The Carousel remained a hungry, devouring tiger. Interest on
loans ate me up: I had fifty-one of them from twenty-two lending institutions, totaling more than $2.5 million from 1959 through 1963. I was liv-
ing pretty high on the hog, too: I spent a great deal of money entertaining, for travel, and I'd bought a $125,000 home for my family in the
posh Spring Valley section, only a hop and skip from LBJ's home as vice-
president. My net worth on paper by 1963 was more than $1.7 million,
but I recall few days when I didn't feel pressed and pressured by notes
coming due, bills coming in, and the constant need for operating cash.
Sometimes when the pressures got me, I drank; it was imperative to get
away from my problems for a few hours, to forget, to play at being
happy. But the next morning reality would come with the dawn and I
would plunge into the next round of hectic juggling and dealing to stay
afloat.

Chapter Twelve

The Beginning of the End

"You would be a Mongolian idiot not to take the fifth amendment. The Senate isn't the place to try your case."

IN LATE August of 1963 the staff director of the House District of Columbia Committee, and a fellow South Carolinan, Clayton Gasque, came to my office in an agitated state. He said, "Bobby, I'm afraid my friend Ralph Hill is about to cause big trouble. He's threatening to file a civil suit against you for damages, and go public with a charge that you're peddling influence."

I think I laughed. "What am I supposed to have done that's damaged him?"

"He claims you're causing him to lose his vending contract at Melpar," Gasque said. Melpar was a Virginia-based company which manufactured missile components, and was a subsidiary of Westinghouse Air Brake Company.

I said, "Clayton, that's pure bullshit. I *got* him the Melpar contract and you know it."

Gasque nodded his head, but he looked so worried it was almost comical. He is a tall, skinny man with a face so wrinkled, as Drew Pearson once wrote, "that it seemed perpetually pressed against a window screen." He was, at the time we talked, an official in Ralph Hill's Capitol Vending Company; his boss, Congressman John McMillan of South Carolina, then chairman of the House District Committee, was a stockholder in the company.

"You'll remember," I told him, "that Hill's contract contains a clause that Melpar can cancel his services on thirty days' notice, which is pretty standard. I know a little about the situation and Melpar wants a vending company that can also operate its employee cafeteria. Melpar thinks that Hill's company isn't qualified to do that. Hill's never been in the food business."

"Well," Gasque said, "Ralph also claims that you've tried to pressure him to sell his vending company to you."

"More bullshit. We made him an offer that Serv-U would buy him out if he wanted to sell. Frankly, when I learned from Ed Bostick of Melpar that he was getting rid of Hill, I thought we'd take his vending machines off his hands—possibly to our mutual benefit. But he rejected the offer and we've put absolutely no pressure on him."

"I'm worried about what he'll do," Gasque said. "I brought him to you and I feel responsible for what could happen."

I said, "He's bluffing. He hasn't got a case. If he charges me with peddling influence, don't you see that he'll be involved too?"

Clayton Gasque said, "Bobby, the guy's about half nuts and he's desperate. I think you should talk to him."

"No! I got him his original contract, then he didn't pay the fee we'd agreed on."

I had known Ralph Hill but slightly until Clayton Gasque brought him into my office in early 1962; I'd seen him at meetings of the South Carolina State Society, over which I presided; I knew he'd once worked in some patronage job under Congressman McMillan and that was it. When Hill came into my office the first time he bluntly said, "I own Capitol Vending Company and we have the concession on the House side. Can you help me get my machines in the Senate?"

I said, "Well, I think it's a bad situation and I don't know much about it, but we can look into it." Hill went on to say that the government might save money by dealing with a single contractor and so on, while I telephoned Senator Robert Byrd of West Virginia, chairman of the appropriate Rules subcommittee. He told me that his clerk would be more familiar with the details than he was. I then called the clerk, who said "Bobby, this is a bit embarrassing but you're a pro and I know you don't want to embarrass the chairman. The truth is, senators and their wives so abuse the Senate restaurant that we run a deficit there of more than $1 million each year. As a way to cover part of the deficit, we subsidize some of the loss through profits from the vending machines. Second, the vending company we use—Canteen—is sponsored by Senator Everett Dirksen and he's insisted that they have a long-term contract. Be discreet in what you tell anybody about this, because it would look like hell in the newspapers." I told Ralph Hill that Canteen had a long-term contract, its services were apparently satisfactory, and in general sloughed him off.

Several months later I was having dinner in the back dining room at the Sheraton-Carlton with Fred Black, Ed Bostick of Melpar, Carole Tyler, and a couple of other young women. Bostick said he was in the market for a vending company to serve Melpar, and he understood we'd just formed Serv-U. We decided, eventually, that the Melpar operation was a small one in which we were not all that interested. I then suggested

Ralph Hill's Capitol Vending Company. Melpar officials were not enthusiastic after meeting with Hill. They feared he was undercapitalized and
thought he wanted too big a slice of the pie. I talked to Ed Bostick, however, and he agreed to give Hill the concession as a favor to me.

Ralph Hill was elated. "You get things done," he said. "I'd like to hire
you as my general counsel. We can clean up in this town." He suggested
a fee of $1,000 per month for a year. Later, Hill would claim that he at-
tempted to give me a case of liquor for my services and that I had
demanded $1,000 per month. It didn't happen that way. Indeed, in his
euphoria that day Ralph Hill babbled about merging with Serv-U at a
later date and almost shook my hand off when he took his leave.

When my first payment came due, Hill said he was shy of operating
capital and asked to pay me $250 per month until he got in better shape.
This continued for a few months and then Hill came to my office again.
He said that because of inflation he needed to raise prices at Melpar, and
he asked me as his representative to negotiate the increase. I got Ed Bostick to agree to higher prices. Hill then paid me $600 monthly for a while
and then ceased payments altogether; he paid about $5,000 rather than
the $12,000 he'd originally suggested.

After Hill had operated at a good profit for about fifteen months, Ed
Bostick called and said, "Bakes, can you find me a food outfit to operate
the Melpar cafeteria? We're getting terrible complaints from our employees and I've just got to get rid of the people we're using." I said, "Ed,
you've been kind to me and I want to return the favor. I don't know anybody off the top of my head but I'll find you somebody." We briefly discussed whether Ralph Hill could handle it. Bostick was dubious, since
Hill had no experience in the food business. I said, "To be fair with you,
I doubt if Hill can cut it. I don't think he's got the resources to feed 4,000
people a day. But I will find you somebody." I got the Marriott Company
and a half-dozen other companies to look at the Melpar operation. None
was willing to take the cafeteria unless they also could have the vending
machine concession. In August, Melpar notified Hill of this and of its in-
tention to invoke its thirty-day cancellation clause. That's when I heard
that Hill was thinking of suing me.

A few nights later while Carole Tyler and her roommate, Mary Alice
Martin, were having drinks with friends at her town house on N Street in
Southwest Washington—which was in my name—Hill dropped in with a
man he introduced as a business associate. He called Carole aside. "He'd
been drinking," Carole later said. "He looked like death warmed over.
He was shaking and half crying and saying that unless he kept the Melpar contract he'd ruin you, because you'd given him verbal assurance he
could operate there for at least three years."

"He knew he had a thirty-day cancellation clause."

"I told him I didn't know the details," Carole said, "and suggested he talk to you directly. He just kept on ranting and raving about blowing you out of the water and ruining you. Then he grabbed my hand and kissed it and apologized for 'whatever harm may come to you.' In the next breath he's warning me that unless you come through for him within a week he'll sue and make a stink."

The experience shook Carole Tyler. She called me very early the following morning and after having related it said, "Honey, that guy's scary. You could be destroyed. Make peace with him, please." I said, "Carole, I'm not giving in. Let him do his worst." Though Carole implored me to change my mind, I refused. Probably it was one of my biggest mistakes.

Later that day I took Ed Bostick of Melpar to the White House Rose Garden to see General Rosey O'Donnell of the air force receive an award from President Kennedy on his retirement. I told Bostick of Hill's threats. He became frightened. "The publicity could be very bad," he said. "Maybe we could help you if you'd work out some financial settlement with him." Again I refused, saying Hill had "a bullshit lawsuit that even Clarence Darrow couldn't win."

Soon Hill went to his investor in Capitol Vending, Congressman McMillan, and told of his intent to sue me. Clayton Gasque called in alarm and asked whether Hill and I might not settle our differences. Again I was stubborn. On September 9, Hill filed suit against me, my law partner Ernest Tucker, and Serv-U Corporation. His suit for $300,000 in damages alleged that he'd paid me $5,000 in payoff money and that Tucker and I had "maliciously conspired" to oust him at Melpar and take over the vending machine concession. The second of the charges, at least, was patently false. I was astonished that he'd actually filed the suit, but thought we'd beat it in the end. I failed to see the terrible storm brewing.

The press did not take note of the suit until September 12, when a reporter going through court records ran across it. A brief story appeared in the inside pages of the *Washington Post*. A few reporters then called or came to see me. I told them that Hill was dealing in vicious slander, and creating a lot of gossip that I hoped would get into print so I could sue him. The resulting stories were perfunctory and didn't excite anybody. I guess it sounded to people as if two guys had gotten involved in a cussing contest and there wasn't much to it.

Lyndon Johnson was worried, however. He sent Walter Jenkins to see me. "The boss would hate to see this thing blown up," Jenkins said. "Reporters have been around asking questions and he's afraid Bobby Kennedy's putting them up to hanging something on you so as to embarrass him." I attempted to reassure Jenkins. Shortly thereafter, however, he approached me and said that LBJ thought I should quietly settle the lawsuit. "Tell him not to worry," I said. "I don't think the guy will dare bring his case to trial. I believe that after a while it will just wither on the vine." I wish now that LBJ had sent for me personally and had used his well-known powers of persuasion. If he had, I probably would have agreed to settle. Senator Mansfield didn't even mention the matter to me.

It was a story in the September issue of *Vend* magazine, a trade journal for the vending machine industry, that blew the lid off. The story told of my investment in Serv-U with lobbyist Fred Black, said that we'd gained many contracts while still a paper company, that we'd replaced many experienced vending companies where government contracts were the primary source of income, that we'd received liberal and instant credit from an Oklahoma bank controlled by Senator Kerr and his family, and cited Serv-U's spectacular growth. Suddenly, journalists came running in a pack. I went running to Abe Fortas and hired him to be my attorney.

Mike Mansfield sent for me; I gave him a report on the Ralph Hill–Melpar situation and filled him in on how Serv-U had come about. Then I said, "If you think this will embarrass you personally, or embarrass the Senate or the Democratic party, I'm prepared to resign. I don't want to, because some might take it as an admission of guilt, but I'll do it if you think it's best." Mansfield quietly said that I was doing an excellent job for him, he had faith in me, and he wouldn't think of asking me to quit before I'd had my day in court. He issued a statement to the *New York Times* saying much the same.

The spate of newspaper stories set off a Pavlovian reaction in Senator John J. Williams, the Delaware Republican who liked to be labeled the "Watchdog of the Senate"; he had made a reputation by exposing the "mink coat and deep freeze" scandals involving General Harry Vaughan in the Truman administration and had contributed to the downfall of Sherman Adams, President Eisenhower's top White House assistant, when it developed that financer Bernard Goldfine had paid for vacation trips for Adams and gifted him with expensive furs. Senator Williams virtually declared open season on me, asking people who knew of my operations to come forward. One who did was my former partner in the Carousel, Geraldine Novak, whom my Serv-U Corporation had bought out with two promissory notes, the second of which was to be paid from future profits of the Carousel. Don Reynolds, the insurance man, came forward with his story of the hi-fi gift to LBJ and the advertising he had to buy on Johnson's TV and radio stations as a condition of writing a life insurance policy on him. Senator Williams was happy to announce such stories to the press.

He also presumably enjoyed breaking the story of how I'd bought the $28,000 town house Carole Tyler lived in. Lurid newspaper accounts spoke of "$7,500 worth of French wallpaper, wall-to-wall lavender carpets, and all-night parties of Washington's powerful and mighty." A great deal of hyperbole was involved. It was a nice enough house, but the furnishings were vastly inflated as to worth and style, as were the reports which sounded as if orgies occurred there with the setting of the sun.

"Ralph Hill's lawsuit against me, about the vending machines, resulted in a spate of newspaper stories which touched off a Pavlovian reaction in the United States Senate. . . . Probably, failing to settle it was my biggest mistake." (*United Press International*)

There *was* an embarrassment involved, however. I had incorrectly and improperly listed Carole Tyler as my cousin when I applied for the loan, in order to satisfy the Federal Housing Authority's regulation that anyone buying an FHA-underwritten home must either live in it or have a relative living in it. At the time I gave the matter little more serious thought than would a groundhog; indeed, Carole and I had shared a laugh about it. "Well," I said to my lover, "at least you're my kissin' cousin. So it's only a little white lie."

In truth, Carole and her roommate made the payments on the house; I was the owner in name only, though I had made a loan to Carole to cover the down payment and the partial costs of the furnishings. Carole and her roomie had attempted to buy the house on their own. In those days, before anyone had heard of women's liberation

"My Serv-U Corporation had bought out Geraldine Novak's interest in the Carousel with two promissory notes. . . . She told the Senate Rules Committee that she didn't believe her husband committed suicide because of business dealings with me." (*United Press International*)

or consumer rights, young single women found it almost impossible to gain credit approval. I thought this unfair. When the young women couldn't swing the financing under those conditions, I volunteered to make application for the FHA loan as their front man. I was not aware of the "relative" proviso until I filled out the FHA loan application, and I both impulsively and whimsically listed Carole as my cousin. It sounded ever so much more sinister in the newspapers, however: I had bought my lady a love nest, a lavish one at that, where people presumably ran around naked with bottles of champagne in each hand and I had conspired to break the law.

Now the hounds were in full cry. Senator Williams, Senator Scott of Pennsylvania, Senator Curtis of Nebraska, Senator Goldwater, and other Republicans demanded a full-scale Senate investigation into my activities. Another Republican who raised his righteous voice in demanding an investigation to restore purity to government was a private citizen by the name of Richard Nixon. I soon learned how easily rumors are accepted as fact when the story is sensational and the target is on the run. Stories appeared that I was involved in an abortion ring preying on unfortunate young women for profit. This was a flat lie.

That it was a lie didn't prevent details being told of how the alleged abortion ring worked, however. Pregnant girls were instructed to stand in front of a given People's Drugstore in downtown Washington, or in front of the Willard Hotel, holding a pair of sunglasses in their hands and wearing some sort of a flower. They would be approached by a middle-aged woman who would tell them to shut their eyes. She then would lead them to a nearby car, blindfold them, and drive them for about ninety minutes to some secluded rural site where abortions were performed. Then the young women, again blindfolded, would be driven back to Washington in the dark of night. I, too, had heard such stories and it may be that such an operation existed. Bobby Baker was in no way involved in it, however, nor do I know who was.

New stories appeared every day, however, no matter how speculative. There were accusations that I'd used Senate chefs and Senate equipment at the Carousel. Untrue. That I received payroll kickbacks or padded my payroll with employees who did not actually perform work. Untrue. That I'd invested in a Jacksonville, Florida real estate development financed with $400,000 from Jimmy Hoffa's Teamsters Union pension fund. In truth, I had declined to invest when I heard that the union was underwriting the development. Geraldine Novak made additional headlines with her comments about having called at my office to pick up bundles of cash. That was true. As I sold stocks, borrowed money to keep the Carousel afloat, and received cash fees through Wayne Bromley, I sometimes gave her cash for operating expenses or to repay her for bills she'd paid from her husband's construction company account. Each new story, of course, fed the fire.

Senator Mansfield could no longer take the heat. Unknown to me at the time, he'd been meeting with Senator John Williams and had been fed each morsel of gossip or any accusation anyone cared to make. In early October of 1963 he told me that he wanted me to meet with him, with Senator Williams, and with Senator Everett Dirksen to go over the charges and accusations. I said, "Senator Mansfield, I'm perfectly willing to meet with you and with Senator Dirksen or with any Democratic senators you can name and I'll abide by whatever decision is reached. But John Williams is out to get me as a way of getting to Lyndon Johnson. I don't think he'd give me anything like a fair hearing." (I didn't know it at the time, and would not learn it until Lyndon Johnson told me when I visited him in Texas after I came out of prison, but J. Edgar Hoover had told Senator Mansfield that FBI wiretaps indicated I was hanging out with "known gamblers," by which he meant Ed Levinson and Ben Siegelbaum. They were, indeed, gamblers. They were investors and operators of hotels and casinos in a state where gambling was legal. I had not thought to check into their pasts: to me they were businessmen and if gambling was their business, so what?) Senator Mansfield got me to agree reluctantly to include Senator Williams in the meeting. He pled that unless I did meet with Williams, the Delaware senator might accuse us of stalling and of a whitewash. He seemed very nervous. We established the confrontation for Monday, October 7, at 3 P.M., in Senator Dirksen's office.

On that day, by prior arrangement, I'd agreed to take some visiting friends from Texas to lunch at the Quorum Club, in the Carroll Arms Hotel near the Senate. The Quorum Club by now was being described by the newspapers as first cousin to a Mexican whorehouse. Most of its members—senators, congressmen, lobbyists, a few military men and executive branch officials—were staying away in droves.

I should have remembered that day what Thurber once said of the martini: "One is not enough. Two are too many. Three are nowhere near enough." I had four Tanqueray gin martinis at that luncheon. All were doubles. Suddenly I heard myself proclaiming to my bewildered guests, "My boss has abandoned me. The goddamn press is having a field day at my expense. There are so many people involved that if this thing keeps going it will drag them down. I'm of the opinion I'm gonna resign. Fuck Senator Williams."

Somehow I got it in my head that should I resign the entire Bobby Baker episode would magically disappear from the front pages and come to a grinding halt. I left the Quorum Club with a swagger in my step. I recall that it was a crisp, beautiful fall day as I stumbled across the park separating the Quorum Club from the Capitol Building and went directly to Senator Mansfield's office. I blurted out to him, "Senator, we've had an unusually decent and close relationship. But if you insist upon my meeting with Senator John Williams, then I'm compelled to resign forthwith." It's my hazy recollection that he suggested I take a leave of absence until matters might be resolved. With tears in my eyes I shook his hand and said, "No, senator, I can't. I've got to resign."

I stumbled down the staircase, my head a jumble of old memories and impressions of the place I'd come to know and love better than any in the world. I went directly to Carole Tyler's town house, called her, and said, "I've just resigned. Come home, baby." I then proceeded to get gloriously drunk. Numb drunk. I recall that Carole cried, and perhaps I did, but I've no recollection at all of how that Wednesday ended or of whether I made it home.

The gin notion that my resignation might somehow stuff the cat back in the bag did not, of course, hold up. It instead prompted "Second Coming" headlines and more insistent demands from politicians and ed-

"The Quorum Club, in the Carroll Arms Hotel near the Senate side of Capitol Hill, was being described as the biggest den of iniquity this side of a Mexican whorehouse. Most of its members were staying away in droves." (*Wide World Photos*)

itorial writers that the Senate get to the bottom of my tangled affairs. Three days after I quit, Senator Williams introduced a resolution to investigate the affairs of "any officer, or employee, or former officer or employee of the U.S. Senate." The Senate whooped it through by voice vote, sparing the embarrassment of a roll call. There were a number of senators who knew that their own hands were far from spotless, and some might have felt a twinge or two had they been forced to vote individually for the probe. Speculation was rampant on the Hill as to whether, having resigned, I might "sing" and put serious crimps in a few careers.

Life magazine put me on the cover, using an old photo of me peering out from under a mask at a masquerade party, looking as if I was getting ready to rob a stagecoach. The cover of *Time* enhanced my likeness by placing behind it a dark backdrop with an entangling spiderweb. I could not pass a newsstand or a magazine rack without seeing my face or my name blinking at me, nor turn on the radio or television without hearing myself reported, seriously debated, or joked about.

Newspapers were dispatching coveys of reporters to Pickens to ask everyone about their local bad boy. I was gratified by the resulting stories in which my former teachers, employers, friends, and associates had only good to say. It was a welcome relief from such as had appeared in *Life,* where a party was described involving call girls, lobbyists, and nude frolics in a champagne bath. Such a party had occurred at the apartment of a lobbyist I knew, but I had not attended it. *Life* neglected to make this point clear. I came off like a world's champion whoremonger. It appeared that the whole of Washington was rotten to the core because of associations with Bobby Baker.

I telephoned my father in Pickens. "You've read some pretty rough stuff about me," I said, "and you'll probably read a lot more. Take it with a grain of salt. If they're gonna put people in jail for drinking, for liking pretty women, and for turning a profit then I guess I ought to be among the first to go. I've done some foolish things and some careless things, but I don't feel like the devil incarnate, and I'm holding my head up. I hope you and mother will, too." My father became very emotional. "Bobby, we love you so much. Some of this is very hard for people to understand. But we are with you, our hearts are with you . . ." He choked up and couldn't continue. I chattered on, asking questions about the local political situation until he regained his composure.

One Sunday evening I was consulting with Abe Fortas at his home in Georgetown when Lady Bird Johnson called. After talking with Fortas she asked to speak with me. Mrs. Johnson said, "Bobby, Lyndon and I just want you to know we love you. You are like a member of the family and we are so grateful for all you've done for us. Our prayers are with you." I thanked her politely and soon she began to talk of the Vietnam trip she and Vice-President Johnson had just completed. I hardly heard her. I was thinking: *LBJ's right there by her side, but he won't talk to me because he wants to be able to say that he hasn't.* I knew Johnson was petrified that he'd be dragged down; he would soon show this by attempting to make light of our former relationship and saying that I had been more the Senate's employee than his own. *He's using Lady Bird to soft-soap me,* I thought. His hope was that he would not become more entangled in my affairs, and while he feared to make direct contact he probably was equally concerned that I might become miffed at his inattention and say something harmful to the detriment of his career.

LBJ already was nervous because of the Billy Sol Estes scandal and the resignation of a Texas friend, Fred Korth, who'd quit as secretary of the navy following conflict-of-interest accusations. So I had not expected to hear much from him. In fact, from the moment I resigned in October of 1963 until I visited him at his ranch to see a dying man, almost nine years later, we spoke not a word and communicated only through intermediaries.

The second call from high places was not as easy to read and was far more astonishing. I was in the law office of Tommy Corcoran—"Tommy the Cork" as FDR nicknamed him when he was a young New Deal brain truster—discussing my tax situation with him and with Boris Kostelanetz, a tax attorney from New York, when a secretary entered to say that the attorney general wanted to speak to me. I thought, *My God, what have I done now?* Robert Kennedy's secretary, Angie Novella—now secretary to Edward Bennett Williams—exchanged pleasantries with me and asked me to stand by for the attorney general. In a moment that crisp New England twang said, "Bobby, my brother is fond of you and remembers your many kindnesses. I want you to know that we have nothing of any consequence about you in our files—except for newspaper clippings which I'm certain you've read. My brother and I extend our sympathies to you. I know that you'll come through this." I was halting and inarticulate in my response because I was taken by surprise and didn't know what to make of the curious call. Finally I stammered, "I'm grateful, Mr. Attorney General. What you've just done required a lot of courage."

Corcoran and Kostelanetz were shocked, because all manner of leaks had been coming out of the Justice Department about me. Why, then, would the attorney general—whom Lyndon Johnson believed was trying to bring him down through prosecuting me—take pains to call with a comforting message? Our attempts at interpretation dealt largely with the political: were the Kennedys afraid of a general Democratic disaster if my case exploded? Did the call signal that the Justice Department intended to drag its feet, call off the dogs, or what? This, naturally, is what I hoped. John F. Kennedy himself, a couple of weeks earlier, had sent word to me through John Lane, former administrative assistant to Senator Brian McMahon of Connecticut, that I should keep my chin up. For all our discussion in Corcoran's office, we discovered no satisfactory explanation of the attorney general's call. Perhaps we should have considered merely the humane rather than the political. Despite our personal differences, Bobby Kennedy knew that I'd been of service in several common causes. Perhaps he meant no more than to convey kindness to a troubled man who might be receiving his last hurrah.

That explanation would have drawn a snort from Lyndon Johnson. A member of the staff of Senator Tom Dodd of Connecticut had told me that in a car between Hartford and New Haven, where LBJ was to speak at an appreciation dinner for Senator Dodd, the vice-president had viciously lashed Bobby Kennedy for trying to make him look like a "crook" and claimed the RFK had "cooked up" the Baker case for that purpose.

Senate Resolution 212—the "'Bobby Baker Investigation" bill—was referred to the Senate Rules Committee, chaired by Everett Jordan of North Carolina. There were quick cries from Republicans that a fix was in, that Jordan had been friendly with me and had kept a large picture of me in his office until I resigned, and that he had been one of ten senators who allegedly were in the palm of my hand on almost any vote. The general suspicion was that Lyndon Johnson had manipulated it so that Senator Jordan, who was something of a bumbler, would tamely limit the investigation. The suspicion was reinforced when Senator Jordan uttered his infamous line "We aren't in the business of investigating senators."

If that was, indeed, the plan, then it misfired as far as I'm concerned. Senator Williams was permitted not only to be the first witness against me, freely tossing up any rumor or gossip that he'd heard, but then was permitted—*though not a member of the Rules Committee*—to question and cross-examine other witnesses. I don't know of any other case in history where that was permitted, even given the tendency of congressional investigating committees to play it looser with the rules of evidence and with one's civil liberties than any court would permit. Senator Jordan sat by ineffectually during squabbles between Senator Williams and the committee's chief counsel, "Major" Lennox Polk McLendon, a country lawyer from North Carolina, who resented the intrusions of Senator Williams. Williams ultimately would dramatically toss his "Baker File" on Chairman Jordan's desk and stalk from the room declaring the hearing to be "a farce."

After the investigation had been completed, I received a call from Senator John McClellan of Arkansas, who invited me to his apartment at the Fairfax Hotel. Senator McClellan, a dour old man who had the image of "the tough cop" for his investigations of labor racketeering, had never cottoned to Lyndon Johnson. However, I'd had good relations with him. He said, "Bobby, it's a disgrace the way the Rules Committee let those hearings turn into a circus. If they'd assigned that hearing to my committee, I'd have done a tough and thorough job—you can count on it—but I wouldn't have permitted John Williams the wide latitude he was given, and I'd have fired any staffer who permitted the leaks they did to newsmen. You know, something's wrong when you can read the testimony in the newspapers *before* it's given. I don't want to accuse anybody, but if Lyndon Johnson thought he was putting you in friendly hands with Everett Jordan, then God deliver me to my enemies and spare me from my friends."

My original attorney, Abe Fortas, after examining my financial records and tax returns, advised that I testify openly and freely when the Rules Committee called me. "The best solution to this kind of political

"Senator John J. Williams, the dour Delaware Republican, virtually declared open season on me. . . . He dramatically tossed his 'Baker Case' files on the committee table and walked out, charging a whitewash."   (*United Press International*)

hearing," he said, "is to tell the truth. Don't try to fuzz anything over." I knew, however, that if I testified to the total truth then Lyndon B. Johnson, among others, might suffer severely. Suppose they asked me whether Lyndon Johnson had, indeed, insisted on a kickback from Don Reynolds in the writing of his life insurance policy? A truthful answer would torpedo the vice-president. Suppose they asked me what I knew of campaign funds for Johnson, or for that matter President Kennedy? Although I sensed that a "gentleman's agreement" had been reached with respect to avoiding the embarrassment of senators, I certainly suspected that John J. Williams would not honor it where the vice-president was concerned. I had been too recently a member of the club, and too keenly felt a kinship with LBJ and others, to turn rat. You may say that I was honoring the code of the underworld if you will, but I didn't want to hurt my friends. That's the context in which I thought of it.

I know that a client is required to be wholly honest with his lawyer. I think I was honest with Abe Fortas about myself and about Senator Kerr—who was, after all, safe from harm in his grave—and about everyone else. Except, of course, Lyndon B. Johnson. I knew that Fortas was close to Johnson, that he truly worshipped him; I therefore avoided mentioning anything derogatory about the vice-president or raising the prospect that the whole truth might hurt him. Fortas did not yet know that Don Reynolds had spilled his guts to Senator Williams on the insurance policy matter, and I doubt whether he then would have believed it. It was perhaps a blessing for both of us, therefore, that upon the assassination of John F. Kennedy I released him as my attorney.

This meant that I had to seek new counsel. Abe Fortas recommended Jiggs Donohue, a former commissioner of the District of Columbia, but I didn't know him or much about his abilities. I had been impressed during the Senate censure proceedings against Senator Joe McCarthy by the demeanor of his attorney, Edward Bennett Williams. I had, and liberals must forgive me, personally liked Joe McCarthy. He was a good man to enjoy a drink or a card game with, though certainly he was a careless demagogue and deserved the censure the Senate voted him. Senator McCarthy was out of control at the Army-McCarthy hearings—a runaway disaster—and he paid little or no attention to the advice of Ed Williams. I had been a close observer of the hearings and I had seen Williams turn white with rage when he counseled McCarthy to cool it and the Wisconsin senator had, instead, indulged in low jackassery that brought about his certain demise. The hard and good work that Ed Williams had done under impossible circumstances in that case had impressed me. In the years between 1954 and 1963, Williams had become one of the more successful lawyers in America. I wanted him.

Bill Veeck, the baseball man, and his business partner, Nate Dolin of Cleveland, were friends of Ed Williams. I knew them because Nate's young son had worked for me as a Senate page. I asked them if they would talk to Williams to see whether he might represent me. He agreed to take my case, after we'd talked for six hours, at the bargain rate of $25,000. (This did not include the $25,000 I paid to the tax attorney, Boris Kostelanetz; the shocking thing about legal costs, however, is not so much the attorney's fees as the terrible cost of court transcripts, witnesses' expenses, investigative expense, the appeals mechanism, and so forth. I paid in excess of $100,000 for these.)

Edward Bennett Williams became my lawyer in December of 1963; hearings in my case began in the Senate in January of 1964, and I was called to testify on February 19. Very early in our preparations Ed Williams said, "You can't win in a congressional hearing, Bobby. You've got no right of cross examination. The other side isn't bound by the rules of evidence. They can throw out any accusation they wish. Innuendo. Gossip. Gutter stuff. They can ridicule you and lecture you and it's easy for them to cite you for contempt or perjury." Williams discoursed at some length about the history of congressional committees, citing abuses in the cases of Alger Hiss, Joe McCarthy, the Hollywood Ten, Frank Costello, and Howard Hughes.

"In short," he said, "a congressional committee can tie your hands behind your back and you can't do anything about it. You would be a Mongolian idiot"—and I never will forget that he repeated the phrase—"a *complete* Mongolian idiot to do anything other than take the fifth amendment. It's your constitutional right. Stand on it. The fifth amendment avoids any prospect of perjury, and perjury's the one thing that will kill a member of the bar. Perjury will get you disbarred in a trice, and the judiciary will be hard on a lawyer convicted of it."

I said, "Taking the fifth will make me look guilty in the eyes of many. There are some things I'd like to get on the record."

Ed Williams said, "Bobby, I think when passions have subsided you'll win your case and you'll have plenty of opportunity then to get on the record. But the Senate isn't the place to try your case and this isn't the time."

"You're my lawyer," I said. "You call the shots."

Senator Hugh Scott of Pennsylvania proved particularly adept at making up headlines when he couldn't produce a witness for that purpose. Scott was facing reelection in 1964 and the polls showed him in shaky shape; it appeared that a Democratic landslide might wipe him out. Knowing that the Bobby Baker story was automatic page one stuff, he went to great lengths to show how tirelessly he'd been fighting corruption. On one such occasion he dramatically announced to the Senate—with the press gallery looking on—that he had lost "eleven and a half pounds" due to so ardently having pursued the Baker investigation.

The topper, however, was when he charged on the Senate floor—knowing he had immunity there to protect him against a slander suit—that I had made threats against senators who dared to pursue the facts. "He's telling people he's kept book on senators," Scott thundered, and then went on to declare himself unafraid in the face of this menace. Outside chambers, shorn of legal protection, Scott became extremely vague about such "threats" to himself or to others. Of course, what he'd said in chambers made the newspapers and I'm sure some people judged me a thug. "I'd be the dumbest man in the world to be threatening people," I told a friendly reporter who called me for a comment. "My lawyer's told me not to say a thing to the press or to senators or to anyone else, and I haven't. But I do believe I'll risk saying that Senator Scott seems to be a victim of his own imagination. I leave it to you as to whether I know the Senate well enough to understand that threatening its members would be the worst thing in the world for me. If anything, I ought to be up there shaking hands."

More than a hundred reporters were jammed around four tables and about twenty-five photographers jostled for position and fought for footholds when I entered the hearing room in the Old Senate Office Building on a cold February morning. TV lights blazed from all available standards and ledges. There was, as Senator Claiborne Pell of Rhode Island would complain, "a hippodrome atmosphere." It was strange, indeed, to come back to my former haunts in the role of the outsider and to see sitting in judgment of me some men who recently had been my friends and some I'd known as partisan enemies.

A week earlier, Edward Bennett Williams had notified the Rules Committee that for many legal reasons I would neither honor the subpoena seeking my records nor respond to the committee's questions. He now rose to remind the senators of this and to add, "If Mr. Baker is to be made to sit here, sir, and to invoke his constitutional rights before this committee . . . I feel that he should not be held up to public obloquy on the television cameras, and I ask, sir, at this time, that the television cameras be excluded from this hearing room, because the sole purpose of this hearing in the light of the stipulation that we are making, cannot be a legislative purpose because we have advised you, sir, that we will answer no questions. . . . I object to any televising of these proceedings because I say, sir, that they are being held solely for the purpose of the television camera."

Though Ed Williams had spoken in soft and deferential tones, the Republicans began to throw conniptions. Senator Scott claimed the committee had been attacked and insulted. Senator Curtis of Nebraska demanded that unless Ed Williams withdraw his statement that "he be expelled from the room, or that he stand charges of contempt." Committee partisans in the audience burst into applause. All of this theater was, of course, being played out before the television cameras in question. I began to appreciate more fully my attorney's remarks to the effect that all advantages rested with the committee and none with the witness. (Chairman Jordan ultimately ordered the cameras turned off: NBC removed its cameras to the hall, focused on the closed Rules Committee doorway, and broadcast the audio portions of the proceedings).

Major McLendon, the committee counsel, then began to inquire of my records. He was covering the same ground we'd gone over in executive session—that is, behind closed doors with the press and the public

Edward Bennett Williams said, "Bobby, you would be a mongolian idiot to do anything other than take the fifth amendment. . . . The U.S. Senate isn't the place to try your case." (*Wide World Photos*)

"The Baker hearings were conducted in what Senator Claiborne Pell of Rhode Island would characterize as 'a hippodrome atmosphere.' It was strange to come back to my former haunts in the role of the outsider." (*United Press International*)

excluded—a week earlier. Laymen may be surprised to learn that before open hearings are held—and I don't care if we are talking about Alger Hiss, Watergate, or Bobby Baker—carefully orchestrated scenarios have been prepared in private. Very little is spontaneous about open congressional hearings. They are like a play, with roles assigned and the actors speaking their predetermined set pieces.

I said, "Major, I have all the documents that were requested in the subpoena, but I stand by my prior statement. You knew what my position was going to be before I was called back here today."

He responded, "I have a right to ask you a second time. Sometimes people change their minds, you know."

I shot back, "You don't know me. Whatever reputation I had in the Senate, my word was my bond and when I told you I was not going to testify, that ended it as far as I was concerned." Only moments before I had invoked the first, the fourth, the fifth, and the sixth amendments to the Constitution and had told the senators, "I do not intend to participate as a defendant witness in a legislative trial of myself where there are no rules of evidence, when my counsel has no right to cross-examine my accusers or summon witnesses in my defense, when no charges have been furnished to me, and when the testimony has been taken both in secret and in the open."

Then I braced myself. Ed Williams had warned that questions might include gossip, rumor, innuendo, and generally come from out of the blue. "Don't answer anything beyond your name, address, your former position in the Senate, and that you resigned it. The committee counsel and senators may try to provoke you into answering. Don't take the bait. A skilled lawyer may get you to answer what appears to be innocuous questions and then claim that your answering them constituted your waiving your right to remain silent. Just bite your tongue and dummy up."

For almost three hours the committee counsel and the senators threw questions at me; I often had to bite my tongue and recall my lawyer's instructions. When Senator Scott asked whether I had had dealings with "one Joe Fabianich, now in Leavenworth Penitentiary on white slavery charges," I ached to declare that I'd never even heard of the man. I had no choice but to sit tongue-tied when Scott asked "Do you wish to state how many persons you referred to a Puerto Rican doctor for abortions?" and "Will you furnish the doctor's name?" The same when asked if I had placed horse-race bets "with one Snags Lewis, well-known to the police of this city" or whether I had supplied call girls to businessmen. I was unable to explain, though there was a logical explanation, why I had ordered a page boy to pay $50 of his monthly salary to another Senate employee, Joe Stewart. Several times when I appeared to be on the verge of blurting out an answer, Ed Williams gave me looks that said *Watch your ass. Only you can protect it.*

Senators Jordan, Scott, Curtis, and Joseph Clark got on record that I might be in contempt of the Senate. At the conclusion of the long and profitless morning the committee counsel, Major McLendon, issued a public statement: "We witnessed a tragedy here this morning because a man who has occupied a high position in Government, a position close to the heart of power, has felt he has to invoke the Fifth Amendment to protect himself from his own version of the truth, not somebody else's version. The effect is bound to be felt by this Committee, by the Congress of the United States and by the people of America. And it may raise the question if the time hasn't come to deny public officials the protection of the Fifth Amendment. I would be in favor of it from now on."

While Major McLendon was urging that I be stripped of my constitutional rights, Ed Williams was telling newsmen that I'd already been denied some of them by government wiretaps; he exhibited for TV cameras a tiny hidden microphone that had been discovered in the telephone in Eddie Levinson's office at his Fremont Hotel in Las Vegas. I stood in the background thinking *Show biz. This is the Senate of the United States, and its all show biz.* Over lunch at Duke Zeibert's, however, Ed Williams reminded me of the realities: "You've got a long way to go. You're far from out of the woods, and you could wander in them for years. Like Moses in the wilderness." No wiser words ever were spoken.

Chapter Thirteen

Wired Informants and the Death of a Lady

When I saw her broken body I cried like a baby.

POLITICAL hardball was being played by those on each side of the partisan fence, and I often felt like the goat of the game. Hearing and reading about myself as a divisive force was a new and unhappy experience. My job had always been to bring people together in a common cause. It was against my instinct and my experience to rock the boat. I found it painful when such old friends as Senators Everett Dirksen and Barry Goldwater made attacks upon me and promised I would be a big issue in the 1964 presidential campaign. I knew they were political pros, doing their partisan jobs, and I once told a reporter who asked me how I felt about their attacks, "When the political pot cools Barry Goldwater will grab me and hug me." Sure enough, after Senator Goldwater lost his race against Lyndon Johnson, he encountered me at a social function and did exactly that. The partisan attacks made me feel bad at the time, however.

(Not all the attacks were by Republicans. Democrats Joseph Clark, Ralph Yarborough, and Ed Muskie also badmouthed me. I was outraged by Muskie's public piety, considering that when he'd once sorely needed campaign money I had raised on short notice $1,000 from Charlie Daniels, a South Carolina financier and political kingmaker, who kicked through as a favor to me. I delivered the $1,000 in cash to former Senator Earl Clements who in turn passed it on to Muskie. Ed knew I had raised it, though not where I had gotten it.)

I also felt strange when watching TV and seeing men with whom I'd long worked—Walter Jenkins, Bill Moyers, George Reedy, and Cliff Carter—to say nothing of such newcomers as Jack Valenti and Marvin Watson, go in and out of the White House gates or confer with Lyndon Johnson in the Oval Office while I remained a distant and isolated figure. I did send some advice and recommendations to President Johnson through Walter Jenkins, largely in the form of memos which I signed "George Lusk II" in case they fell into the wrong hands, and Jenkins sometimes called me to solicit my opinions. These contacts became fewer as time went on, however, and I won't pretend that I did not yearn to be a part of the excitement and bustle. In the absence of my troubles, I knew I would have had an active role in the Johnson administration and probably would have been the president's liaison link with the Congress.

Now, however, my name inspired sound and fury. Senator Hugh Scott sang that I should be placed under permanent subpoena "because I don't know if he's inclined to wanderlust." There were stories I had stashed a fortune in Swiss banks. I wish that they were true. Even Moscow got in the act. *Izvestia* charged that the Bobby Baker case proved that "bipartisan corruption, honor lost, and dirty customs" made the stuff of American politics. Republicans howled that with Johnson as president, a whitewash and cover-up was in prospect and inferred that LBJ was attempting to impede the investigation. Democrats, acutely aware that more of their number might be harmed should the investigation spread, dragged their feet while at the same time accusing the Republicans of mean partisanship.

Senator John J. Williams presented a resolution demanding that the entire membership of the Senate be investigated, intimating that he knew of senators who were less than pure. The touchy senators rebelled at this slight against the club; Senator Mansfield, in an uncharacteristic burst of public anger, demanded that Senator Williams put up or shut up: "Let him name names." Others castigated the Delaware Republican as a rumor monger and rebuked him for the use of sly innuendo, before shouting the Williams resolution down. This result should have been foreseen by Senator Williams. Too many cans of worms would have been opened on both sides of the aisle had his resolution carried the day.

Senator Williams continued to pump Don Reynolds, the insurance man, in search of new fodder. In August of 1964 he forced the Rules Committee—which had closed shop and was writing its report—to reopen the Baker case. In a speech to the Senate he said that in writing insurance on the performance bond of McCloskey & Company—the Philadelphia outfit constructing the new District of Columbia stadium—there had been a $35,000 kickback which was to go to the 1960 Democratic campaign fund. Matthew McCloskey, president of the construction firm and long a big wheel in Democratic politics—he'd served as national chairman and as ambassador to Ireland—told senators that he had not personally handled the transaction and knew little about it. "These things, somebody goofs once in a while," he said. The senators did not hold his feet to the fire. They appeared to be satisfied with his promise that he would seek recovery of the funds in question, and with his claim that no more than oversight or a clerical error had been involved.

It is perhaps significant that he never tried to recover the money. I was the man who had put Reynolds and McCloskey together, so I know what the understandings were. As an official in the Reynolds insurance firm, I received a $4,000 loan from profits the firm made on the D.C. Stadium transaction. This was not the only business I had brought Don Reynolds. I had placed with him insurance on myself, the Carousel, the Serv-U Corporation, and had directed LBJ, Carole Tyler, and Fred Black to him for insurance coverage.

Not satisfied with having told the truth with respect to the LBJ insurance policy and kicking back a stereo set to the Johnsons, and on the D.C. Stadium deal, Reynolds now launched wilder and more inventive tales. Among these was that I'd once flashed a black bag full of cash—reportedly $100,000—and had indicated it was payoff money from General Dynamics to buy the TFX contract. I never took a dime for myself, for LBJ, or anyone else in connection with that contract. And, if I had done so, I certainly would not have gone around flashing the cash and bragging about it like a schoolboy. The test of credibility here, I think, is that no one ever saw me exhibit that kind of conduct before or since. Reynolds also claimed that he'd paid me $140,000 over the years; this was simply preposterous. For years, however, IRS agents tried to find these nonexistent funds. Only within the past few months has the IRS conceded that they never existed.

As Reynolds continued to make charges, one of which was that Lyndon Johnson had misused foreign counterpart funds during his government travels, it irritated the new president. Johnson then did a dumb thing. He leaked to his friend columnist Drew Pearson, and to other favored newsmen, FBI and Pentagon reports which accused Reynolds of having been forced out of West Point for improper conduct, of having dealt in the black market while overseas in the army, of having brought unfounded charges against others in the past, and of a general instability. This not only was illegal and improper, it also created sympathy for Reynolds—One Man takes on the Establishment—and provided fodder to Scott, Williams, Curtis, Karl Mundt, and other Republican senators eager to prove White House meddling and a whitewash in the Baker case.

It was amusing, however, to note that at a given point Senator Hugh Scott began to soft-pedal criticism of me and to sing hosannas to the new president: "I have so much desire not to damage the Republic. I think Lyndon Johnson is a fine, can-do president, a man of action. I believe he is sincerely advancing a program he believes is in the best interest of this country." There was good reason for Senator Scott's conversion, as I

"Logic tells me he did everything possible, within the bounds of caution, to limit the investigation . . . LBJ's fear was that a broad, sweeping probe might harm himself, his administration, and his political party."   (*Roarlias of Capitol Hill*)

learned through the White House grapevine: LBJ had threatened to close down the Philadelphia Navy Yard unless Senator Scott closed his critical mouth.

I was not in direct contact with Lyndon Johnson and so I truly don't know how much effort he expended in trying to mute the hearings. Logic tells me that he did everything possible, within the bounds of caution, to limit the investigation. Not for Bobby Baker, however. LBJ's fear was that a broad, sweeping investigation would harm himself, his administration, and his political party. He went so far as to lie at a White House press conference on January 23, 1964, when he said, "There is a question raised about a gift of a stereo set that an employee of mine made to me and Mrs. Johnson. That happened some five years ago. The Baker family gave us a stereo set. We used it for a period, and we had exchanged gifts before. He was an employee of the public and had no business pending before me and was asking for nothing, and so far as I knew expected nothing in return anymore then I did when I had presented him with gifts. That is all I have to say about it and all I know about it."

Well, it may be all LBJ had to *say* about it—but it was far from all he *knew* about it. He took the stereo, and he required Don Reynolds to buy that $1,208 worth of advertising on his Austin radio station, as a condition of Reynolds's writing his insurance. It was a kickback pure and simple, though Reynolds himself had originally volunteered to waive his cash commission on the policy and then had reneged. The stereo was to be in compensation for that. Don Reynolds told a congressional committee that he supplied a catalogue from which Lady Bird Johnson selected the type of stereo she wanted; when it was delivered, to LBJ's home, the invoice clearly showed that it had been paid for by Don Reynolds—not by the "Baker family." Reynolds produced the receipt. LBJ also arranged that Walter Jenkins would not have to appear to give sworn testimony to a Senate committee about the Reynolds advertising on his Texas radio station, but could submit a fuzzy written statement which, in effect, denied any knowledge of the advertising arrangement.

So certainly there is a body of evidence indicating that LBJ "covered up," and I'm sure a whitewash of the Baker case would have pleased him. He could only go so far, however, or he would have found himself in the same endless morass as the Watergate gang when they tried to cover up. My rejoinder to those who insist that LBJ whitewashed my case is this: Lyndon Johnson's Justice Department investigated me, indicted me, tried me, and convicted me. If he did me any favors, or in any way attempted to protect me, I am unaware of it. Years later, when I visited LBJ at his Texas ranch after he'd left the presidency, he said that he personally had yearned to turn off the investigative machinery but he had feared the political as well as the legal risk.

My name stayed in the headlines. WIFE OF BAKER PROBER FOUND DEAD IN BATHTUB, ran one. If you got past the headline and into the fine print, it became aparent that the poor lady, married to a Senate staff man, had been stricken by a heart attack. I got the feeling, however, that the headline implied much more of mystery. BOBBY BAKER KIN HELD IN AUTO CHASE. That was when an in-law got arrested for speeding. BOBBY BAKER'S BROTHER DRUNK IN TREE. Honest, that's what it said. My brother Charles wasn't drunk, however. He had experimented with LSD while on the West Coast; the drug inspired him to strip off his clothes and climb a tree, which brought the cops, and when his identity was established it became a big story. Once when my wife and I passed a blind man selling pencils on the street, she asked why I hadn't bought one. "Because," I said, "sure as hell something would go wrong and there'd be a headline saying BOBBY BAKER SHORT-CHANGES BLIND MAN."

In late 1964 the Senate Rules Committee filed its report and conclusions resulting from the Bobby Baker hearings. It said, in part:

Baker's official position and his opportunity to be informed with respect to pending legislation made his acquaintance and friendship desirable and useful to many people, including some who were engaged in performance of defense contracts for the Government, and knowing this, he engaged in business activities which, by the very nature and the circumstances, were highly improper for a public official. He engaged in business ventures involving corporations doing business with the U.S. Government, under circumstances justifying the conclusion that, directly and through others, he had compromised his freedom to always act in the public interest. . . . Baker, and to a less extent, possibly other former employees of the Senate, abused positions of trust.

Though it and the resulting headlines (BAKER ACCUSED OF GROSS IMPROPRIETIES) did not provide pleasant reading, the Senate committee made no recommendations that I should be prosecuted. It found a number of charges made against me by Don Reynolds to be without foundation. It found that I had not dictated that North American Aviation be given certain defense contracts, that I had not influenced the TFX contract, that I had not obtained or attempted to obtain any government contracts for Riddle Airlines, that I had not attempted to influence government inspectors at Fort Monmouth, N.J., in behalf of a contractor doing business with the Signal Corps, that I had not used inside information about the future location of a federal highway to establish a motel-restaurant near it, and that I had not been involved in a scheme to profit off wheat speculation through alleged inside information from the Commodity Credit Corporation.

The report stated that the FBI had investigated each of those Reynolds charges and found them without substance; the FBI also reported that Reynolds had made certain unfounded charges against Lyndon Johnson, Senator Mansfield, some Immigration officials, and others. Neither did the Rules Committee decide to hold me in contempt for having taken the fifth amendment, though the minority—or Republican— members dissented and cried of a whitewash. After almost a year of investigations and hearings, the Senate committee recommended but one pallid reform: that a special select committee be established to deal with future conflict-of-interest cases. Shortly thereafter, the full Senate voted against its members' being required to make financial disclosures or make public their tax returns. So much for reform. It would be business as usual.

But if I had come out of the Senate hearings relatively unscathed, my problems were far from over. I was being investigated by the FBI and the Internal Revenue Service; a grand jury was convened in Washington and began to take testimony from anyone who'd ever had any business dealings with me. As we later would prove, my telephones and those of many of my friends and associates were being tapped. I first learned of this when a telephone company employee, whom I'd know slightly years earlier when my small children played with his youngsters, sought me out to say that my home phone, that of my law partner Ernest Tucker, and Carole Tyler's phone had been bugged. "I'll lose my job if anyone learns I told you," he said, "but I thought you ought to know. They're violating your constitutional rights." There were taps on Fred Black's suite at the Sheraton-Carlton and in the Las Vegas offices of Cliff Jones and Ed Levinson. I found myself proceeding as if all telephones that I used regularly, or any in the names of my associates, were bugged. A time or two I was tempted to talk sheer gibberish or nonsense into the telephone, or to allude in elaborate code to what federal evesdroppers surely would have taken to be dark and sinister matters, but I decided that I had enough real troubles without manufacturing or compounding them.

All manner of pressures were applied to my associates. Wayne Bromley proved the more susceptible to these. Hoping—as he later testified—that the investigation "somehow would go away without involving me," he originally lied to several investigators and kept getting in deeper and deeper. Sometimes he was well intended. He falsely told a grand jury that in writing a given letter he'd typed in the initials "G.A." after his own initials, to indicate to clients that he had a secretary when he did not. In truth, he was attempting to protect a young Capitol Hill secretary, Germaine Angel, who had innocently typed the letter at Bromley's request. Bromley falsely told various investigators that he had never had any business dealings with me, that he'd never split fees with me, that he owned no stock in MAGIC, and other foolish fables. He talked with me, and with Cliff Jones, about what to say in order that we might keep our respective stories straight. Everyone involved was under investigation and in danger of being indicted and so these conversations often were wary and calculated.

At a given point, when Bromley learned that Cliff Jones had told investigators different versions of events than Bromley had attested to, Bromley decided that he was deep in the soup and might go to jail. He consulted his attorney, who feared that his client might become involved in an obstruction of justice. Unknown to me, Bromley and his attorney then met with William O. Bittman—who eventually would prosecute me, and who earlier had sent Jimmy Hoffa to jail—and a Bittman aide, at Bromley's home on Seven Locks Road in Bethesda, Maryland. This occurred on the evening of March 22, 1965.

The prosecution scared Bromley to death. Bittman told him that unless he fully cooperated then his ass belonged to the government and he would go directly to jail. Under this threat, Bromley agreed to telephone me from time to time with federal investigators listening in on the calls; he also agreed to permit himself to be wired with electronic gear so that it would transmit our conversations when we were together. Wayne Bromley later testified in court that Bittman approached FBI Director J. Edgar Hoover with a request for permission to put a body recorder on Bromley in order to entrap me. But Hoover, a close friend of Lyndon Johnson's, and so close to Walter Jenkins that he sent him a bouquet of roses after Jenkins had been busted on a morals charge in a Washington men's room, denied the request and angrily ordered Bittman out of his office. Bittman was wily. He got agents of the Bureau of Narcotics to agree to wire Bromley. Hoover had no control over the narcs, since they worked under the supervision of the Treasury Department.

Not knowing that Bromley was wired, I talked to him in utmost candor—as I always had done; we'd been friends since we were teenage page boys. During the time that Bromley was wired, and because he had lost his job with the National Coal Council due to publicity attending his association with me, I made him personal loans totaling about $5,000.

Once when Bromley was wired for sound and I was staying at the Beverly-Rodeo Hotel in Beverly Hills, he visited me under the guise of being out West to confer with Cliff Jones. I took Bromley to a party attended by Marlon Brando, Anita Eckberg, and other movie stars, and got him a date with a cute starlet. At one point that weekend, because I feared my hotel room might be bugged, I asked Bromley and Cliff Jones to step out into the hallway with me. I think Bromley's conscience began to hurt him, because he evidently cut off the recorder and told his control agents that it had malfunctioned. Eventually, Bromley's old feelings of friendship or his conscience got the upper hand in his inner struggle, and one night after having a few drinks he privately confessed that he had allowed himself to become "a walking microphone" in my presence.

I was not pleased, to say the least. Because Bromley feared trouble should the prosecution learn he had tipped me off, I agreed not to hold my tongue. "But eventually," I told him, "if I'm indicted, then Ed Williams will file a motion to dismiss charges against me because of illegal electronic surveillance. And your name is bound to come out, Wayne." Bromley unhappily agreed, but asked that I postpone the action as long as possible so that he might escape indictment by currying favor with the prosecutors and pretending to go along with them. Though he never was indicted he was named as "an unindicted co-conspirator"—just as, years later, both Richard Nixon and my prosecutor, William O. Bittman, would be named unindicted co-conspirators for their roles in the Watergate scandals. To compound the rich ironies, incidentally, the last time I heard, Wayne Bromley was himself a prosecuting attorney in Louisa, Kentucky.

I originally had thought that even though my legal troubles might take years to unravel, I would eventually overcome them and grow rich. My MAGIC insurance stock was becoming more valuable by the day, as was my Serv-U stock; I had plans to enlarge the Carousel and, perhaps, to build luxury condominiums at the ocean resort. These plans did not take into account the realities. As the government continued to investigate me, filing tax liens and tying up my resources, my credit sources began to dry up. Even my wife's Senate paychecks were seized. With Senator Kerr dead, the Oklahoma City bank called in its note and I began a desperate search for new money. My request for a loan from Albert Greenfield, the wealthy Pennsylvanian I'd helped with a $10 million tax problem, was turned down in a cold, curt letter taking no account of past favors. Like the Murchisons and other men of means, he no longer had any use for Bobby Baker. If I could not call in old debts, then certainly I had no chance of finding new sources of credit—people were not exactly lining up to do business with me anymore. Consequently, to pay notes and my ongoing legal expenses, and to have operating money for the Carousel, I frequently found it necessary to sell off my Serv-U and MAGIC stock.

When not occupied with my own attorneys or hounded by government investigators, I became a full-time innkeeper at the Carousel. My wife came down each weekend to help out, and my children who were old enough worked as bellhops, busboys, or assisted at the front desk. I ran the operation, from taking care of purchasing and receipts to booking shows for the dinner theaters we featured, to pinch-hitting as a bartender; often I donned work clothes to perform chores of plumbing or other necessary tasks. People from all over the country frequently stopped by the Carousel, their curiosities whetted by my notoriety—and, face it, I had my manager, Gordon Houser, erect a huge and ostentatious sign on the highway near the Ocean City outskirts advertising my place. My theory was that if I had to live with a certain infamy, then as a businessman I'd just as well cash in on it. Once, when I was attending Carousel chores in a greasy pair of coveralls, a lady tourist asked me where she might find Bobby Baker. She wanted to look him over, she said, to determine for herself whether he might be guilty of all the bad things she'd heard. I told her that I probably thought as highly of Mr. Baker as anyone in the world and she had my assurances that he was a nice guy. Later that evening, when I was overseeing the bar and dining room in a suit and tie, the woman introduced herself to me without recognizing me as the workman she'd earlier consulted.

Carole Tyler had resigned from her job in the Senate shortly after I had quit mine; as I did, she took the fifth amendment before the Senate Rules Committee. For a while she returned to her home in Tennessee, but after the headlines cooled off she returned to Washington to work for me—which, of course, made new headlines. We had continued our romance. I loved Carole, but I refused to leave my family for her. This led to stormy scenes in which she sometimes cried or threatened to commit suicide. Despite such scenes there were moments of fun and sharing. Certainly I was not prepared for what happened to her on a Sunday in early May of 1965.

Carole was at the Carousel, where she was working as my book-keeper. On Sunday morning she and her roommate, a young woman named Dee McCartney, began having drinks with a West Virginia man, Robert O. Davis, who had been vacationing at the Carousel for about a week. She originally had intended to take a sightseeing tour over the eleven-mile-long island on which the Carousel was built, in Davis's private plane, but the morning weather was judged too soupy for flying. They continued to drink; observers later told me the pilot appeared to be pretty tipsy. About 2 P.M., Robert Davis and Carole Tyler drove to the Ocean City airport, the weather having turned bright and sunny, and went up in his airplane. Witnesses later said that the single-engine aircraft approached the Carousel, buzzed it a few times at low altitudes, and then began to pull up sharply as it banked into a turn taking it out over the Atlantic. The aircraft failed to come out of the turn. It hit the water nose-first at high speed and sank like a stone, only a couple of hundred yards from the Carousel.

I was in Washington when someone called to tell me the bad news. My wife and I, and my physician, Dr. Joseph Bailey, chartered a small airplane and flew to Ocean City as quickly as we could. It was nearing nightfall by the time we arrived. I boarded one of the Coast Guard boats searching for the wreckage, and I was on hand when the plane was pulled from the deep shortly after 1 P.M. When I saw Carole's body, dressed in a green pants suit I had bought her, I broke down and cried like a baby. Dr. Bailey told me that she and the pilot had died instantly of massive head injuries. The hardest thing I ever had to do was call Carole's mother and tell her that her daughter was dead.

Dorothy and I were among twenty-odd of Carole's Washington friends who accompanied her body on the train to Lenoir City, Tennessee, for burial. Through those long, dismal rites I felt that I had bottomed out for sure, that life never would be good again, and I knew that not for a long time—if ever—would I care for anyone as deeply as I had cared for Carole. She had stood by me with unswerving loyalty and affection when others had cut and run. *She was only twenty-six,* I thought. *She had only started to live. God, what a waste of beauty and goodness.* I began to wonder, sitting there in the flower-banked little red-brick church among Carole's friends and relatives, if I might not be somehow jinxed or star-crossed—perhaps cursed in some dreadful way, so that all who came near me might be destroyed.

No matter the difficulties I had experienced with my wife, or later would experience (we were divorced in 1977, after a long separation), I shall never forget what a tower of strength she was during that entire ordeal. Dottie was aware, of course, of all the publicity about my love affair with Carole Tyler and she had been deeply hurt. It could not have been easy for her to attend that funeral and hold up her head. Brave is not a strong enough word for what she was that day.

Carole Tyler's was the second shocking death of someone I'd loved within a span of little more than two years. Senator Kerr had been stricken with a serious heart attack in early December of 1962. Though this should not have been surprising, given his age, weight, and eating habits, it always takes you by surprise when you are close to the person involved.

I was at home on Christmas Day of 1962 when my telephone rang and Dr. Jim Keating, the senator's personal physician and a former naval doctor assigned to Capitol Hill, told me that Senator Kerr wanted to speak to me; he was calling from Doctor's Hospital in Washington.

"Merry Christmas, senator," I said.

"And to you and yours, Bobby," he responded. "In fact, I'd like to make this your most memorable Christmas ever. I'm grateful to you for all that you've done for me and I know you've been having a tough time. I'd like to make you a gift of the $50,000 I loaned you this year."

I was dumbfounded. "Senator," I said, "I love you dearly and I appreciate what you're saying. But you should not be using the phone. The important thing is for you to recover your health. We'll talk further about the $50,000 when you've recovered."

"No," he said, "I want you to wipe the slate clean with me. Report the gift as a legal fee. This is a wonderful time of year and I've had reasons to reflect lately on my friendship with you and with Lyndon Johnson and I want to do this for you."

I thanked Senator Kerr from the bottom of my heart; we again wished each other Merry Christmas; he spoke briefly of our going into the cattle business in Kansas after he'd recovered, and then he rang off for the last time. A week later—on New Year's Day, 1963—I was driving back to Washington from the Carousel when I heard on the car radio that he had died of cardiac arrest. I pulled my car over to the side of the road and wept. No man had done more for me.

I had not realized it at the time, but that telephone call from Senator

"Carole Tyler also took the fifth amendment. She resigned from her job shortly after I had quit mine and returned home to Tennessee until the headlines cooled off." (*United Press International*)

"When I saw Carole's body, dressed in the green pants suit I had bought her, I broke down and cried like a baby. . . . The aircraft had hit the water nose first at high speed and sank like a stone, only a couple of hundred yards from the Carousel."

"My wife, Dorothy, and I were among twenty-odd of Carole's friends who accompanied her body on the train to Lenoir City for burial. . . . I felt that I had bottomed out for sure." (*United Press International Photos*)

Kerr was the most important of my life. Later, in connection with my trial preparation, I asked Dr. Keating for a simple affidavit to the effect that Senator Kerr had, indeed, made such a call. But he had developed a strong case of amnesia, and could remember nothing. I was shocked. "Surely you remember that call," I protested. "You obviously dialed my number and then gave the telephone to Senator Kerr after I came on the line." Sorry, but he simply had no recollection of it; it had been a long time, and so forth. I've often wondered if Dr. Keating sincerely had forgotten; perhaps he'd placed many calls for Senator Kerr and had paid scant attention to them. Obviously, the call was not as important to him as it was to me, and it may have had little impact on him. Or, I've thought, perhaps Bob Kerr, Jr.—who was always jealous of me and hostile to me—*wanted* the doctor to forget. Maybe Dr. Keating simply wanted no hassle from the IRS or other government investigators. Whatever the reason, his lapse of memory would in time leave me wallowing dead in the water.

During the preparations for my trial I went to Oklahoma to learn from Senator Kerr's only son whether he had left any record of having made the $50,000 loan to me. I was frankly dubious that he had. I knew that only thirteen days after Senator Kerr's death, the authorities had discovered almost $2 million in cash in his office safe and in various lockboxes. No records existed as to where that great amount of money had come from.

Bob Kerr, Jr., was cold and abrupt; no, the only loan recorded to me was a $500 one from 1959 and the books showed it had been repaid in full. Young Kerr also pointedly said, "My father kept faithful records. He once loaned me $18.18 and even that transaction was put down in his ledgers." I thought, *But some transactions he obviously did not record. At least $2 million worth.* So I said, "Well, were you aware that your father kept large sums of cash?" His son said shortly that he had not been aware of it until after his father's death; I think he resented my close relationship with Senator Kerr. The senator had been a stern father, one who dictated the lifestyles even of his relatives by marriage, and I had the idea that his only son had been kept at arm's length emotionally. He knew, too, that Senator Kerr often had likened me to a son and this had to grate on him. Young Kerr went on to complain that his father had died leaving an outdated will, and said that the IRS was attempting to "ruin" the Kerr family by confiscating much of its $22 million fortune through use of the inheritance tax. Then he abruptly dismissed me.

Back in October of 1964 I had settled the law suit with Ralph Hill, the Capitol Vending man whose $300,000 action had started my legal trou-

bles and led to my resignation. We had met with our attorneys in the
Warner Building, for the purpose of taking pretrial depositions, when
Hill's attotney—David Garliner—asked Ed Williams for a private confer-
ence. They went into the men's room together.

In a few minutes Williams returned and beckoned me aside.
"Bobby," he said, "Carliner wants to settle. He's not sure they've got
much of a case. He asked for $50,000 but I talked him down to $30,000,
provided you agree."

"Well," I said, "I hate to give that bastard Hill one thin dime. I did
him no harm. On the other hand, he torpedoed me for filing a bullshit
law suit."

"It's your money and your decision," my lawyer said, "but if you can
get out for $30,000 I think you ought to do it. Hell, the trial will cost you
more than that. I think you ought to be practical about it."

In the end, I agreed. I paid Ralph Hill the $30,000—including
$10,000 sneaked to me by Ed Bostik of Melpar—locking the barn door
long after the horse had gotten out.

On January 5, 1966, a federal grand jury sitting in Washington returned a nine-count indictment against me; if convicted, I could be
forced to pay $47,000 in fines and go to prison for as many as fifty-seven
years.

There were two counts alleging income tax evasion for the years
1961 and 1962; five counts alleging that I had defrauded the California
savings and loan moguls of the $99,600 in "Kerr cash"; one count alleg-
ing that I had aided and abetted Wayne Bromley in his filing a false tax
return; and another count alleging that I had conspired with Bromley
and Cliff Jones to defraud the government through false tax returns for
the years 1963 and 1964.

The indictments did not surprise me. After more than two years of
hearings, investigations, headlines, wiretaps, pressures on my friends
and associates, and having had the financial screws applied to me, I had
not thought the mess would disappear in a happy puff of smoke. I did
think, however, that I would be acquitted and I actually looked forward
to my day in court. That day would not come for more than a year.

Chapter Fourteen

Charged, Tried, and Convicted

*"This case hangs on the Kerr cash. You've got
no choice but to tell it all."*

MY TRIAL began in Washington in early January of 1967 before Federal District Judge Oliver H. Gasch. He was sixty-one at the time, a big, long-faced man who was a former prosecuting attorney. Though Lyndon Johnson did not know Oliver Gasch personally, he had appointed him to the federal bench in 1965 on the recommendation of Abe Fortas. Ironically, mine would be the first big case over which he would preside.

When Edward Bennett Williams learned that Gasch would preside over my trial, he came to me in low spirits. "Bobby, Judge Gasch literally hates me. We've had a personality conflict from the first. I don't really know the reason but we've got bad chemistry between us. I think you should get another attorney. I'm afraid that Judge Gasch will rule against all the vital motions I make, and you'll be the loser."

I said, "Ed, I've got the attorney I want. You just do your job to the best of your abilities." Later, due to decisions rendered by Judge Gasch not only in open court but in chambers—*especially* in chambers—I had reason to recall what Ed Williams had told me and to wonder if I'd made the right decision. I've also wondered if we made a mistake in not trying for a change of venue. There were good reasons we did not at the time: (1) the cost of staying away from home for attorneys and myself seemed prohibitive and (2) we'd hoped that by putting on black character witnesses, ranging from Congressman Adam Clayton Powell to men who had worked for me, that we might favorably influence Washington jurors. Bill Bittman knocked that strategy in the head, however, by threatening to expose my affair with Carole Tyler to the jury.

Not long before the trial was to begin, Ed Williams was driving me home from his office one night when he suddenly blurted, "Bobby, the prosecution made an offer this afternoon and it's my duty to report it to you. The decision has got to be yours and yours alone."

"Lyndon Johnson had appointed Oliver Gasch to the federal bench on the recommendation of Abe Fortas. Ironically, mine would be the first big case over which Judge Gasch would preside." (*Wide World Photos*)

"I knew that my prosecutor, William O. Bittman, would be a tough nut. He had hard, cold eyes and was by his own admission humorless. . . . Later, Bittman would be named as an unindicted co-conspirator in the Watergate case—just like Richard Nixon." (*Wide World Photos*)

I said, "So they want to make a deal."

Williams nodded. He said, "Bill Bittman proposes the following: if you'll plead guilty to any one of the nine counts against you—and you can pick it out—then he'll drop the other eight charges. He also promises to be very lenient in his recommendations as to punishment."

"Ed," I said, "if I felt guilty then I'd jump at the chance. But I don't feel that way. I feel that if I plead guilty I'd be part of a farce. That I would be pleading to a lie."

"I want you to fully realize the consequences of what can happen if you are convicted," my lawyer said. "You could get a ton of years. I got the impression from talking to Bittman that if you'll plead to a single count, you'll get no more than ninety days to six months. I can't guarantee it, but that's my gut feeling."

I said, "But if I plead guilty to one count then the assumption's gonna be made that I'm guilty of every goddamned one of 'em. It will appear that I stole money from my friend and benefactor, Bob Kerr. I didn't do that, and I've got too much pride for people to go on thinking that I did."

"I believe we're in good shape on the tax questions," Williams responded, "but it's tough to say whether a jury will believe you about the Kerr money. He's dead and he's not here to speak for himself. That could backfire on you."

"Hell, I don't have to prove I *didn't* take it. The government's gotta prove that I *did*."

Edward Bennett Williams said, "Bobby, you can never figure what a jury will do. It's a roll of the dice. Think about it. Bill Bittman's tough. Bobby Kennedy put him on the Jimmy Hoffa case because he's like a bulldog, and he put Hoffa in jail. There's a lot of press hysteria connected with your case and the political implications are grave."

I thought about it while Williams silently drove the car and then said, "Ed, absolutely under no circumstances do you have authority to tell Bittman I'll plead guilty to one damn thing. If I do, the press will play it that I got my wrists slapped, that I copped out, that a fix was in. The assumption of total guilt will be with me the rest of my life."

"Well," he said, "it will be with you if a jury finds you guilty, too."

"Maybe they can kill me," I said, "but they can't eat me. I'll go to trial."

"I concur with your decision," Williams said. "I didn't want to influence you, because if something goes wrong then you're the guy who will have to pay the piper."

I knew that William O. Bittman was a tough nut. He had hard, cold eyes and by his own admission was humorless. A bulky former linebacker for Marquette University, he wore his hair in a crewcut and reminded me of a man the nation would later get to know—H. R. Halderman of the Nixon staff. I knew from his wiretapping, electronic buggings, and the pressure he'd applied to potential witnesses that Bittman would play hardball all the way (I learned that when the FBI bugged Fred Black's Sheraton-Carlton Suite for six months, one of the periodic visitors there was a congressman named Jerry Ford. He was friendly with Black, but I don't know what he used the suite for). Yet, I could not bear the thought of being labeled as a guy who'd stolen from his best friend. I wanted to get my relationship with Senator Kerr on the record and was willing to run risks in order to do that. Edward Bennett Williams had been preparing my case for almost two years; I had confidence in his ability to get my story across.

At this stage in the proceedings I began to pay the penalties of past indiscretions. I instructed Ed Williams to place as many black people as possible on my jury. I recalled that Williams had produced the great former heavyweight champion boxer, Joe Louis, to bear-hug Jimmy Hoffa in front of a black jury and refer to him as "my friend." Hoffa's subsequent acquittal in that trial, rightly or wrongly, was attributed by the news media—encouraged by the prosecution—to that incident. Though I intended nothing quite so heavy-handed as being embraced by Joe Louis, I did have in mind calling as character witnesses a number of blacks ranging from Congressman Adam Clayton Powell to staffers I knew on the Hill, some of whom I had placed in jobs. Williams did a fine job and the racial makeup of my jury comprised eleven blacks and one white. It was then the prosecution dropped what I thought to be a dirty bombshell.

Bittman apparently saw through my strategy. He approached Ed Williams and said, "Ed, do you intend to offer character witnesses?" Williams said that he did. "Well," Bittman said, "if you do we're prepared to impeach your man's character. We've got hotel and motel records from all over the country showing Bobby Baker to be registered with 'Mrs. Baker' at the same time he was telephoning 'Mrs. Baker' in Washington or 'Mrs. Baker' was telephoning him from Washington. We won't introduce those records provided you don't call character witnesses."

I was furious when Ed Williams related this conversation and I made the hot-headed decision to go ahead and call character witnesses. "I've got to disagree, Bobby," Williams said. "Those people on that jury aren't sophisticates. They're working men and women, with family ties, and unless somebody's been tampering with their religion I imagine several of them are serious Baptists. It won't help to have you tarred as a sexual dilettante." After I cooled down a bit I reluctantly agreed. I *did* have enough problems without adding to them, and what could be the profit in embarrassing my wife anew? Dorothy and I had tried to pick up our lives after the "Baker scandal" broke; she had been supportive, during the long years of my troubles, even to the extent of accompanying me to Carole Tyler's funeral in Tennessee after the airplane crash that took my lover's life.

In retrospect—and believe me, I've had plenty of time to mull it over—I think that the type of jury I had asked Ed Williams to choose was a factor in my conviction. The jurors were working-class people and far from sophisticated. They could not identify with the huge sums they heard thrown about during the trial—$300,000 loans; $200,000 payoffs; $100,000 profits—and could not comprehend that Senator Kerr of Oklahoma might "forgive" a $50,000 personal loan to me just as Nelson Rockefeller later would do for Henry Kissinger. I'm of a mind, now, that I inadvertently outsmarted myself in shaping that jury. I also wish I'd been a little more discreet when signing hotel registers.

My eyes began to be opened early in the trial when Judge Gasch denied a motion to dismiss the charges against me on our contention that evidence had been tainted by illegal wiretaps and electronic snooping. He made this ruling despite the fact that in an early bench conference he himself had said these conversations had been "illegally taken," and Bittman, the prosecutor, had responded, "That is correct your honor. We have made that admission and I again make that admission." Obviously, in planting listening devices such as had been found in the offices or hotel suites of Cliff Jones, Ed Levinson, Benjamin Siegelbaum, Fred Black, and others of my associates, federal agents had been guilty of surreptitious entry—or, to state it bluntly, burglary. We now know in these post-Watergate times that such crimes were commonplace among federal agents. I did not know it at the time. More to the point, neither did my jury.

Judge Gasch also ruled against our motion that complete transcripts of all bugged conversations bearing on my case, or the tapes themselves, be made available to us. He allowed the government to submit only such summarized excerpts of federal agents' notes as the prosecution wished to place into evidence. This meant the government could base its case on selective evidence and incomplete information. Whatever might have been on the tapes that tended to support my contentions thus did not come to the jury's attention.

A ruling that Judge Gasch made in his private chambers was equally damaging. It was based on national security considerations. Sound familiar? But it was Lyndon Johnson's man, not Dick Nixon's, who wrote

Judge Gasch a letter and asked that tapes involving me be suppressed in the interest of "national security." On a morning early in the trial, Judge Gasch summoned the attorneys into his office. The judge said he had a letter from Secretary of State Dean Rusk, asking him not to permit it to be revealed that federal agents had bugged the embassy of the Dominican Republic. It would embarrass the U.S and do great harm to our national security, Rusk had written, should it become known that America eavesdropped on the Washington quarters of foreign governments.

I had been taped several times when talking with Oscar Genera, the finance officer of the Dominican Republic. We talked frequently because I had been hired to land for the Las Vegas group—Levinson, Jones, and Siegelbaum—a contract to operate the hotel and the casino of the largest hostelry in the Dominican Republic, the *Ambahador.*

It was important to me to be able to introduce the tapes, or transcripts thereof, because they would have directly refuted one of the government's charges of fraudulent income tax reporting. I had rented a small apartment at the River House in Arlington, Virginia, just across the Potomac, which I sometimes used for business and entertainment. Consequently, I claimed a partial tax deducation on the apartment. IRS disallowed the deduction and charged fraud. Had I been allowed to produce the government's own records, my telephone calls to and from the Dominican embassy would have proved conclusively that I had talked for business purposes and, therefore, had not defrauded the government but had claimed a legitimate business expense. Judge Gasch, over the vehement protest of Edward Bennett Williams, ruled that because of the national security factor we might introduce no evidence that would have shown the Dominican embassy to have been bugged. "You are tying my client's hands behind him," Ed Williams told the judge. "He loves his country and wants to help it, but this issue goes to the heart of our defense. You and the secretary of state are effectively leving us powerless to disprove one of the counts against the defendant." But Judge Gasch was adamant: he must serve the cause of the greater good, which was America's national security considerations.

Later, over dinner at Duke Zeibert's, Edward Bennett Williams said to me, much as he would say to the jury in his final summation, "We're fighting a phantom. How do you come to grips with it? We're in a position of not being allowed documents and information vital to your defense. The prosecution has suspended the concept of equal justice under the law. They've used wiretaps, perjury, and threats. How the hell do you come to grips with them?"

We did not worry much about the tax cases. Boris Kostelanetz, my tax lawyer, thought we were in good shape on most. The 1961 tax case, as an example, was based on my having failed to report $278 in income from an investment with Senator George Smathers. I didn't report it because someone in my office had mistakenly filed the letter transmitting the check in the alphabetical folders I kept on all U.S. senators, placing it under "Smathers" instead of in my personal file where it properly belonged; had it been there, I would have discovered it at tax time and would have reported the income. Perhaps I might be accused of carelessness and sloppy bookkeeping, but we didn't think a jury would find fraud in such circumstances.

I had been careful to report as income the $50,000 gift, in the form of a canceled debt, that Senator Kerr had made to me. It had been listed as a legal fee, just as the senator had suggested. There were more troublesome tax charges, some involving money Wayne Bromley had reported as income when we had split fees, but we felt that some involved matters of interpretation of a complex law and that others might be so called into dispute as to cause a jury to harbor the necessary "reasonable doubt" which would prevent conviction. What bothered us was the Kerr cash.

"This case hangs on that money," Edward Bennett Williams repeatedly told me. It bothered him that it was my word against a dead man's silence—and against the word of a powerful group of men who would not be eager to admit they had indulged in bribery. "No assurances of immunity have been given to those savings and loan sharks," Williams reminded me, "and you can bet they'll be out to save their asses. They'll say whatever Bill Bittman wants them to say." My lawyer also feared that a jury of working men and women would be skeptical about the possibility of anyone making a gift of $50,000. "To most of them," he said, "a thousand dollars is big money and $5,000 is a fortune. They could go through life without ever seeing that much money in one lump sum. They simply can't conceive, I'm afraid, of a man giving away ten times that much." Williams didn't have to draw me a picture: if the jury failed to believe that Senator Kerr had (1) first loaned and (2) then made a gift of that money, it was likely to believe I had stolen it as charged.

We put Fred Black on the stand and he testified that Senator Kerr had told him in late 1962 that he'd made a $50,000 loan to me and had wondered whether I would ever be in a position comfortably to pay it back. Black said he told the senator he doubted that I could. I couldn't produce anyone or any records, however—Dr. Keating having suffered a memory lapse about placing Senator Kerr's Christmas Day telephone call to me—to give direct evidence that I had come by the money legally. That it had, indeed, been a gift.

Now, here is where we might have been immeasurably helped had we but known that my original attorney, Abe Fortas, had since late 1963 sat on an admission by former Senator Allan Frear that Senator Kerr once had made him a gift of big money; Kerr had told me it totaled $200,000. If the jury could have eyeballed Frear, admitting under oath that, yes, Senator Kerr had given him that huge sum of money, then surely it would have had far less trouble believing that he might have given a quarter of that amount to me. At any rate when I released Mr. Fortas as my attorney on November 22, 1963, that memo was not forwarded to my new attorney, Ed Williams. Not until years later, after Fortas had left the Arnold and Porter law firm and a lawyer there shipped to Ed Williams an old box of "Bobby Baker files" he had come across, did the Frear admission come to light. I still lose sleep over knowing it existed, stuck away in the files or carelessly tossed into a box, at a time when it could have been vital to my defense. As a witness before the grand jury and at my trial, Senator Frear swore that he had had no business dealings with me.

"You've got no choice but to tell it," Edward Bennett Williams said. We were sitting in his office, late at night in one of the innumerable conferences we'd had in preparing my defense, pouring over financial statements and telephone records and the mounds of documentary clutter indigenous to a complex law suit. This was many months before my trial, and Williams was telling me that I had no choice but to brand Senator Kerr as a man who willingly and knowingly took bribes. "The truth can't hurt him now," Williams said. "He's safe from harm in the grave. I know it's not popular, and I know it's tactically and psychologically risky, to badmouth the dead. But you've got no choice. You've got to tell the truth, in the fullest detail you can recall, if the jury's going to believe you."

I agreed with my lawyer. This didn't mean that I would enjoy besmirching the reputation of my dead friend, however. I don't want to sound pious or two-faced, so I won't claim that for a single moment I considered *not* telling the harsh facts about the $100,000 bribe. When the government is after you with its vast investigative resources, when it can bring intimidated witnesses and illegal wiretap evidence against you, when you realize that there's literal truth in the wording of the case style—*The United States of America*(!) v. Robert G. Baker—and that the whole buckled and badged law enforcement apparatus of the federal government is against you, then likely you aren't going to roll over and play dead. Not if you value your freedom. No, you are going to look after your own ass and your own reputation, and you are not going to shed crocodile tears over anybody else's. As I saw it, telling the hurtful truth about Senator Kerr was a distasteful necessity, nothing more and nothing less.

The prosecution painted me as the biggest con man to come along since Ali Baba had slick-talked his way into the cave of the forty thieves. "Motivated by greed," Bittman told the jury, "spurred by an insatiable lust for money and power, he built a financial empire so huge he had to steal to save it from destruction and so destroyed himself in the process.

That is why he is here."

The savings and loan moguls, who'd contributed to the Kerr kitty, paraded to the witness stand to claim that I had solicited $100,000 from them in a strong-arm manner and that I had claimed it would go to various senators and congressmen who, thereafter, could be expected to look upon their industry's legislative wishes with great favor. They told that story because they could not admit to having bribed Senator Kerr. To admit it would have left them open to prosecution for having violated the Corrupt Practices Act.

Only a few weeks earlier, during the taking of pretrial depositions, the savings and loan officials had claimed not to recall the names of the congressmen and senators I allegedly had collected the money for. Not a single name could they provide. Suddenly, however, their memories unfogged and they magically recalled eight names. The government then produced Congressmen Wilbur Mills and Senators Carl Hayden, Thruston Morton, Wallace Bennett, Frank Carlson, William Fulbright, Everett Dirksen, and George Smathers—all of whom happily denied that they'd received a dime from me. Of course they hadn't. The issue was a straw man, set up and knocked down by the prosecution.

Ed Williams fought back by telling the jury, "These were six flinty-eyed bankers. They were not gullible farmers, slack-jawed bumpkins. Do you think that these marble-hearted bankers would for one moment have put out $100,000 if they didn't know where it was going? . . . [Do you believe] that these tycoons would turn over $100,000 to senators whose names they didn't remember thirty days ago, about whose politics they knew nothing, and about whom they'd never spoken to one another? Why, you could steal the *Mona Lisa* by walking out with it under your arm easier than [you could get them to do] that." He also asked, "Have you ever before heard of a larceny case where the victim made no complaint? These sophisticated bankers didn't voluntarily rush in here to testify. The government compelled them to do it."

Williams ridiculed the testimony of Kenneth Childs, the savings and loan biggie who'd said that he'd only talked about such inconsequential matters as gin rummy when he'd met with Senator Kerr in an anteroom off the Senate chamber on September 24, 1962. "The very next day," Williams said, "the congressional conferees [headed by Senator Kerr] agreed to tax stock and mutual companies the same." This, of course, had been what the bribe was all about.

My lawyer made the pertinent point that when Senator Kerr's lock-box at the National Savings and Trust Company in Washington had been opened only thirteen days after his death, there should have been at least $41,300 in it from the S&L bribe according to my calculations—and that, indeed, a total of $42,950 had been discovered. I had earlier testified that I'd been with Senator Kerr on October 22 and on November 5, 1962, when he'd deposited in his lockbox a total of $41,300 which I'd brought him.

We had received what appeared to be an incredibly good break. John Powell, general counsel of National Savings and Trust, tele-phoned Ed Williams to say, "You've just won your case. I've checked the records at our bank and Senator Kerr visited his lockbox on the exact two days Bobby Baker said he did. Kerr rented a lockbox from us in 1952, used it in 1955, and didn't enter it again until October 22 and November 5 of 1962." Yes, Mr. Powell said, he would so testify under oath and he would produce the records.

We were elated. Here, at long last, was corroboration that I had not made my story of whole cloth. We back-slapped and hugged all around. I said to my wife, "Honey, we've crossed the Rubicon. Once the jury un-derstands that I didn't pilfer the Kerr cash, it will cast doubt on the remainder of the government's accusations." I was accused of having not only misappropriated the Kerr cash, but of having avoided paying taxes on all of it save the $50,000 which I'd reported as a legal fee after Sena-tor Kerr had made me a gift of it. It seemed to me logical that once the jury realized I hadn't stolen the money, but had surrendered it to Kerr, then the allied tax charges, too, would evaporate.

William O. Bittman did not easily quit, however. He claimed the defense had "tailored" its testimony. In other words, we'd somehow learned the dates on which Senator Kerr had entered his lockbox and then had contrived a story to fit those facts. This begged the question of how I would have known Senator Kerr had visited his lockbox in the first place if I hadn't been with him. And why would I have been with him at that particular place, unless I had delivered the money as I'd testified? "The evidence fits Mr. Baker's testimony," Ed Williams said. "We couldn't have tailored it if we'd tried. It is too much to be a coincidence."

[EDITOR'S NOTE: *Michael Tigar, then a young lawyer for Edward Bennett Williams and now in private practice for himself, in 1977 told Bobby Baker's col-laborator on this book, "I'm convinced that Baker told the whole truth about the Kerr cash. I investigated it. Clients sometimes lie to their lawyers, but Baker in that instance certainly didn't. When Senator Kerr died, and his lockbox at Na-tional Savings and Trust was opened—in the presence of the recorder of deeds for* the District of Columbia—the 'yellow sheet' the recorder made out verified the money found there was just as Baker had described it to us.

"The important thing to remember is that the yellow sheet, a routine form the recorder of deeds was required to make out, was in the recorder's custody and Baker never saw it before he told us his story. There was no way he could have seen it or have known what it would reveal. He had no opportunity to alter it, nor could he possibly have tailored his testimony to fit it. There's no possible way Baker could have guessed what that yellow sheet would show. So he had to know—which means that he told the truth.

"Senator Kerr's son claimed the lockbox contained a few $1,000 bills. This was not what the yellow sheet showed. The recorder himself had no independent recollection of that, he said, but it seems to me a man would remember if there had been any $1,000 bills. You don't see them every day.

"Since Baker said he had delivered the Kerr cash in $100 bills, young Kerr's testimony was devastating to him. The jury could not know, as I knew, that Bobby Baker had no way of knowing the total in that lockbox unless he'd been with Senator Kerr when Kerr put the money in there.

"When I first saw that yellow sheet the recorder produced, which jibed with Baker's claim to us before he possibly could have seen it, I thought, 'We're home free. We've got it knocked.' Because, you see, you can't lie about what you don't know. The yellow sheet was independent corroboration of Baker's story! But the jury thought we were defense attorneys with a narrow cause and that we'd tailored Baker's testimony to fit the facts as best we could."

Mike Tigar also said, "Judge Gasch killed us when he refused to sever the Kerr cash charge from the other charges. That really did Bobby Baker in. When the state can come in with a scattergun approach—'This man's on trial for nine felony counts'—then the odds against the defendant leap dramatically. The jury thinks, 'Well, he must be guilty of something or they wouldn't bring nine counts against him.' A jury not knowing he was charged with other counts might have put more credibility in his story of the Kerr cash had that been a one-shot charge. The judge made us try the whole thing in a package and each charge tainted the next.

"Once the jury chose to disbelieve the Kerr cash story, labeling it a slander against a defenseless dead man, it was almost automatic that the jury would punish Baker by finding him guilty on the lesser charges: that gave them comfort, gave them confidence in their original decision. In short, the jury disregarded the specifics and settled for a general pattern of guilt.

"I think the Baker trial was political to this extent: (1) the prosecution chose to prosecute him while ignoring his superiors who'd conducted themselves in much the same manner, and it labeled him as a wayward bad boy, not as part of a generally corrupt system; (2) in order to protect the government's reputation and image, the government chose to regard Baker as someone who was atypical and not

worthy of being in government: it made a concerted effort to get him at all costs;
(3) the government chose to make Baker the subject of scrutiny it would not risk
bringing against others; and (4) Bill Bittman used the case to catapult himself to
the highest possible status in the federal prosecuting system."]

During cross examination, Bill Bittman approached me—as a newspaper man wrote—"with all the compassion of a mortally wounded rhi-
noceros." Jabbing a pencil as if he intended to puncture not only my
story but my physical person as well, he said: "No one was ever present
during the periods that you gave the money to Senator Kerr?" I responded, "Yes, sir." Bittman: "You're the only person alive today who
can testify that story is true?" I then responded, "You are absolutely
right." I had anticipated the first of those questions and had wanted to
respond "You don't hand over bribes in a crowd," but Ed Williams had
cautioned me against getting into a pissing contest with Bittman. "He's
tough and he's a pro," my lawyer had said. "He'll eat you alive if you give
him the chance."

Bittman also sneered at my story that someone in my office—probably Carole Tyler, who usually handled such matters—had misfiled the
letter from Senator Smathers which had caused me to overlook reporting $278 in 1961 income: "Again, the blame is placed on a dead person."
He also said, "Whatever wrongs Mr. Baker has committed in his life,
they are small compared to what he has attempted to do to his former
friend, Senator Kerr." I sneaked a look at the jury; I don't think I was in-
dulging in paranoia when it appeared that I received a couple of dirty
looks. Indeed, after my conviction, one of the jurors would say that he
and other jurors had not appreciated my accusing my dead friend, Senator Kerr, of taking a bribe. Jurors had concluded that my defense attorney and I had concocted and rehearsed my alleged meetings to pay him
off, despite my testimony jibing with his lockbox visits.

In this respect, I had been hurt by the testimony of Marvin Gaut, an
official of the Otis Elevator Company, who had contradicted my contention that I'd received a cash loan from Senator Kerr at a breakfast meeting in Oklahoma. Gaut said he had been with us throughout the entire
breakfast and had not seen me or Senator Kerr leave the room, as I said
we had. I can't account for his testimony. Since there's evidence that
prosecutor Bittman put pressure on others to testify in a manner convenient to the government's case, and since Otis Elevator—like many other
companies—had spread some money around Capitol Hill, it may be that
Mr. Gaut felt vulnerable to official displeasures. He'd had Wayne Bromley on a retainer and the IRS was investigating him.

At any rate, the old fears of my lawyer proved accurate: "We just didn't believe," a juror told newsmen, "that Senator Kerr would give anybody that much money."

My trial lasted about three weeks. I was ill with the flu much of the time and on the final day of my direct testimony had to rush from the courtroom to the men's room, where I lost my breakfast. Reading old newspaper accounts of those days, I am astonished at references to how loose and relaxed I appeared: bantering with newsmen, talking politics, guiding a lady who hadn't recognized me to the proper courtroom when she'd asked where they were holding the Bobby Baker trial. I remember tensions and fevers not hinted at in the news accounts.

Edward Bennett Williams orated for almost three hours in his final summation. He is a wizard of words and I found his performance compelling. The jury, too, appeared extraordinarily attentive. I took hope from this. The summations ended about sundown on Friday, January 27, 1967; the jurors received Judge Gasch's instructions the following morning. They retired to deliberate about noon on that Saturday.

Though it may have been a self-serving wish, I felt that my chances of acquittal were good. Certainly "reasonable doubt" had been established. The government seemed not to have supplied much corroborating evidence of felonious wrongdoing, either by documentation or untainted witnesses. I had always worked within the system, was of the system, and had confidence in the system. I could not fathom that it might fail me.

I got up early on Sunday and searched newspaper stories for clues as to what journalists thought my fate might be. They were cautious accounts, however, and I gained no clear insights. I still felt light-headed from my bout with influenza and several times dozed in my chair. About 10:30 A.M. word was flashed that the jury was ready to state its verdict.

My wife and my two oldest children, Bobby Jr. and Cissy, joined me in a courtroom that held only a corporal's guard of newsmen and spectators. I searched the faces of the jurors for some inkling of what they'd done with my future. None looked directly at me. This, I had been told, was a bad sign for the defendant. *Please, God!* I thought. *Please, God!* In a filmy haze I saw and heard the jury foreman, a government computer programmer named John Buchanan, intone: "Guilty . . . Guilty . . . Guilty . . . Guilty . . . Guilty . . . Guilty . . . Guilty . . . Guilty."

Newspaper reports said that I sat through the monotonous litany "stone-faced," "stoic," "without visible emotion." Probably that's correct: I have always reacted to dangerous or adverse situations with the outward appearance of calm. Whatever my appearance, however, a hot ball of lead roistered through my gut. My hands shook when I put fire to a cigarette. *Guilty!* There is no uglier word in the English language.

"After the jury's 'guilty' verdict my wife and I blinked back tears. Newspaper reports said that I sat through the monotonous litany 'stone-faced and stoic.' . . . Whatever my appearance, a hot ball of lead roistered through my gut and my hands shook . . ." *(United Press International)*

But if I was numb and stunned, Edward Bennett Williams appeared to have been hit with a brick. On Saturday, the jury had questioned the judge as to whether I might be guilty of criminal activities in transactions involving my law partner Ernest Tucker, and Bob Thompson of the Murchison interests. Judge Gasch had instructed them that no criminal action was involved in either case, and that they should cast such thoughts aside. Williams had been elated. His theory was that a positive response from the judge at that point had to work to our psychological advantage. We thus had gone through Saturday night and Sunday morning in something of a euphoric state. Now, however, the jury had slapped us down, stomped us, and left us with the look of zombies.

My wife and I blinked back tears on the ride home from the court-house. Cissy invoked a little girl's option by unabashedly crying. Trying to put a good face on a traumatic occurrence I said, "Baby, this is just the first step in a long process. We'll make a motion for a new trial, and we've got our appeals ahead of us. Our day will come. Keep your head up and remember that church ain't over 'til they sing." I believed it, too.

Ed Williams and other lawyers of my defense team appeared at my home on Van Ness Street about an hour after the verdict. Williams had red, swollen eyes. The instant he attempted to speak to me he started crying again. He did not cry a silent, gentlemanly stream of tears; his thick body shook and jerked almost convulsively as he sobbed. Mucus ran from his nose. I wiped it off, mixed him a stiff drink, and tried to comfort him. "Ed, I could not have been better represented. You worked your ass off. We were victimized by circumstances and it wasn't your fault." Williams was inconsolable, as was the kindly Boris Kostelanetz, the brilliant tax attorney, and CPA Milton Hoffman, each of whom had dedicated himself to my defense.

I don't think Ed's grief was so much for me personally, or because he'd lost a highly publicized case, as it was for the perversions of justice he saw in the prosecution's tactics. He is, and has always been, a stickler for the constitutional niceties and he's outraged when they are violated. When finally he could talk on that dismal Sunday afternoon at my home, he raged not against the verdict so much as how it had been obtained. The jury's having failed to believe the Kerr cash story continued to bother him. *"Nemo dat quod non habet,"* he kept saying. It was a Latin phrase he'd quoted to Judge Gasch during a bench-conference discussion of the Kerr cash and is loosely translated "No one gives what he ain't got."

On February 13, 1967, Ed Williams filed for a new trial on the grounds that the jury foreman, John M. Buchanan, had concealed that he was a lieutenant in the reserve unit of the District of Columbia Police Department. He had remained silent when Ed Williams had asked prospective jurors "Is anyone connected with the police department or the fire department? Is any one of you a special police officer?"

Defense attorneys almost automatically dismiss policemen as prospective jurors, on the grounds that they tend to identify with the prosecution and not the accused. Williams said, "I would have used a peremptory challenge to exclude Buchanan from the jury had he disclosed his police connection." On March 21, however, Judge Gasch denied our motion. He held that Mr. Buchanan's police work was "completely voluntary and without compensation," that he'd served as a police officer "only on specific occasions," and that he "had not intentionally concealed" his police connections.

Ruling on another motion, Judge Gasch again denied our request for a new trial on the grounds that my conviction had been improperly tainted by the use of illegal wiretaps and electronic snooping.

Now began the long, costly, and sapping appeals process. More than three years would pass before the U.S. Circuit Court of Appeals for the District of Columbia upheld my conviction. The long delay, not uncommon to complex law suits, became a political issue. Two women reporters—Sara McLendon and Miriam Ottenburg—seemed to make a personal crusade of getting Bobby Baker's ass behind bars. They led the chorus singing that my powerful political cronies were protecting me. *What* powerful political cronies? They had long ago cut and run.

In late May, Ms. Ottenburg wrote in the *Washington Star* a biting, four-column article on how, despite my conviction, I was living high off the hog and employing batteries of high-powered lawyers to keep me on the street. I don't know if her story had any effect on the Court of Criminal Appeals. I *do* know that within forty-eight hours of its publication, that court had upheld my conviction and Judge Oliver Gasch had ordered me to jail. I posted bond and Ed Williams took the next legal step: an appeal to the Supreme Court of the United States.

Judge Gasch had sentenced me to from one to three years. The *Washington Star* was among newspapers crying that my sentence was excessively light, that I'd not received as much time as a rookie car thief. It is true that Judge Gasch could have sentenced me to much more; I felt relatively lucky not to have had the judicial book thrown at me. What the editorial writers had not taken into account, however, was that the Justice Department Parole Board interprets a one- to three-year sentence to mean the maximum period, and that no white-collar criminal involved in political cases up to that time had ever received as much as three years—and would not, until Judge John Sirica laid the heavy hand on noncooperative Watergate burglars. Still, I could have gotten a lot worse. I've sometimes thought perhaps Judge Gasch, having leaned on me so heavily with his adverse rulings and decisions in chambers during the trial, had attempted to compensate by sentencing me to much less than I might have received. He had been quoted in the press, "If Baker was to be believed, I could see a verdict of acquittal. If he was not to be believed, then I could see a verdict of guilty." I read this as meaning that the judge had seen the case as touch and go, rather than clear-cut.

In December of 1970, near the Christmas season, I telephoned my secretary from the airport in Atlanta, to learn that Ed Williams was attempting to locate me and had said the matter was urgent. I immediately called him. "Bobby," he said, "this is the saddest message I've ever had to transmit." I said, "What's happened?" "The Supreme Court has refused your petition of *certiorari*," he said. "I just can't believe they wouldn't give you a hearing. But that's it. We're locked out." I, too, was surprised. I had frankly thought that my friend Justice William O. Douglas, and other friends of Edward Bennett Williams on the big court, would at least give us a shot. Perhaps I was still reacting as the wheeler-dealer politician to have entertained such thoughts. I said, "Well, I guess that's it. When do I go to the big rodeo?" Ed said that we didn't yet know; almost immediately Judge Gasch ordered me to prison effective as of January 2, 1971, although I eventually would get a postponment of two weeks in order to close out my private affairs.

The impact of what Ed Williams had told me did not hit me until I had boarded an airplane for Washington. I ordered a double Tanqueray gin and thought, *What a hell of a Christmas present!* In the middle of my second double gin, I felt tears on my cheeks. A compassionate lady sitting next to me—a college professor, it developed—asked whether she might do anything for me. Suddenly very small, I spilled it all out: who I was, what had happened, and what I faced. I wish I had been more of myself, more alert, so that I might have gotten her name and address, because she held my hand and said many comforting things: don't lose your spirit, hang on to your spunk, persevere. She quoted Faulkner's Nobel Prize speech: "I believe that man will not merely endure: he will prevail." When I was alone and needed somebody, she had been there.

When the plane landed at Washington National Airport, I went directly to the Admiral's Club, where I had long been a member, and tied into a couple more Tanqueray gins. I telephoned my wife from there and said, "Dotty, I've got some news that isn't the best in the world but I don't want a wake tonight. I want to celebrate being alive and being free." Perhaps it was the liquor talking, or maybe my mood had to do with the lecture I'd received from the lady on the plane, but I had already decided to live my remaining days of freedom to the fullest. Freedom becomes the more precious once you realize you are about to give it up.

We went to the Jockey Club, had dinner, and for the first time talked about what I had always studiously avoided: the imminent shadow of jail. Up to that point Dotty had been a fantastically loyal and supportive friend. I told her that I respected and loved her for it, and hoped that once I'd done my time I could repair the damage she'd been done over the past eight years. We agreed that we must carry on as best we could, and survive the immediate uncertainties a day at a time.

All five of my children were on hand when we arrived home, three of them visiting from college during the Christmas holidays. To the last in number they embraced me, assured me of their love and of their respect. I said, "I'm the wealthiest man in the world." Then I couldn't talk anymore.

Chapter Fifteen

Surviving in the Slammer

"Stay away from that man. He's a killer.
If he tells you to kiss his ass, you'd better pucker."

A FTER a final family dinner on January 13, 1971, I said good-
bye to my children, to my secretary Georgia Liakakis, and to
a few close friends. Though I had no way of knowing it at the time, one
of the persons bidding me an affectionate farewell long had been
planted as an IRS spy under orders to pilfer my documents. With my
wife, her sister, and her brother I made the cold, cheerless drive to
Pennsylvania to surrender to U.S. marshals.

Completing tests and the orientation program at Lewisburg Prison
took about ten days. Despite Jimmy Hoffa's urgings that I remain at
Lewisburg, I jumped at the chance to be assigned to Allenwood. About
thirty miles west of Lewisburg, it was a minimum-security facility, a
haven for white-collar offenders. I felt I would be more at home there,
more among my kind, than at the rougher prison where Jimmy Hoffa
had been incarcerated. Allenwood was not a place of locks and bars. The
first impression was of an army camp; inmates lived in barracks surrounded by a high wire-mesh fence about two miles' distance from the
center of the prison. At Lewisburg I had been depressed by the max-
imum-security-type tensions and regulations. As Hoffa had told me,
Lewisburg averaged about a killing a month. Homosexuality was rampant among long-term prisoners. Lovers' quarrels leading to violence
were commonplace. Violence was a way of life. Frankly, I was terrified
there.

The guards, always fearing the possibility of an explosive riot, were
suspicious and brutal. They ruled by shows of power or a blank, personal indifference. They looked at you without seeing you. You were
worth nothing to them. I hated being marched in lockstep to meals or
anywhere else I went, hated the grating sounds of clanging metal doors
and the grating rasps of locks, hated the confinement in a solitary barred
cell, hated the threatening atmosphere, the bad food, the entire cattle-

like operation. Very early on Inmate Number 37266–133, formerly known as Bobby Baker, decided that he would go bananas and develop a bleeding ulcer if forced to remain there. Allenwood simply *had* to be an improvement.

I managed to meet a few times with Jimmy Hoffa before being transferred; he gave me instructions for the future. "They don't have medical facilities where you're going," he said, "so you'll come back here for treatment. Develop some chronic complaint. When you come for treatment, one of my guys in the infirmary will arrange for you to meet me in the library or somewhere." That would be no problem, I said, because I truly had a bad back—a slipped disc—and it would require periodic attention. "What's your religion?" Hoffa asked. I said that I had been raised a Baptist but had long ago given up church. "It looks good to the parole board if you attend," Hoffa said. "They don't have a Catholic priest at Allenwood, so tell 'em you wanta attend Catholic services and they'll have to let you come back here. We can talk in church." Again, no problem: my wife and children were Catholic.

When we met we talked of politics, the economy, of good times and personalities we had known, and of life in prison. "Every fuckin' lawyer should have to do ninety days in jail before being admitted to the bar," Hoffa said, "and every fuckin' judge oughta do at least six months. The bastards oughta know what it's like in here, what shit holes they're sending people to, and what goddamn reforms oughta be made."

Hoffa was the toughest man I've ever known. Determined that the authorities would not break his spirit, and unwilling to show the slightest sign of weakness, he insisted on working one of the hardest jobs in Lewisburg—standing on his feet all day in a mattress factory. Even in the presence of hard-eyed guards he never lost his sense of himself or, indeed, his attitude of command. Whoever killed him, if we can safely make that assumption, must not have had an easy time of it.

Just before I shipped out to Allenwood he had me memorize the names of three Italian inmates—I'll call them Larry, Curley, and Moe— and he told me, "They're my guys over there where you're going. They'll get you a good job and pass the word nobody's to fuck you over. I don't think many people in that goddamn old-folk's home would hurt you, but being connected with me oughta keep the bullies and queers off your ass."

Larry, Curley, and Moe received me as one of the family. My job was to wipe trays in the mess hall during each meal, and to supervise the cleaning of the mess hall after ward. This left a great deal of spare time to read, sleep, walk, or—when my sore back permitted it—to play tennis. I didn't mind getting up early and reporting to the mess hall by 6 A.M., because I'd always been an early riser. Only occasionally did I take naps even when given the opportunity, however, because veteran convicts warned me that prisoners who used sleep to escape reality eventually became apathetic and zombie-like. I was determined, in my own way, that prison would not defeat me; I stayed as physically active as possible. Many days I walked twenty miles or more, within the "in-bounds" markers which stopped at safe distances from the prison fence, so that I might tire myself enough to sleep well. I would walk from the dining hall to the church and back, a distance of about a mile, then retrace my steps, and retrace them again and again. Time hung heavy on my hands, though I took an accounting course for a while and read everything I could find. I'll always be grateful to an inmate named Richard McCaleb, who was doing ten years on a gambling rap. He brought me the *Washington Post* each day; it was like getting a letter from home.

Because the authorities leaned over backward to see that I was granted no special favors, and to protect themselves from charges that Bobby Baker was being coddled on orders from on high, I was the only prisoner at Allenwood on the restricted mailing list. This meant I was limited to ten persons with whom I might correspond, even though I had a wife, five children living at widely separated points, seven siblings, parents, business associates, and lawyers with whom I needed to correspond. Occasionally I risked loss of good time by getting someone to smuggle letters out for me, but I couldn't control incoming mail. Only after I had been released from prison did I learn that many old friends had written me or had wired me or had sent reading materials or other gifts. Sometimes this mail was returned to sender, and sometimes it simply was held at the prison and I never was told about it.

I don't know which powerful politicians wanted me "coddled." Richard Nixon, with whom I'd never been close, was the president. He had mentioned me unflatteringly from the campaign stump on numerous occasions. During my entire imprisonment, however, a few inmates, almost all guards, and the prison administrators seemed to resent my former high station and to be determined that I wouldn't get special treatment. I didn't expect it or ask for it and so their attitudes really bothered me. Any breaks that I got came not from the authorities but from the prison underground ruled by Jimmy Hoffa.

Because I knew I was under special scrutiny, I was careful not to break the rules or, if I bent one, to do so carefully. I wanted no loss of good time, no trips to "the hole"—solitary confinement—at Lewisburg, no trouble or complications that might give the authorities a chance to refuse me parole. Consequently, I eschewed the drinking bouts and grass-smoking parties which sometimes occurred in Allenwood. If you had access to money and took care of certain guards, and were willing to take the risks, you could get almost anything you wanted: liquor, dope, special foods. Everything but a woman. Administrative personnel really cracked down on those found with contraband goods, and I didn't consider momentary pleasures worth the risk.

The guards, who had more day-to-day contact with prisoners than did the office or administrative personnel, seemed divided between those who enjoyed busting or hard-assing their wards and those who profited by providing their wards illegal goods or services. The white-collar personnel, on the other hand, did everything by the book and seemed strangely blind to the conduct of the guards. I think the prisoners knew more of how the guards operated than did the administrative officials. In short, prisoners were at the mercy of two different sets of masters who operated under conflicting sets of rules.

When Christmas came and I'd been in prison almost a year, I unbent to take a couple of drinks, and once—celebrating news that my parole was coming up—I joined an inmates' party and got all vomity drunk on the terrible combination of champagne and Chivas Regal scotch. Friends who feared that my drunkenness might be discovered, to the detriment of my parole, cleaned me up and took care of me until sobriety returned.

I lived in fear of a particular guard—or "screw"—we called "Sneaky" because of the mean joy he derived from unexpectedly shaking down prisoners and their personal effects in hope of finding contraband items. Sneaky looked as if he'd been assigned to his job by central casting: a semiliterate cuss who had a disposition somewhere between that of a devout sadist and a stinging scorpion. Sneaky's political heroes were George Wallace and Ronald Reagan; he hated Lyndon Johnson and transferred that hate to me because I'd been "Lyndon's boy." He enjoyed sneering at LBJ in my presence, calling him all manner of vile names, as if hoping I might fly off the handle and give him the opportunity to discipline me. The way I felt at the moment, however, LBJ had not come to my defense and I damn sure wasn't about to go to his. I lived in fear that Sneaky, or one of his inmate stoolies, might plant contraband in my locker or otherwise create mischief.

Sneaky did cause me trouble once. I had been furloughed to attend my grandmother's funeral; on the evening I returned, he supervised my changing from civilian clothes back into prison garb. I had on a $400 mohair suit that had been made for me at Saks Fifth Avenue, a rich-looking fabric that inspired several insults from Sneaky. When I attempted to hang the suit on the wire hanger that had been provided, there was nothing in the material to grip the hanger and it several times shot off the hanger and fell to the floor. "Got drunk did you?" Sneaky said. He demanded to sniff my breath. I had consumed three beers in Washington, hours earlier, but I was in no way drunk. "You smell like a brewery," Sneaky charged. "I'm gonna write you up for reporting in drunk. You know that's a violation of the rules, don't you, Junior?" I said, "Then I demand a sobriety test." Sneaky laughed and said, "I don't give a fuck *what* you *de*-mand. You can *de*-mand any fucking thing you want. But what you *git* is up to me."

I was always amazed at hardened veteran cons, most of them black or what we loosely called "Mafioso types," who routinely defied the authorities. They were long-termers with scabby records who had little hope of parole, and they might rebel without warning. Many refuse to take the routine psychological tests, simply saying, "Fuck you; stick your mother-fuckin' tests up your ass. Go study a bug if you gotta study something." I felt that the tests were simplistic and a waste of time and taxpayer's money, but how you scored—and your periodic psychological profiles—went into your medical file and was made available to the parole board. I tried to tell a couple of tough nuts they were cutting their own throats in refusing the tests. One black dude said, "Shit, they ain't do shit for me. They take one look at my record and say 'Uh-huh, this dude a menace to society' and forget me. But if I can bug the Man, you unnerstan', make him think I'm proud crazy and mean as ol' King Kong, he gonna leave my ass alone. He gonna walk a goddamn circle to avoid my path, and that's all I want from the motherfucker."

I got along well with most blacks in jail because of their near reverence from Lyndon Johnson's dedication to civil rights. Their attitudes amazed me. Most of the blacks in prison had been discriminated against in every way: they had been born in the slums, neglected, unemployed, left to wallow unskilled and uneducated in their poverty, and there's no doubt these factors had contributed to their tendency toward crime. They knew, too, that the courts were tougher on them than on whites. Yet, they sincerely thought LBJ "a good dude" who'd tried to help their people; few seemed bitter that his good intentions had not personally lifted them up by their bootstraps. "I like the man," one black said, "because you knew he was gonna come on with that 'heavy heart' shit, all that down-home cornball shit, but he was pushing and tugging Mr. Charlie and Miss Ann like nobody had ever did it before. The cat tried, you know? He cared about people, man, and this Nixon muthafucka wouldn't piss on a black man's ass if his guts was on fire."

If any one group changed my political perceptions in prison, it was the young men who'd been jailed for refusing to fight in Vietnam. When I went to prison I was as hawkish as Barry Goldwater, Bob Hope, and General Curtis LeMay rolled into one. I had always believed that the

U.S. military could do no wrong and deserved the support of every citizen. My country was automatically right in its international disputes. Indeed, the only time I attempted to communicate directly with LBJ after I'd fallen from grace was when I wrote him a letter in 1968, while he was under fire as the Vietnam War went badly and people were rioting in the streets for peace, to tell him that he was one hundred percent right in his vigorous pursuit of that war and that I was proud of him. That neither President Johnson nor any member of his staff bothered to acknowledge my letter may have been personally disappointing, but it detracted not one whit from my support of his policy.

Yet, prisoners I originally considered "draft dodgers" convinced me I had been wrong—that our policy in Vietnam made no sense, that we were giving up lives and money to support a corrupt regime and at the cost of suffering even to the people of South Vietnam, that we were meddling in the internal politics of another nation at no profit to ourselves, that it was an illegal war because the Congress had never followed the constitutional requirement of declaring war, that it was an immoral war. The stubborn courage and sincere convictions of those young men turned me around. The prisoner authorities assisted in my conversion through the maltreatment of those young men. They were given the scummier jobs, more arbitrarily and harsly dealt with if caught in rules infractions, routinely ridiculed or brutalized. As President Nixon's contempt for the antiwar young was so well advertised, they had virtually no chance for parole. It was open season on them.

Originally, the antiwar kids had been as suspicious of me as I was of them. To them I was "LBJ's man" and to their minds he was the devil incarnate. If the black prisoners felt warmly toward LBJ, and transferred those feelings to me, it worked the opposite with the antiwar young. What originally made me curious enough to want to talk to them was observing their courage. I'd presumed them to be less than manly because of their refusal to fight for their country. But they showed me a stubborn dedication to their beliefs that I had not often encountered in the political life or in the business world. They had integrity and stood up for their individual rights, come what may.

Once they rebelled against the prison authorities. Weary of their shoddy treatment, they surrounded a bus leaving the prison compound and wouldn't permit it to move; they literally put their bodies under the wheels. The warden reacted in a panic. Within moments he'd flashed the alarm to Lewisburg, and here came the good squad: special cops in helmets, hoods, steel vests, and carrying deadly nightsticks which they used to crack heads. The protesters were hauled off to the hole at Lewisburg, some receiving only perfunctory medical treatment or none at all before being thrown into solitary. Leaders were rapidly dispersed to various other prisons in the system. From that moment on, I was on the side of the kids.

Because I had a legal education I often was sought out by other prisoners for help in composing their letters, briefs, or other documents seeking redress from the courts or stating their grievances. I had been warned by prison authorities not to stir up trouble as a jailhouse lawyer, and was forbidden to write legal documents for them. The best I could do was advise them on the proper persons to contact, the proper form in which to make their motions, and in general steer them through the bureaucratic channels. I did supervise the drawing up of documents, but due to the specific warning the authorities had given me I feared to write them personally. The end result was that the appeals or motions of poor semiliterates were slowed down, as they had to struggle with composing their own papers under my surreptitious guidance.

Once I'd been accepted by my fellow inmates, one of my biggest problems was inmates who meant well and who brought me gifts of extra food, blankets, clean sheets, clothing, and so forth. This caused me trouble with resentful guards and the administration, as well as some few antisocial and jealous inmates. The strain this could bring about was illustrated by the visit to Allenwood of my son, Lyndon John Baker, on the occasion of his tenth birthday in November of 1971. The kitchen chief, a strong Mafioso, baked a birthday cake for my son. To insure our privacy, Mr. Hancock, the civilian kitchen boss, permitted us to eat it in the officers' private dining room at an hour when it was not in use; kitchen inmates gathered 'round to sing "Happy Birthday" to my son. I was touched by this and did not stop to consider that it might cause trouble. But guards who got wind of this "special treatment" raised the ugly prospect of causing a major stink about it.

Hancock appeared to be in danger of losing his job. He set a clever trap, however, for a guard known to steal food from the prisoners' rations, and caught him in the act in front of witnesses. A trade of convenience was made: if the guards would dummy up about the birthday party, the inmates would dummy up about the food-stealing guard. Those of us involved in that successful negotiation shared in a moment of rare camaraderie. When you have a few rights, even a minor victory takes on the significance of a major triumph.

A more major successful rebellion was staged by Black Muslims, who refused to eat the regular prison food because of religious considerations. The administration in Washington greeted this news with a knee-jerk reaction: By God, they could eat it or they could starve! But soon word got around that the Muslims meant business and would do what they had to do, including rioting, if that's what it would take to focus public attention upon the denial of their religious rights. Word apparently was flashed from the Bureau of Prisons to keep the lid on at all costs, because the authorities quietly reversed themselves and made the requested dietary changes. It always seemed insane to me that prison authorities automatically responded in the negative to complaints by prisoners, and made festering conditions worse by their oppressive, knee-jerk reactions. Though they may pay lip service to the alleged rehabilitation role of prisons, their locks and bars are used to administer punishment and little else. That's the reality.

I can give some helpful advise to the president, to the high mucketymucks of the Bureau of Prisons, to judges and legislators and governors, and to those well-meaning blue-ribbon panels of plain citizens involved in working for prison reform—though I doubt if it will be heeded. Stop advertising your visits to prisons in advance. Don't give the wardens and their lackeys time to polish, fumigate, prepare special meals, put on showcase productions, and trot out their tame inmates to tell you how wonderfully well they are being treated. Instead, make surprise visits with all the stealth and swiftness of a commando raid. Then you'll truly see what sink holes of despair are being operated to the detriment of the prison population and, in the end, to society at large. You'll see the rats and the vermin and the roaches, the grubby food, the idleness, the petty brutalities, the underpaid and ill-educated guards who operate in an atmosphere of fear and corruption. You'll find inmates willing and eager to tell you hard truths, because the prison authorities will not have had time to safely remove them from circulation in advance. Just a few such surprise raids, followed up by the appropriate firings and publicity and ass kickings, and you'll see new, better, and more humane attitudes begin to emerge. The policing must be unceasing, however, or the prison system soon will sink back to its present levels of ineptitude and uncaring. That's the main problem. People are locked up, forgotten by society, and abused by their keepers—and nobody cares. Nobody. Absolutely nobody.

It's a mistake for wardens and their top guns to be career civil servants. They are small-minded bureaucrats petrified about anything that comes out of Washington, and they are determined to put a good face on their operations no matter the realities. They will lie, cover up, or sweep humans as well as dirt under the rug in order to protect their own asses and careers. They will turn their heads and fail to acknowledge violence or bribery, either by their guards or by inmates. Another shortsighted policy is that of hiring unskilled guards because they'll work cheap. This invites corruption. Many of these guards are as antisocial and as resentful as the inmates they supervise. The potential for explosions is built in.

Reform must begin with the guards, the people who have the most direct contact with prisoners, and—next to the prisoners themselves—the low men on the totem pole. Young, bright men should be selected, and they must be well paid. They should be schooled in psychology and criminology. This would lead them to understand that ninety percent or more of the people in jail *are* guilty, and by nature or by circumstances are rebellious toward society. (It is an outsider's myth that most prisoners claim to be innocent. Nine out of ten openly admit their guilt.) If these offenders are to be changed, it will not be by dumbass, crooked old guards but by professionals who are knowledgeable men. Wardens should be selected from among the elite and best of this trained cadre, so that in time the prison system will be operated by officials who know the realities and how to respond to them. Enough of political hacks and career civil servants afraid of their own shadows ignorant of the realities of their jobs and unwilling to learn.

All this would take much time and money. The alternative, however, is what we now have: a corrupt system where inmates are offered only minimal protections by their so-called keepers, or may be exploited by them, before being sent out to repeat their crimes. The prison subculture—the underground—in truth controls such discipline as exists in most prisons, and it is far from even-handed. Certain rules are ruthlessly enforced: welch on a bet and your head will be cracked; rat on the wrong man and there's a knife in your ribs. But this is rule by terror, and only the fittest survive. I may have survived and even have profited from my association with Jimmy Hoffa, the underground power of Lewisburg and Allenwood, but this doesn't mean that it was fair or even that I liked it. Hoffa knew this. When he came out of jail he devoted much of his time to personal appearances and television appearances in which he told the harsh truth about the prison system, and he was sincerely dedicated to changing it. I doubt that we will make significant changes, however. In America we lock 'em up and throw away the key.

Prisoners transferring into Allenwood were permitted to bring in no papers, letters, or notes. One day a new arrival, introducing himself as Dr. Donald Plotnik, called me aside and produced a crumpled note from his shoe. I recognized the handwriting as Hoffa's: *"Bobby, the Italians are resentful of my Jewish friend. They're jealous. I hope you'll look after him."*

Dr. Plotnik was a physician from Columbus, Ohio. He'd once been voted that city's "Outstanding Young Man" by local Jaycees. A gun collector, he added to his collection a machine gun—and it's against the law for any private citizen to own one. One night, under the influence of drink, he test-fired his machine gun by blowing the tops out of all the trees in his yard. For this a no-nonsense federal judge sentenced him to ten years. Though I can't vouch for it, I heard—not from Plotnik—that he'd been involved in political activities distasteful to the judge and that this accounted for the severity of his sentence.

I took Dr. Plotnik under my wing and got him a job working with me in the mess hall. We became close friends and tennis partners. Often he joined me on my marathon walks around the Allenwood yard. I never knew why Larry, Curley, and Moe so hated him, but Hoffa had been right. One day the three Italians told me that Plotnik was "a rat and a scumbag"—a particularly serious pejorative among Mafioso types, I'd learned—and that I henceforth should have nothing to do with him. I was unaccustomed to incurring the wrath of hard cases in prison, and had always tried to avoid it, but I stood up to them: "Jimmy Hoffa sent me that note asking me to take care of Plotnik, and unless he tells me to the contrary then Plotnik will continue to get most favored treatment from me." The Italians then began to give me the silent treatment. They neither spoke to me nor looked at me for several days. This under-standably made me nervous. I didn't sleep well and looked over my shoulder a lot.

I went to Lewisburg for treatment of my slipped disk and arranged to meet in the chaplin's office with Jake Ursini, who was nearing the end of a twenty-five-year term for bank robbery, and who was Jimmy Hoffa's main man in prison. I told him of the rebellion by Larry, Curley, and Moe and asked him what I should do. "Wait here," Ursini said. "I'll go see Jimmy." When he returned he quoted Hoffa as follows: "Tell those fuckin' Italians to come here for medication on the next bus and to get their asses over to see me. And tell Bobby Baker when I send an instruction the first time, that's the rule until I repeal it."

On returning to Allenwood I appraoched Larry, Curley, and Moe and attempted to talk with them. They turned their backs and started to walk away. I shouted after them, "Jimmy doesn't want you guys questioning him anymore. In effect, he said you can go fuck yourselves. And you're to get your asses over to see him on the next medical bus." They looked at each other in astonishment, but all of them made the bus. When they returned, they were docile and acted as if nothing untoward ever had happened between us. Never gain did they harass Donald Plotnik or put the badmouth on him. I don't know what ultimate power Jimmy Hoffa had, and I'm not sure I want to know even now; whatever it was, it was damned effective.

The protection of the Hoffa group may have kept me from serious harm on at least one more occasion. A huge, black Cuban—who'd been doing a long stretch in Leavenworth for murder—was transferred to Allenwood to see whether he had so tamed his antisocial instincts as to be considered for parole. He was a magnificent physical specimen, tall and strong, and in appearance reminded me of Muhammed Ali. He spoke only broken English, however, and since I am not bilingual we had something of a communications problem. It was my feeling, too, that Big Al—we'll call him—was not real bright. There was a dullness in his face, no light behind his eyes, and an overall sort of bovine sluggishness.

Big Al was assigned to my kitchen detail, and right away began to grunt dissatisfaction with the way I'd organized the cleanup crew. I don't think he understood that because of my bad back I couldn't always do my share of the heavier work, and my supervision seemed to irritate him. He took to bumping into me, dragging his mop across my shoes, sloshing water on me, or anything to provoke me. I tried to talk to the man but he only glared or ripped off bilingual curses. One morning I was not in the greatest mood myself and told him, among other indiscretions, to go fuck himself and to kiss my Democratic ass. This deeply offended his sense of macho. Another of the cleanup guys, rumored to be a hit man for the Mafia—we'll call him Nick—intervened to smooth ruffled feathers. I though the incident was closed and after my work was performed I went back to my barracks. A few minutes later I looked up to see Big Al looming over me with a murderous look in his eyes. He said, "You motherfuck. Me gonna kill you." There then began the race of the tortoise and the hare as I scrambled about looking for something heavy to hit the big bastard with. Fortunately, Jake Ursini, the Hoffa confidant, had heard of the dispute and rushed into my barracks to intervene. Again, I thought a certain uneasy peace had been made. A couple of days later, however, Big Al got on my case again. He muttered threats through the noon work shift, gave me the hard eye, and finally a throat-cutting gesture. I'd had enough, so I called him a Spanish word I loosely understood to mean cocksucker. Apparently, that's exactly what it meant. Big Al went up in flames. It took a half-dozen inmates to restrain him. I armed myself with a stack of heavy metal trays until he'd been calmed and led away.

Jake Ursini looked me up and he was fit to be tied. "For Christ sakes, Bakes, cool it. Big Al's gone apeshit. I've managed to keep you alive because I keep telling him that you're tight with Hoffa, but even that won't work if you keep on insulting him." I said, "Look, I'm afraid of that big bastard. I know he's a killer. Hell, he's proved it! But I can't let him abuse me and kick me around like a dog. What am I supposed to do?" Jake said for me to stay out of the guy's sight and he'd keep working on him.

That afternoon late I put on my sweatsuit and started jogging around the "in-bounds" markers. I ran and ran and ran and it was after dusk, approaching dark, when I returned. As I neared the barracks I heard distraught voices and somebody crying. In the dim light I thought I recognized the bulky form of Big Al, and my heart skipped a beat. Then I heard Jake's voice calling to me. "Bobby," he said, "I told Big Al that you're sorry and want to shake hands. Shake." I hesitated and Jake hissed, *"Shake, goddammit!"* Big Al and I gingerly shook hands; he muttered something in broken English. Jake patted him on the back and led him away, talking in a consoling manner.

In a few minutes Jake came into the barracks and said, "Bobby, somebody tipped me that Big Al was hiding in the grass waiting to knife you. I took this off him." He showed me a wickedly long knife with a curved point. I stared at it, dumbfounded. "It took me ten minutes to talk him out of the knife," Jake said, "and another ten to convince him that if he killed you, then Hoffa would have *him* wasted. He cried and said 'I want no trouble with Hoffa, but Baker insult me.' I explained that you don't understand life in here, that you're a goddamned innocent, and convinced him to leave you alone. I'm gonna see Jimmy about what we can do, but in the meantime you stay away from that man. And if he tells you to kiss his ass, you'd better pucker." The next day I learned that Nick, the hit man, told Big Al that he had been ordered to rip his tongue out if he said another word to me. Under these pressures, Big Al left me alone. Much to my relief, it soon was decided that Big Al wasn't ready for rehabilitation and he was transferred back to a maximum-security prison.

About the time a bank robber was saving me from a mad killer hiding in the grass with a fistful of wicked knife, the gentlemen of the Board of Governors of the Columbia Country Club, in Chevy Case, Maryland, wrote me a most formal letter quoting from its Constitution: "In case the Board determines that any member of the Club has engaged in conduct unbecoming a gentleman or which may endanger the good order, welfare, and character of the Club, the Board . . . may expel such member from the Club." That, it seems, was exactly what the Board had done in the case of Robert G. Baker. The gentlemen were kind enough, however, to extend the right of appeal: all I had to do was appear, in person, before the Board on a given date and I would be permitted to argue my case. Somehow, it did not seem like a thing to trouble the warden about.

God never visited my cell, as He apparently did Charles Colson's, but I became a faithful churchgoer for more reasons than to visit with Jimmy Hoffa or to impress the parole board. The guards were convinced that we regular churchers attended so it would look good on our records, but I can't imagine that so transparent a device would impress the authorities. There was very little of true religion in my church attendance, though I did urge some young fellows to accompany me because I thought it might aid their rehabilitation. But I largely attended church, as did so many others, because of the social opportunities. In church one might talk with the priests, the nuns, and other visitors from outside. These conversations were a great relief from the usual prison bullshit. Those of us who attended regularly might occasionally be permitted to attend a civilian church in the free world as a special visitor. I suppose you would have to have been confined to understand what a treat that was—just to get away, even for a few hours, from the monotony of prison life and to enjoy such simple pleasures as seeing women walking on the streets, or children playing in a yard, or talk with someone without looking over your shoulder to see if a guard or a stoolie might be eavesdropping. Given enough notice that we would be permitted an "outside" church visitation, it was possible to alert one's family and to enjoy a brief reunion outside of the regular visiting channels.

For these same reasons, and at Jimmy Hoffa's suggestion, I became active in the Allenwood chapter of the Jaycees. Imagine Jimmy Hoffa, the two-fisted tough guy, recruiting for the apple-cheeked young Jaycees! But he told me, "Bobby, the little things mean a lot. You'll get to talk with someone from the outside, and in time they'll probably arrange for you to visit a Jaycee chapter or two outside the walls. It will be like a breath of fresh air. Anytime you can break up the routine, anytime you can claim a moment of freedom, jump at the chance. It can help you keep your fuckin' sanity. You'll brood less about what's happened to you and what shit you may step in tomorrow."

I also got to make a couple of brief trips outside the walls with the Allenwood tennis team, when it was permitted to compete in tournaments. It was at such a tournament, indeed, that I began to realize that things were badly amiss with my wife, Dotty. She failed to show up as she had been doing when I could infrequently get outside the walls for short periods. As time wore on she found more and more reasons not to be able to make it on the regular visitors' day. Soon word came to me through friends in Washington that she was being seen around town with a former FBI agent then working for a Senate committee. I suppose it was inevitable. She'd been through too much with me, including the hurt of my affair with Carole Tyler, and she was only human.

My parents, both of whom were in ill-health, visited once at Allenwood over my protest. I hated the notion of their seeing me in prison garb and feared that they might become emotional. Actually, since Al-

lenwood had no bars and failed to fit the layman's concept of a prison—
to the naked eye, anyway—I think the trip actually boosted their spirits. I
put on a good front for them, telling them what a healthy life I led and,
all in all, making prison sound incongruously close to life in summer
camp. My mother, who had been an invalid for years, did not have the
strength for other visits, and soon my father's health would break. Before it did, however, he loyally petitioned Senator Strom Thurmond,
Congressman William Jennings Bryan Dorn of his home district, and
Judge Clement Haynsworth—whom Nixon had unsuccessfully tried to
appoint to the Supreme Court—for their assistance in attaining a parole
for me.

I would not be eligible for parole until I served at least one year. My
first parole hearing was held in November of 1971. I told the board I felt
I'd been convicted of something I didn't do, that mine had been a political trial and a trial by the press, that certainly I planned no life of crime
and was eager to become a useful and productive citizen. I heard no
word for weeks. One morning I picked up the *Washington Post* and there
was another headline with my name: BOBBY BAKER DENIED PAROLE. No
reason was given. I had simply been turned down. Neither then, nor
later, was any official decision relayed to me.

After I'd gone around with a long face for a couple of days, a
friendly guard beckoned me aside. He said, "Baker, I've been in the
prison system for thirty years. I think I can read it pretty good. I'll bet
money you're out of here by the first of June." It was by now around the
first of the year; the guard was talking about six more months. He said,
"The habit is to take a new look about every ninety days. It's my guess
they'll reconsider your parole around April, and probably release you in
May or June. Just be sure you keep your nose clean." June seemed far
enough away, but the guard's prediction was the first fresh hope after
my disappointing turndown, and I clung to it.

I knew that nothing was certain, however. I'd also learned that even
if I kept my nose clean, others might dirty it for me. Let me explain that:

About the time I had been ordered to prison, I was visited by officers
of the Metropolitan Police Department of the District of Columbia. "Do
you know Paul Enten?" they asked. "Yes," I said, "I've known him for a
number of years." Enten was a Georgetown decorator whose clients included the fashionable and the rich; I'd seen him socially on a number of
occasions, and he'd been a guest at the Carousel. The officers asked
whether I'd ever bought anything from him. Again I answered in the af-
firmative: "I bought a set of silverware for about $300, if I remember.
Enten said he had bought the silverware at an auction, along with a
number of antiques, but that he had no particular requirement for it and

would let me have it at a small profit." Had I bought anything else from him? "No." Had he stored any items in my house? "Yes, as I recall he asked my wife if he might store some antiques in my basement. I think he said he'd bought more than he had storage room for, and she gave him permission to use our basement. He said he'd call for items as he needed them and had space for them." How long had they been down there? "Oh, a year or more I guess, if they're still there. I haven't been down there in months myself. My wife would know better than I do." Did I know what was there, or had been there? "I saw a big old clock and a bunch of boxes, but I didn't look in the boxes. What's this all about, anyway?"

It was all about burglary, that's what. Paul Enten was accused of being the fence—that is, the disposer of stolen goods—for a ring of burglars that included Georgetown policemen. The policemen tipped the burglars off when certain wealthy citizens would be out of town and had asked the Georgetown police precinct to keep an eye on their homes. According to the government, the ring had stolen from such prominent citizens as George Preston Marshall, owner of the Washington Redskins football team, Judge Roger Robb of the U.S. Court of Appeals, and Lady Norman Lewis, a Georgetown socialite who was married to a man who'd been knighted by the queen of England. The loot had amounted to $250,000 worth of antique valuables—including the silverware I'd purchased, and items stored in my basement. This inventory included a grandfathr clock that originally had belonged to Daniel Webster, fine china, silver teapots, and similar items.

I could not believe it. Harboring stolen goods in my basement, some of which had belonged to an Appeals Court judge, was something I needed like a hole in the head. My wife and I appeared before the grand jury, told them the circumstances, and cooperated in turning over the stolen goods to the authorities. Dotty volunteered that Paul Enten had been "good" enough to permit her to put several valuable vases and candy dishes on display in our living room. The authorities thanked us for our cooperation and that seemed to be the end of it.

I'd been in jail but a short time when I was told that one of the burglars, a man I'd never met, claimed that I once had visited Enten's apartment to pick and choose from the illegal loot. I was incredulous. "That man is trying to buy his freedom at my expense," I told the investigating officers. "I'll take a paralyzed oath that this whole thing happened just as Dorothy and I said it did." Paul Enten, to his credit, admitted that my wife and I had no inkling of his operations, and testified that we'd never been in his house. But there soon was a new headline for my scarpbook: BOBBY BAKER LINKED TO THEFT RING. The story was played prominently in the Washington newspapers, and I knew that it had to have at least a subliminal effect on Justice Department officials. "Damn if I don't seem to be snakebit," I told Jake Ursini. "One of these mornings I'll wake up and find a headline BOBBY BAKER SHOOTS SANTA CLAUS."

It was no laughing matter, however, as I found when I was temporarily transferred from Allenwood to the Montgomery County Detention Center near Rockville, Maryland, to be called as a witness in Paul Enten's trial. In the interim, it developed that several policemen had been involved in the burglary ring; the leader of the rogue cops had shot himself to death just before the trial. Incredibly, though I had never been charged or indicted in the case—and had a letter from the investigating officers thanking me for my cooperation—the prosecutor, an assistant U.S. district attorney, Harold J. Sullivan, alleged in his opening remarks that I had knowingly bought stolen goods from Paul Enten. New headlines. New reasons for me to worry about parole.

Two black federal marshals came from Washington to transport me from Allenwood to the Montgomery County Detention Center. Under rules established during the Nixon administration, no federal prisoner could be transported unless handcuffed and in leg irons. It was a silly, inhumane rule: ninety percent of federal prisoners are in for nonviolent crimes: embezzlement, stock fraud, auto theft, gambling, tax evasion, dope convictions, draft dodging. There's simply not all that many federal prisoners who would try to break away. Nonetheless, I shuffled out of Allenwood wearing so much hardware you'd have thought I was a killer rapist—even though I was to be a witness for the *prosecution!*

A few miles down the road from Allenwood one of the marshals said, "Mr. Baker, can we trust you?" I said, "Yes sir, I believe you can." He said, "We hate this goddamn cuff-and-iron rule. It's a pain in the ass and it's not necessary. But the administration is enforcing the rule in a tough way, and it would be our asses if anybody knew we'd unchained you. I'll do it, if you'll give me your word not to say that we did, but we'll have to put you back in locks just before we get to the detention center." I said, "You got a deal, pal." Before we got to the point where the officers again stopped to put me in chains for appearances' sake, they had spilled out their bitterness toward Nixon and Attorney General John Mitchell for their apathy toward the plight of blacks and for the chicken-shit rules coming out of Washington. "It's making a bad system worse," one of the marshals said. "When you keep cracking down and cracking down on people, treating them like animals, they've got to explode at some point. Nixon and Mitchell, they're gonna fuck around and cause a bunch of prison riots and get a lot of peace officers killed as well as inmates."

I was horrified by the existing conditions of the Montgomery County

Detention Center. Not only was it ever so much worse than Allenwood, it was even worse than Lewisburg Prison. The first night I was there, they kept me in a barred cell with about thirty other people, most of whom were drunks or had failed to pay their alimony or were accused of other minor violations, in such crowded conditions that you'd have trouble duplicating it outside a New York subway at rush hour. Iron bunks were stacked three tiers high and contained only thin plastic-foam mattresses; my bunk didn't even have that. I got a blanket, period. Prisoners vomited and cursed and flushed the single commode and talked all night. They were just settling down, at 6 A.M., when my name was called and I was removed to a holding tank. Through the night I kept thinking, *Montgomery County is one of the three or four wealthiest counties in America, and yet this putrid jail is something straight out of Charles Dickens.* It was crowded, it stank, the facilities were primitive. All in the middle of grand affluence.

The holding tank was a tiny, individual cell with a bare concrete floor and no chair or anything else to sit on. Because I'd dressed in a suit for my appearance in court, I couldn't very well sit on the floor; it was so dirty in there, it looked as if someone had butchered hogs. Consequently, I stood on my feet from shortly after 6 A.M. to 9 A.M. when a deputy U.S. marshal came after me—just in time to insure that I got no breakfast.

Talk about your luck of the draw. The deputy was a redneck with a capital *R*. From the moment he stepped into the holding tank, I knew it would be a long day. "Cain't stay outta trouble can you?" he sneered. He trussed me up as if I might be John Dillinger: handcuffs, double chains running from a corset-like garment around my waist, and leg irons. As soon as we left the detention center for Washington he said, "You're my prisoner and don't you forget it. One funny move and you're no better than a cripple." I decided to say not a word on the entire drive. "I'm a George Wallace man," he volunteered, "and we got no use for son-of-a-bitches like you. We're gonna teach you goddamn criminals what the prison system's all about. Them chains feel good, boy? You learnin' your lesson?" I kept my silence. The wizened little peckerwood kept up his torrent of verbal abuse almost to the U.S. Courthouse. It seemed to enrage him that I wouldn't answer his questions, though they largely consisted of his repeating "Whatta ya think of that?" For a while I had something close to murder in my heart, but as my silence made the deputy more and more frustrated, I almost got to enjoying it. At the end of the day, however, I was greatly relieved that a more humane officer claimed custody of me. At least he didn't curse me or jerk me around by chains.

Judge John J. Sirica, not yet made famous by Watergate, presided over Paul Enten's trial. I testified that Enten had stored items at my house, that I'd bought a set of silverware from him, and that I had not known the items were hot. No, I had not known what-all Enten had stored in my basement, or its value. For one thing I had more personal and more troublesome matters on my mind, and as far as the basement went, "I stay out of there. I'm scared my wife will give me work to do down there." A newspaper account described me as "relaxed, almost jovial." Well, why not? After prison and being carted around in chains, even a courtroom looked good.

I was wiping trays during the noon meal when an inmate ran up and said, "Bakes, you made it! I just heard on the radio they're paroling you the first of June!" Inmates crowded around to congratulate me and shake my hand. Everyone wore smiles, and I'm sure mine was the broadest. The guard who had accurately predicted when I would be released looked me up to proudly claim credit, and I was happy to give it to him. That night, I violated my policy of not getting drunk in prison. The Chivas Regal and champagne did me in, but thanks to inmates who looked after me I did not get put on report. Even though I had the granddaddy of all hangovers the next day, my face wouldn't stop grinning. Now it was merely a matter of keeping my nose clean for a few weeks, of counting the days, and the nightmare would be over. What could go wrong now?

Well, something did. One morning I was told to report to the administration office. There two tight-lipped U.S. marshals awaited me with handcuffs and leg irons. I said, "Gentlemen, what's this all about?" They grunted that I was wanted in New York; that's all they knew. *Wanted in New York?* "There's got to be some mistake," I said. "I'm not charged with anything in New York and I never have been." One of them said, "We don't know shit about it. Just following orders." They trussed me up and drove me to New York City in a heavy silence. I was amazed, frightened, puzzled. It seemed an experience straight out of Kafka.

I was driven to the West Street Prison, an old converted warehouse with virtually no windows and plenty of vermin. I think it was a Friday. Through the entire weekend I could find out nothing about why I was there. I stood in line almost three hours to use a pay telephone and call collect to my brother-in-law, Robert Comstock. "Tell Dotty to find out what the hell's going on," I told him. "I asked the guards when they came by with food, but nobody will tell me shit. And tell her to come up here and bring me money. I don't have a dime for soap or cigarettes or anything else." (I had quit smoking shortly after going to prison, because cigarettes substituted for money as a means of exchange; to smoke cigarettes was the same as smoking dollar bills. Now, however, in my new confusions, I was dying for a cigarette.) I waited all day long in the scabby visitors' center. Dotty did not show up. I still did not know why I had been hustled out of Allenwood and brought to New York. There had been many moments when I thought I had bottomed out emotionally in the past few years, but I think I hit a new low that night. I couldn't understand what had happened to me, or why my wife hadn't responded to my call for help.

The next day I lined up to use the telephone again and suddenly heard someone shout "Bakes!" just before he grabbed me and hugged me. It was Sy Pollock, a New Jersey businessman whom I'd known back in my glory days, and who then had been active in the National Republican Club and often came to Washington. Now he was in jail, charged with having engaged in securities fraud. "Play sick," he told me. "Get to the hospital so we can talk." I soon developed a migraine headache and went to the hospital.

Pollock's case was before the grand jury, and we figured out that possibly I had been called to appear before it because of my acquaintance with him. But why, other than that I knew him? I knew absolutely nothing of the case in which he was involved. When I got before the grand jury, I so testified; I said, "I don't know why I've been brought here. I know Sy Pollock, yes. In the past I tried to help him on a couple of business deals in Puerto Rico. But as to the matter at hand, I'm totally ignorant. I would guess the prosecutor is going on a fishing expedition, but I can tell you under oath and under penalty of perjury that I can't help him land his fish." The grand jurors quizzed me in detail; I continued to repeat that I knew absolutely nothing. Finally I said, "I know so little about this that I have a hard time understanding the questions, because I'm not familiar with the terms of reference you're using, or the people involved, or anything else. I'm due for parole in about a month and if I could tell you anything, I would. I've already learned, to my sorrow, that it doesn't pay to protect other people and if I knew anything I'd tell you." Ultimately, the grand jury appeared to be convinced.

Back to the West Street Prison. There I languished, idle and in the dark. Again, no one could say or would say why I continued to be held. Conditions at the West Street facility were the worst I'd encountered— even worse than the Montgomery County Detention Center—and there was constant violence: fights, stabbings, sexual assaults. I was terrified. To come this close to having done my time unscathed, and then to be victimized by random violence within the last few weeks, was a terrible prospect. By this time I almost was convinced that something dreadful would happen.

I managed to get my wife on the telephone. "Dotty, I can read the handwriting on the wall and I guess it's all over for us. But if you have one flicker of feeling left for me, even as a friend, I need your help now. I'm going crazy in this hell hole and nobody will respond. Go to Congressman Dorn and Senator Thurmond and see if they can find out why I haven't been transferred back to Allenwood." She made the contacts, and soon I was back. I had been away from Allenwood for three weeks and now had only three weeks to serve before I would be paroled.

Not long before I had been jerked up and transported to the West Street Prison in New York like a side of beef, I had been assigned as a clerk to the administrative officer at Allenwood. During my absence, however, the job had been abolished. I spent my final days administering I.Q. tests to newly arrived inmates. It was depressing to see their despair and confusion and realize the many tough days and nights they would go through before they, too, would be face to face with parole.

I spent my spare time saying good-bye to friends I'd made in jail, like Blinky Palermo, a former top-flight manager of professional boxers, doing fifteen years for having fixed a boxing bout; Blinky, who worked in the prison commissary, had fluttered over me like an old mother hen, worrying about my health and well-being, and his good advice had helped me adjust when I first arrived in prison. And like Carmine DeSapio, the aging and ill former political boss of much of New York City, now a sickly old man whose pride was hurt because he sometimes required the assistance of other inmates to accomplish the slightest chore. Or a coal operator and contractor, who'd persuaded his tax accountant to write off his girlfriend's swimming pool as a tax deduction—earning a year for himself and for the tax man as well. And Jake Ursini, the Hoffa man who served as my protector when Big Al been on the verge of carving me with his wicked knife. I would miss these men. Society considered them misfits, and surely they'd brought havoc on themselves, but each had befriended me in his own way and I was grateful. They'd actually proved more loyal and selfless than many of the Washington big shots I once had claimed as friends.

There was one more troublesome flurry before I was to be permitted to breathe free air. A new headline told it: BOBBY BAKER LINKED TO MAFIA. "Man, Bakes," an inmate joshed, "I knew you was uptight with Lyndon Johnson and Jimmy Hoffa and all them top cats, but goddamn if I knew you ran the mob, too." I'm afraid my answering banter and smile was a little strained. The new publicity, I feared, might cause the Justice Department to have second thoughts about my parole. Indeed,

the story had been leaked by someone *in* the Justice Department. Somebody up there didn't like me.

The trouble was over a man named Salvatore Badalamente. Or,
more accurately, *two* men. I had known a Salvatore Badalamente,
though only slightly and briefly; he was a sometime associate of Sy Pollock. As it turned out, the authorities and the newspapers wound up
with egg on their faces: they had confused the Salvatore Badalamente I
knew with a man of the same name who, years earlier, had been a big
Mafioso. Unfortunately for their purposes, though fortunately for me,
that particular Salvatore Badalamente had been dead for about thirty
years. There was no way I could possibly have known him, or have been
associated with him, as soon became evident. That final bureaucratic
goof seemed the ultimate comic irony of my experiences, but I was too
exhausted to laugh.

On the morning of June 1, 1972, my prison ordeal was over. I slept
little on my final night and arose in great excitement. It was touching
that so many inmates called out cheerful congratulations to me as I went
through the final administrative processes. Several slipped me notes ask-

"The day I got out of prison, old friends surprised me with a welcome-home
luncheon at Duke Zeibert's restaurant in Washington. It was good to see Duke
and the boys again after a lot of bologna sandwiches." (*United Press International*)

ing me to call this or that person, or do some other favor for them, once I'd "hit the bricks" again. You can believe that I took care of each and every one of those errands, because I'd learned how important it is to have free agents looking out after you on the outside. Several inmates refused to go to work that morning because they wanted to see me off with their cheers. I heard them behind me as the gate swung open, and though I was extremely glad to go I had a lump in my throat. *There's some good in everybody,* I thought.

The press knew I was coming out of jail; a covey of reporters and cameramen awaited me. I said to them, "Sixteen months and fourteen days ago, I told you I would do my duty and do it with honor. I have. Thank you." I did not respond to their questions, but ducked into the car driven by my wife and set out toward the free life. In fact, given the pillorying I'd taken from the press, I rather enjoyed being in a position of not giving a damn that they stood on the side of the road and howled for more particulars as we sped away. Once we arrived in Washington, there was a pleasant surprise: old friends—not elected politicians but people I'd worked with, drunk with, done business with, gone to football games with—had arranged a "welcome home" party for me at Duke Zeibert's restaurant. They gave me a standing ovation when I walked in. Did it make me feel good? You're damn right it did! I'd been a little short of standing ovations for quite a while.

I had no way of knowing that only seventeen days later a band of burglars would break into an office in the Watergate complex in Washington and that their capture, in time, would cause the Nixon administration to apply the screws and threaten me with yet another stretch in jail.

Chapter Sixteen

New Troubles with the Watergate Gang

"What do you know on Larry O'Brien?"

W AKING up free is a precious gift. I could hardly wait, back at my home on Van Ness Street, for each new dawn. I was high on the world. To enjoy the simple luxury of dressing as I pleased, padding to the kitchen to eat what I wanted for breakfast when I wanted it, opening the door to claim the *Washington Post* off the front step—and knowing my name would not leap out at me—constituted a bit of heaven. I reveled in being able to go for a walk in my tree-lined neighborhood, or drive where the wind or whim took me, while most of the city slept or its people sullenly climbed from their beds, coughing and groaning and bickering, reluctant to resume their daily routines and understanding nothing of how lucky they were.

Not that my life lacked real worries. It became evident early on that Dotty and I would not be able to go back to that long ago when we'd trusted each other and had shared young dreams. A massive misunderstanding had occurred shortly before I was released from prison. Dotty wrote me a long letter in which she enumerated her grievances, admitted to faults of her own, and hoped that we might mutually strive to prevent doing further damage to each other; there was even the hope that perhaps we might let bygones be bygones. Somehow, this letter was not delivered to me. Not for several weeks would her letter be returned by prison authorities and the misunderstanding cleared up; in the meantime, we'd each proceeded on the assumption that the other was cold, uncaring, and had given up on the relationship. Dotty and I continued to share the same house, though that's about the most you could say of it.

The Nixon administration in its public pronouncements was continuing to treat the Watergate case as "a third-rate burglary," though the world now knows that frantic efforts were going on behind the scenes to limit the investigation, to stonewall it, and to cover up. Despite the early diggings of Carl Bernstein and Bob Woodward of the *Washington Post,* or the complaints of Senator George McGovern and other Democrats, the public was paying only scant or perfunctory attention. About the time that Republicans were convening to renominate the Nixon-Agnew ticket—which would put the time at August of 1972—I received alarming news from an attorney, Paul Sachs, a fellow graduate of American University Law School. Sachs was accused of having given illegal advice in connection with a securities fraud case involving Sy Pollock. Sachs's attorney, Benton Becker—later President Ford's lawyer, who would work out the agreement pardoning Richard Nixon—had prepared a memorandum for Sachs, the guts of which was that the government would not be interested in plea bargaining with Sachs unless he could provide crucial evidence to convict Bobby Baker or some other prominent Democrat.

"Convict me of *what?*" I asked Sachs.

"Anything," he said. "Tax evasion or securities fraud or whatever."

Like most people, I then had no idea of how deep were the Watergate waters or how deep the Nixon administration's fears. I was puzzled. I also was scared, so I ran to my attorney at the time—James (Meiggs) Reilly—and asked him to go see the U.S. attorney, Harold Titus, who was an old friend of Reilly's, and inquire what in the name of God might be going on. I was literally petrified at thoughts of new legal nightmares. "I've been through nine years of torment," I told Meiggs Reilly, "and I just can't face it again. I think if I had to go back to jail I'd shoot myself."

Reilly returned to report that Harold Titus had appeared to be cordial; my lawyer thought I had little to fear. Shortly afterward, however, newspaper stories reported that Bobby Baker was one of several people being investigated in a securities fraud involving a company called Control Metals, Inc. I knew this leak had to come from the Justice Department, and this knowledge inspired new fear; I could feel footsteps behind me and hot breath on my neck. I told my lawyer, "Meiggs, I have never owned one single share of Control Metals or had anything to do with it. I know absolutely zilch about that case. I'll willingly testify to that under oath before the Securities and Exchange Commission, or a grand jury, or anyone else. Get me an appointment with Harold Titus so I can assure him of this. Let's nip this thing in the bud and end all speculation. It wouldn't take much to get my parole revoked and I can't stand any loose talk in the newspapers or anywhere else." The U.S. attorney was evasive, however; he told Meiggs Reilly that he would be tied up with the Republican National Convention for a while and that I should sit tight.

The Watergate investigation then was being conducted by the original Justice·Department team of Seymour Glanzer, Robert Ogred, and Earl Silbert; later, newspapers and the Watergate investigating committee—chaired by Senator Sam Ervin—would harshly criticize these men for having dragged their feet. This would lead to the appointment of Archibald Cox as special Watergate prosecutor. Meanwhile, however, leaks kept coming down from the original team of prosecutors that my indictment in the Control Metals case might be handed down momentarily.

I went to Ralph Hutto of Senator Jim Eastland's staff and told him, "Ralph, I think the Nixon administration has in mind blowing off a new round of Bobby Baker publicity just before the November election so as to take the sting out of the Watergate thing. I've heard that the assistant attorney general in the criminal division, Henry Petersen, is an honest cop. I'd appreciate it if Senator Eastland would get me an appointment with him so I can head this bullshit off at the pass." Hutto, an old friend, spoke with Senator Eastland and the appointment was made. I told Mr. Petersen my story and said, "I think it would be a crime if I got indicted by a grand jury that wouldn't even call me as a witness. I've *begged* to go before that grand jury and tell it under oath that I know nothing of Control Metals, that I've never owned its stock or sold it or recommended it." Henry Petersen was polite, attentive, and noncommital. I was never called before the grand jury and I was never indicted (though Sy Pollock, Paul Sachs, and others were), which made it clear it had been a fishing expedition all along.

Enter Robert Vesco, the securities manipulator. Sometimes I think that when I die—and my entire life flashes before my eyes as the myth tells—then I'll watch a brain movie of every thief, con man, and rogue who walked this earth in my lifetime. My connection with Robert Vesco was, thank God, only marginal. It came about through a Beverly Hills friend, Roy B. Loftin, a transplanted Texan I'd met years earlier through Clint Murchison.

Shortly after I left prison, Loftin was negotiating a business loan for his air conditioning company in the Los Angeles area from one of Robert Vesco's many companies. Loftin got to know Vesco, who then was the object of SEC civil actions—and who was plenty worried. With great reason. Vesco in 1970 had hired as his administrative assistant a nephew of President Nixon, a young man who was the son of the president's brother, Donald. Vesco and Loftin also knew—as I did not—that Vesco had contributed $250,000 in hard green to President Nixon's 1972 re-election campaign, and that the money had been corporate money and therefore was illegally given. Vesco, Nixon, and all Republican top dogs

"Enter Robert Vesco, the securities manipulator. Sometimes I think that when I die, and my entire life flashes before my eyes as the myth tells, then I'll watch a brain movie of every thief, con man, and rogue who walked the earth in my lifetime." (*United Press International*)

who knew of this were scared witless that the SEC civil actions would blow the lid on their connection. Roy Loftin, during this period, called me as often as twice a day to seek my judgment and advice on how to keep the lid on something that he hinted was terribly explosive. "Roy," I joked, "if I knew how to do that, would I be a former jailbird?"

"This is serious, Bobby," Loftin said. "Vesco's putting pressure on me to learn what I can from you. He feels he's got to get to somebody. If you'll go along, it could help me get that loan from him. I need it badly." I agreed to meet with Loftin, a lawyer named Tom Richardson—who was Vesco's securities advisor—and a Vesco bodyguard named Bobby Hull. (Hull later was mysteriously killed in Beverly Hills.) They flew to Washington and I met them at Page Aviation, at Dulles Airport, where they presented a memorandum outlining their explosive problems. I read it while they figeted and squirmed, and saw immediately that Robert Vesco was trying to frighten the Nixon administration into calling off the SEC dogs. I said to myself, *Careful, Baker. Get involved in any conspiracy and you'll be back in the Crossbar Hotel.* At last I was learning.

I said, "Well, the only man to go to is Bebe Rebozo. He's the one man in the world Dick Nixon fully trusts. I've known Bebe myself for years, met him through Senator Smathers of Florida. He's always been tight with the Smathers group, and he's friendly toward me. I think you can count on him to get this memo to the president."

Loftin said, "Well, we don't know Rebozo. Can you handle it for us?"

I said, "I'd rather not. If the newspapers got my name in it, it would help you about like a dose of the clap."

"Well," Loftin said, "we don't know any other source we're sure of. Just be real careful how you do it."

I flew to Florida, in early October, and registered at a Key Biscayne motel under the name of William Thompson. This was the name of a deceased mutual friend of mine and Bebe Rebozo's. Bebe understood immediately who I was, because we'd made contact in that name in the past; indeed, scarcely a month earlier, we had done so—about which more later. Bebe told me to come to his office at the Key Biscayne Bank and Trust Company after normal business hours. There I handed over the Vesco memo; it's my recollection that, under Bebe's urgings, I wrote down on a yellow legal pad some suggestions as to how the matter might best be handled. Frankly, I think I wrote a hodgepodge of gobble-dygook. My main goal was to please Bebe, and his powerful connections, so that the Justice Department might be dissuaded from attempting to zero in on me as the Democratic fall guy during their Watergate uncertainties. As always, Bebe volunteered very little of himself.

Shortly after I returned to Washington, Roy Loftin again called in behalf of Robert Vesco. He wanted to arrange a Washington meeting with me for Vesco, himself, and the securities lawyer Tom Richardson. Vesco and his party flew into Washington National Airport in the Lear-jet he'd bought from Frank Sinatra; I again huddled with them at the Page Aviation terminal. Loftin had tipped me off that Vesco was in the market for a top-notch criminal lawyer. My first instinct was to send him to Charles Colson, but Colson was more a fixer than a defense attorney and by this time there were inside suspicions that his hands might not be clean in the Watergate matter. I therefore recommended to Robert Vesco that he hire Edward Bennett Williams and I volunteered to make the introductions. "I need to see him immediately," Vesco said. "We're doing everything possible to prevent any SEC hearings before the November election."

I arranged the meeting in Ed William's office in the Hill Building, at the corner of 17th and Eye Streets, N.W. We met with Williams, a lawyer in his firm named Vincent Fuller, and another lawyer—described as a securities specialist—whose name I no longer recall. I was getting a bit cautious in my old age, having been burned before, and so after the exchange of pleasantries I carefully said, "Ed, I really don't know much about Mr. Vesco other than what I've read in the newspapers—and I know how inaccurate *that* can be. Without prejudging his case, it appears from a private communication that he possibly may have a criminal problem with an alleged illegal campaign contribution from corporate funds. I'm here strictly as a service to my friend Roy Loftin, who's doing business with Mr. Vesco. I want everybody to know that I'm not taking a fee, nor will I accept one, for this service. If it ever broke that I was here,

I'm sure I would be subpoenaed and I'd have to take the fifth amendment again. So if I may be excused, I'll wait in the bar downstairs." I simply didn't want to know any more than I already knew.

Tom Richardson, Roy Loftin, and I went to the bar and drank while
Robert Vesco was counseled by Ed Williams and his assistants. About two
hours later Vesco slipped in to join us. He appeared much more worried
than previously, nervously drumming his fingers on the tabletop and
flashing a taut smile which was a first cousin to a grimace; I received the
impression that for the first time he realized he was in serious jeopardy.

Vesco said he'd told Williams that he was represented by a firm in
New York in connection with his civil action, and that Williams had
responded, on hearing the firm's name, "You could not be better represented in the securities field. Our speciality is criminal law, if you think
you have a need for that." I could not resist asking whether Vesco had
hired Williams. He shot me a quick look and said, "Yes, it appears so";
later, a member of the Williams firm would tell me that Vesco had paid a
quarter-million dollars to that firm against any future criminal contin-
gencies.

I don't know what Ed Williams did for Robert Vesco, if anything.
After the election, of course, all hell broke loose; Robert Vesco soon fled
the country under charges that he'd bilked investors out of $250 million;
since then, he's lived in Costa Rica in a garrison state, surrounded by
bodyguards, and reportedly in fear of contracts out on his life. When big
money is involved, believe me, the rules are rough. Inside or outside
prison, the percentage of gentlemen is very small when the stakes are
high and hardball is called for. The codes and the penalties are strikingly
similiar.

I was taking the holiday air at my old haunt, the Carousel Motel in
Ocean City, over the Labor Day weekend in 1972, and had just returned
from a walk along the beach when the switchboard operator told me that
she had two "urgent" telephone messages for me. The first was from my
family home in Pickens. I returned it and learned that my mother had
just died. This should not have been a surprising message, given her
long history of bad health, but I suppose we are never fully prepared for
the shock. My grief was dry. I didn't shed a tear, but felt a numbing loss.
I told my brother that I would be in Pickens the following day, to stand
in the receiving line at the funeral home, and in the trauma of the
moment I forgot the second of the "urgent" calls. After a shower, while
changing clothes, I came across the second message slip, which I had
stuck in my pocket. It instructed me to immediately call a Mr. Gregory in
Key Biscayne, Florida. Staring at the unfamiliar name a while, I had a

"When Bebe Rebozo called me, he did so as 'Mr. Gregory' and I used the name 'Bill Thompson'. . . . 'What do you know on Larry O'Brien?' Bebe blurted." (Rebozo in center, between Robert Abplanalp and Richard Nixon) (*United Press International*)

hunch. I then called the Miami operator and found that the phone number "Mr. Gregory" had left was that of the Key Biscayne Bank and Trust Company. Since I knew no one there except Bebe Rebozo, I knew he had to be "Mr. Gregory."

I went to a safer phone than I thought my Carousel room might provide and called the Key Biscayne number. Though it was a Sunday afternoon, Bebe Rebozo's secretary answered. I told her to tell him that "Bill Thompson" was calling. Bebe came on the line and said, "We need to talk about that business venture and I'd like you to fly here immediately." I said, "Well, Mr. Rebozo, can it wait? I just got word that my mother died and I've got to be home by tomorrow afternoon." He said, "I truly hate to bother you in such a sad time, and I extend my condolences, but this is a matter of the greatest importance. If you can arrange to get here late tonight, we can meet for breakfast. I'll have you on your way by noon." He said he would make reservations for me at the Key Biscayne Hotel, and would see me there at seven o'clock the following morning.

We had breakfast in my suite. As soon as he entered, Bebe pressed one finger against his lips until he'd turned the television set on to a high decibel level. We sat close together. Bebe Robozo said, "Bobby, I know you're a Democrat, but how do you feel about Senator McGovern?" I said, "I think he's a very decent man, but he's not my cup of tea. I believe the nut liberals have captured him, and I'm afraid of some of their wild schemes. I don't think he'd be good for the country." While I figured that this was what Rebozo hoped to hear, it also represented my true feelings. I did not, however, tell Bebe that I was far from overjoyed at the prospect of four more years of Richard Nixon.

Rebozo nodded. He tapped me on the knee and said with a half smile, "Good! Would you like to help our president?"

I gave careful thought to my response and then said, "Well, I'm not real sure how I'd go about it. I'm not exactly the most popular man in America, you know. As a matter of fact, I've been wanting to talk to you about how I'm being treated by the Justice Department. I telephoned you at the White House and left word that 'Bill Thompson' had called."

"I know that. That's why I called you and asked you here."

"Bebe," I said, "I don't know what's going on. Justice is leaking it that I may be indicted in that goddamn Control Metals case, and I don't know a nickel's worth about it. My lawyer can't get anybody to say what the hell is happening. I can't get to Harold Titus, and when I talked to Henry Petersen he didn't tell me shit or give me any clue."

"What do you know on Larry O'Brien?" Bebe Robozo blurted.

I said, "Bebe, I don't really know anything on him. I don't like the bastard and I know enough about politics to figure he's probably vulnerable in the campaign contribution category, but I couldn't prove a thing."

"Try," he said.

"I just don't have the goods," I said. "Honest. I was never close to the man; we never operated in the same ballpark even though we were on the same team."

Rebozo wrinkled his brow and looked disappointed. He said, "What Democrat can you give us? They're trying to kill us with this Watergate fiasco. We gotta fight back."

What Democrat can you give us? If I'd had any doubts that my new harassments were tied to Republican fears of a Watergate explosion, they flew off on quick wings. I thought it over for a moment and said, "Well, let's talk about Cy Anderson. Maybe he can give you something."

Cyrus Anderson was a representative of the railroad unions and other industries with government problems. In short, a lobbyist. He was a decent man, I thought, with a fine family and he had a serious heart condition. He'd been indicted along with Senator Daniel Brewster of Maryland for being a conduit of funds from Mo Speigel, of the mail-order house, to Senator Brewster when Brewster had been a member of the Senate Post Office Committee. In an effort to get out of his troubles, he'd gone along enthusiastically with George Meany's decision that labor should do nothing to help Senator McGovern. I said, "Bebe, I've heard that Cy Anderson is willing to provide some terribly incriminating information about the Kennedy brothers, and to testify against Danny Brewster, if he can avoid going to jail. He's got a bad heart and he's petrified that a trial will kill him or that he'll die in prison."

Bebe said, "The Kennedys are dead. I'm not sure that information would help us much. What does he know on them?"

"Campaign money, I think."

"That's not strong enough," Rebozo said. "We need to nail O'Brien. Have you heard anything about what really happened at Chappaquiddick? Did O'Brien play a big role in that?"

"Bebe," I said, "I was out of fashion among Democrats *long* before Chappaquiddick. Except for Jack Kennedy himself, I was never even reasonably close to the Kennedy people. I'm afraid I just can't help you."

Rebozo said, "Well, keep your ears open. Think about it. I want you to come to my office and repeat what you've told me here."

I followed him to the Key Biscayne Bank and Trust office in a rented car, and at a decent distance; once in his private office I organized my thoughts and wrote them down on a small, monogrammed scratchpad I picked up from his desk. Bebe then turned on a Dictaphone machine and had me repeat the Cy Anderson–Maurice Hutchinson information. He indicated that the Dictabelt would be sent to President Nixon or sources close to him. We shook hands and as I left he said, "I'll be in touch with you." I thought, *Yeah, I'm afraid so.*

I scooted to the airport, only to find that my Miami-to-Atlanta plane was delayed by mechanical problems. Its tardy arrival in Atlanta caused me to miss my connection to Greenville, South Carolina. I rented another car and raced toward Pickens. My thoughts were a jumble of my mother's death and my new dilemma: obviously, the Nixon crowd intended to force me to the wall in their desperate effort to dig up new dirt on prominent Democrats. I was fatigued and disspirited when I arrived in my home town, just in time to take my place in the funeral home receiving line that night. The funeral was on Tuesday. I went through it in a fog and then, after a day spent with relatives who'd gathered for my mother's last rites, I hurried back to Washington.

Almost immediately, I had another message from "Mr. Gregory." It asked that I call him at an unfamiliar number in Key Biscayne. I did this from a pay telephone and was instructed to call President Nixon's personal attorney, Herb Kalmbach of Newport Beach, California, who then was staying at the Regency Hotel in New York. "Call as Bill Thompson," Bebe Rebozo instructed. "Use a safe telephone."

Once I'd reached Herb Kalmbach, he asked me to meet him the next day in the main lobby of the Waldorf Astoria Hotel in New York City. "There's a big clock there," he said, "or I think it's a clock. It's a round ornament imbedded in the tiles in the center of the lobby. There are divan-like seats on all sides of it. Sit facing the Lexington Avenue entrance."

I had never met Herb Kalmbach and knew little about him; Watergate had not yet catapulted him to infamy. Almost on the dot of the appointed hour, a distinguished-looking impeccably dressed man entered the lobby of the Waldorf and after circling the centerpiece clock a half dozen times, like Indians zeroing in on a wagon train, he stepped forward and said, "Mr. Bill Thompson?" I said, "Yes, good to see you." We shook hands. Mr. Kalmbach seemed frightened. In a low voice he said, "Follow me about twenty paces to the rear and we'll find a quiet place for lunch." We went downstairs—the Waldorf main lobby is on the second floor—and I kept the required distance as Herb Kalmbach turned right to walk parallel with Lexington Avenue and then crossed 49th Street. He turned right again, then turned sharp left to enter the Barclay Hotel. It wryly occurred to me that I'd spent many wonderful nights there with Carole Tyler, in the suite maintained by U.S. Freight, back in my salad days.

Over lunch, Herb Kalmbach seemed almost desperate to uncover dirt involving Larry O'Brien. "As I told Bebe," I said in hushed tones, "I just don't know a thing on the man." I was at a loss. Then Kelmbach said, "Tell me about the TFX fix." Halfway through my recitation of how big politicians and big defense firms reach mutually beneficial accords, he impatiently waved his hand and said, "I know all *that*. Did O'Brien have anything to do with the TFX decision?" I said that I doubted it; that, in the period we were talking about, O'Brien had been more Indian than chief. His prominence had come at a later date. "Hell," I said, "until Larry O'Brien latched on to Jack Kennedy's coattails, he was just another Boston wardheel who'd failed at running a second-rate hotel. I doubt if President Kennedy thought enough of his abilities, outside of O'Brien's political grunt work and a minor talent for tactics, to bring him on the inside. I can guarantee you he wasn't on a level with Bob McNamara and the other biggies who made the TFX decision. O'Brien didn't amount to much more than a popcorn fart until Lyndon Johnson made him postmaster general."

"Well," Kalmbach said, "do you have anything on him from the Johnson era?"

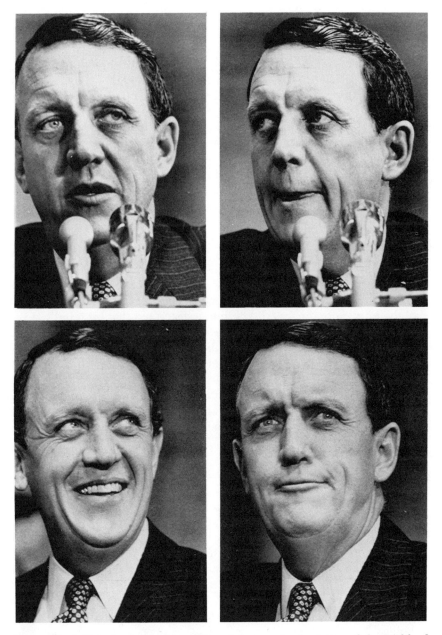

"I met Herb Kalmbach, President Nixon's lawyer, in the lobby of the Waldorf. He seemed frightened. In a low voice he said, 'Follow me about twenty paces to the rear . . .'" (*United Press International*)

"No," I said. "Mr. Kalmbach, you've gotta remember that by the time LBJ got to the White House I wasn't around anymore."

This old news made Herb Kalmbach morose. He toyed with his food, pushing it around on his plate, barely nibbling at it. I had the notion he didn't particularly enjoy what he was doing, though maybe this was because he was failing to bring home the expected bacon. After a bit he said, "Well, it might be convenient for you should your memory improve." It was then I knew he was tough: not at all the goody-goody he later would represent himself as being during the Watergate hearings and at his subsequent trial. I said, "Look, Mr. Kalmbach, I'm damn near desperate to live my life without additional complications. If I had what you wanted, I'd give it to you. My martyr instincts are pretty damn well depleted by now. But I don't think it would do anybody any good for me to make up bullshit information."

"Oh, no, no," he said, hastily. "That would be counterproductive. We've got to be certain of our facts. But we *do* hope you'll continue to search your memory." We talked politics for a bit in general terms; I then launched into a long discourse about my recurring problems with the Justice Department. Mr. Kalmbach's eyes seemed to glaze over; I had the impression he was pretending to listen but that his mind was on vacation in a distant place. *This is a smart man,* I thought, *but he's a cold fish.*

Herb Kalmbach soon called for the check, paid cash, and suggested that I linger at the table until he'd left the restaurant. Throughout our meal, his eyes had darted and searched the room as if someone might be coming after us with a bench warrant. Kalmbach gave the room a final sweeping search, nodded abruptly, and took his leave. The next time I saw him he was on television, describing himself to the Ervin Committee as a duped and innocent man.

In 1974, shortly before his death, I received astonishing news from Clyde Tolson, the ill and aging assistant director of the Federal Bureau of Investigation, who had been J. Edgar Hoover's lifelong best friend; Hoover had preceded him in death a year or so earlier.

Virtually on his death bed, and for motives that I am at a loss to explain unless it had to do with settling accounts in his soul before the end, the old man told a private nurse—who had attended each of my children during their infancy—"Your friend Bobby Baker should know that his secretary, Georgia Liakakis, is a paid government informant and has been for years. She has supplied many of his documents to the government."

I cannot too strongly state my degree of disbelief when this word was passed on to me. I had known Georgia Liakakis for years. When her boss, a car dealer named George Hodges, had died in the mid-1960s, I got her a job with Sy Pollock; when Pollock later went to jail, I hired Georgia Liakakis as a part-time secretary and girl Friday. She had asked permission to store several boxes of Sy Pollock's files and records in my basement, and I agreed; I guess this was in 1968. Over the years, Georgia Liakakis had become like a member of the Baker family: she had a key to my house, the run of my files, so my life was an open book to her; my children loved her and affectionately called her "The Greek." She picked them up after school, prepared their snacks, helped them with their homework, and played games with them. I could not have been more astonished had someone told me that one of my sisters was a government spy.

My initial reaction was that old Clyde Tolson must have lost his marbles. I simply did not want to believe his accusation. I telephoned a friend, Billy McKeon, who had been a House page boy when I was a Senate page; Billy had been in partnership with Georgia's late boss and I knew that he maintained an extremely close relationship with her. In addition to working for me, Georgia Liakakis sometimes sold automobiles for Billy and was reported to be a whiz at it. He met me at an apartment house near Captiol Hill, which I was rehabilitating for rental purposes; we stepped outside to escape the ears of workmen. I told Billy what Clyde Tolson had passed on and added, "You know her better than anyone. Do you think it's even marginally possible she might spy on me?"

Billy's answer shook me to my heels. He said, "Frankly, it wouldn't shock me that much." I stood aghast. "Why in hell would you say that, Billy?" "Well," he said, "I heard she may have tax problems. That would give 'em one hell of a hold on her. She'd be at their mercy." This, too, was astounding news. "Billy," I said, "I had no idea. She never once let on she had tax problems." McKeon said, "If the government wanted her to turn on you, then she wouldn't be likely to confide her problems to you, would she?"

Once I'd accepted Tolson's truth on the surface, there seemed much within my experience, and the national experience, to corroborate it. The government had willingly produced witnesses who committed perjury at my trial. It had wiretapped me and my friends and associates. It had pressured me, under loosely veiled threats of jail, to deliver a prominent Democrat to offset Watergate embarrassments. Then *why wouldn't it* turn my secretary into an in-house spy, if given enough leverage to get away with it?

Bobby Baker aside, and such paranoid fantasies as he may have accumulated in nine confusing years, it had become public knowledge that the FBI long had engaged in burglary, illegal wiretaps, infiltrations, and manufactured evidence. That its acting director, on orders of top White House aides, had willingly "deep-sixed" incriminating materials which he improbably claimed he'd not been curious enough to examine before burning them in his fireplace. That the Central Intelligence Agency and the Pentagon, with the blessings of at least four presidents, had knowingly engaged in illegal acts and then had lied about them. That two successive attorneys general had broken the law and lied under oath. That even the man who had prosecuted me, Bill Bittman, had been labeled by a grand jury of citizens as an "unindicted co-conspirator" for his part in paying blackmail money to Watergate criminals—and that even the president of the United States himself was a crook, a liar, and had misused and abused his power in so many ways as to tax the imagination of even a novelist. Superimposing this knowledge on top of all the abuses I'd personally seen, heard—and sometimes participated in—during my own time at the top, then why should I have any trouble believing my government capable of one more dirty trick?

I telephoned Sy Pollock, who was on the verge of going to trial in a securities fraud case in Newark, New Jersey, and said, "Sy, it appears I've had a trojan horse within the gates for a while. And, since she worked for you, I'd guess that you did, too." Pollock was as astounded as I originally had been. His attorney immediately moved to compel the government to make available all illegally taken documents, and to reveal how they had been obtained. He also demanded that Georgia Liakakis be subpoenaed and compelled to testify. The defense also issued a subpoena to me. I was not only willing, but eager, to testify. My bones told me that at long last I would not again be forced to slink away from a courthouse bearing a loser's brand.

Federal Judge Frederick Lacey was a former U.S. attorney in New Jersey; as do an unfortunate number of judges with similar backgrounds, his record indicated that he had a prosecutor's mentality. We therefore expected no big breaks from him. After *in camera* hearings, however—closed conferences in the judge's private chambers, where basic nut-cutting goes on without being impeded by the formalities of open court—he ruled that before I appeared to testify the government must burp up any and all documents pertaining to me.

And lo, the government did surrender a Justice Department microfilm labeled "Baker-Pollock"—containing more than 700 documents obviously pilfered from my files. J. Edgar Hoover himself had perhaps gone through my garbage. The file contained a mighty hodgepodge: my personal checks, telephone calls received and made, personal letters both written and received, business contracts, notes my children had written asking Georgia Liakakis to pick them up after school, Christmas cards, scratchpads, newspaper clippings, on and on. Looking them over, I became convinced that not all of them had been turned over to the feds by Georgia Liakakis. She'd surrendered many documents, sure. But to the trained eye that obviously wasn't the whole story. There were in the government's file old records dating back to Lyndon Johnson's 1960 campaign and earlier, tax and business records from the long ago. I knew my filing system; I knew that many of those files had been stored in places where Georgia likely could not have found them without outside help and, indeed, that even had she found them she couldn't have gotten into them on her own because they were under locks for which she had no keys. In preparing my defense for my trial—long before Georgia came to work for me or would have had access to my records—I'd been puzzled that many documents I *knew* I had were nowhere to be found. We'd turned the house upside down to no good end. Now these missing documents had turned up in the government's files. The conclusion was inescapable: the feds had performed against me what the FBI calls "black-bag jobs"; you and I would call it burglary.

The government went to great lengths to prevent Georgia Liakakis from being compelled to testify: Pollock and Baker, well-connected with the Mafia, gave her reason to fear for her life; she should be spirited away to an unknown city, given a new identify, and protected for the rest of her life. Judge Lacey, bless him, ordered that Ms. Liakakis be brought to him for a secret hearing in his chamber. No, she told him, she didn't fear Sy Pollock or Bobby Baker. If she feared anybody, she feared agents of the government. Yes, she'd agreed to furnish documents to the authorities after they'd scared her about taxes. Where and how had the government agents copied the documents? They'd come to her home on several occasions and she'd also delivered documents to agents at motels and restaurants; the agents then filmed them. Had she also supplied the agents with recordings of telephone calls? Yes, she had. Did the agents also copy these? Normally they listened to them and took notes. Had she been paid for her information? Yes. Had the agents encouraged her to produce all possible documents? Yes.

Government witnesses reluctantly admitted to Judge Lacey in *in camera* proceedings that Georgia Liakakis had, indeed, delivered documents to an FBI agent, Tom Sullivan, and to an IRS agent, Francis J. Cox, and that she'd met on occasion with an assistant U.S. attorney, a Mr. Clark—but by their account Georgia Liakakis had sought them out: they'd never pressured her, her information hadn't been worth much anyway, she was afraid of Bobby Baker and feared for her life, and so on. To hear them tell it, the whole thing was merely a tempest in a teapot and they'd just as soon have not bothered with it.

After I had testified to Judge Lacey as to Ms. Liakakis's access to my files, the trust I'd reposed in her, her admission to me when confronted that she'd been a paid informant but had been coerced into it and so forth, the judge said that he was "concerned about and flabbergasted by" the government's tactics. He asked the chief prosecutor, "Based on what we have heard here, who is to be believed?" And the chief prosecutor, looking a bit abashed, finally said, "Based on Mr. Baker's testimony, he is to be believed." I had begun to think no prosecutor alive ever would put those words on his tongue.

Sy Pollock also testified that in 1970 Internal Revenue agents and postal inspectors had offered him $250,000, a new identity under the government's hush-hush "Alias Program," and reduction of charges against him provided he would deliver derogatory information leading to the conviction of Bobby Baker on any charge I hadn't already been convicted of. (When Pollock's wife brought me this information shortly after the offer allegedly had occurred, I told her, "Mrs. Pollock, tell Sy to take the money and run like a burglar. He can make up anything he wants if it'll help him—and if he'll split his fee with me.")

The press got wind of the government's *in camera* admissions and for once I liked the headline appearing in the New York *Daily News:* FEDS STOLE BAKER PAPERS. This embarrassment inspired the U.S. attorney for the New Jersey district, Jonathan Goldstein, to rise in open court and denounce the tactics of the government he represented—denounce, in other words, his own investigators. Great was his wrath—for the record, anyhow—as he thundered of fair play and justice and pledged an investigation to get to the bottom of the pilfered papers caper; he also asked that Sy Pollock's trial be postponed until after the investigation had been completed. No stone would be left unturned, vigorous inquiries would go forward, culprits would be brought to accountings, blah-blah-blah, and la-de-dah. As of this writing, that was almost two years ago. No one—not Mr. Goldstein nor anyone representing him—has contacted me, or has contacted any of the involved parties, to the best of my knowledge. In short, there was no investigation. The government, caught with dirty hands, quietly buried the matter.

Chapter Seventeen

The Prodigal Son Returns

*LBJ said, "Everything within me wanted to come
to your aid. But they would have crucified me."*

O NE AFTERNOON in September 1972, not long after Bebe
Rebozo and Herb Kalmbach had held my feet to the fire, I
received a telephone call at my Washington home from Walter Jenkins.
It was the first time I'd heard from LBJ's old Texas staff chief since he'd
telephoned me in 1964 to say that President Johnson would like my
thoughts on whom he should choose as vice-president. (I had argued for
Senator Eugene McCarthy, who probably would have proved a disastrous selection. As the Vietnam War worsened, Johnson and McCarthy
would have had the worst fratricidal split since Franklin D. Roosevelt
and his V-P, John Nance Garner, fell out over the third term issue.) Not
many months afterward, Jenkins would resign from the White House
staff following his arrest on a morals charge, and would disappear to
Texas.

"Bobby," he said, "keep this strictly in the family. President and Mrs.
Johnson would like to invite you and Mrs. Baker to spend a weekend at
the LBJ Ranch soon—if you're interested."

"Of course I'm interested, Walter. Tell the leader I'm at his beck and
call. I couldn't be more delighted."

We agreed on a date in early October; Jenkins said he'd get back to
me with details and again cautioned, "This is to be very private. No publicity before, during, or after." I said that was fine with me and then
asked, "Walter, do you know if the leader wants to see me for any particular reason?" Jenkins hesitated while I listened to the telephone wire
hum across the miles to Texas. Then he said, "Well, Mr. Johnson isn't in
the best of health. He's been seeking out old friends lately. I think he's
mending fences."

It was a beautiful sunny October day when my wife and I flew into
Austin. Walter Jenkins met us at the airport and quickly ushered us into
his car as if eager to hide us. En route to his office, where I would meet

an old friend and former assistant of mine—Rein VanderZee—and motor to VanderZee's rock ranch near Banderia, to spend the night, Jenkins said, "Mr. Johnson has to take a siesta every day. Doctor's orders. So you should not arrive at the ranch before 3 P.M. tomorrow." I said, "Walter, level with me. How ill is he?" Jenkins said, "I'm afraid he's worse off than people know. He's absolutely preoccupied with his death and talks about it far too much. He's drinking and smoking again. I worry about him."

When Dorothy and I drove up to the gates of the LBJ Ranch the following afternoon, a Secret Service man told us to wait in the library because the former president was taking a nap. A few moments later, however, a buzzer sounded and another Secret Service agent bounded into the back part of the Johnson ranch house. He soon returned, beckoning us to follow.

I was so unprepared for LBJ's appearance when we entered his bedroom, I'm afraid my face registered shock. Lyndon Johnson was very fat, most pale, and white-haired; he'd aged far more than his infrequent newspaper photos had led me to expect. There was an oxygen mask by his bed, which he frequently used to aid his breathing; he was removing it from his face as we walked into the room. He put on a big smile, however, and after kissing my wife he gave me a warm embrace. "Bobby," he said, "It's been a long time. Too long."

I was experiencing a series of rapid, conflicting thoughts and emotions: *It's not my fault its been so long; I didn't turn my back on you.* Then, right behind it: *Jesus, the poor man looks terrible. This isn't the Lyndon Johnson I knew.* Aloud, I said, "Mr. Leader, we're overjoyed to see you again, but I respectfully ask permission to leave the room until you've completed your rest."

"Oh, no," he said. "Sit down. I've got my nap out of the way. It's not good for old men to sleep all the time."

Lying through my teeth I said, "Why, Mr. Leader, you look like you could spot the world three rounds and still lick it."

"No," LBJ said. "My brain might lie to me but my body knows better."

With that, he launched into a discussion of his health woes. "I went to see Dr. DeBakey down in Houston about open-heart surgery, and I consulted Dr. James Cain and others at the Mayo Clinic, but they all thought the operation would be a waste of time and that I might die on the operating table. I've got cancer, too, you know." I was astonished: nobody knew that. LBJ had another surprise ready: "When they removed those throat polyps when I was president," he said, "they found out they were malignant. Of course, we didn't make that public. And when I had my gall bladder removed and the press jumped on me for showing my scar—well, hell, I did that on purpose so rumors wouldn't get started I'd had a cancer operation. If the damn president has much more than a hangnail the stock market goes crazy." He gulped from the oxygen mask and his color began to improve.

"Lady Bird's in Austin on a shoppin' spree," he said, "but she'll be back soon and I know she'll be proud to see you. Look here—" he rose from the bed, opened a closet door, and revealed a row of trousers which appeared to be double-knits—"I pay about $20 for these. I used to think a man had to parade around in four-hundred-dollar suits but hell, these twenty-buck britches are all a man needs. A man can get along a lot cheaper than he thinks he can. Trouble is, most folks don't realize the difference between what they *want* and what they *need*. Money's not all that important to me now. I don't let it rule me." Then, as if to prove again his talent for contradictions, he said, "Bakes, that lil' ol' television station of mine?" (When he was in public office, it was always "Lady Bird's station.") I nodded "Well, the Los Angeles Times Company's paying me nine million dollars plus for it."

I said, "That'll buy a lot of twenty-buck britches."

LBJ dressed in a Western-style outfit, his shirt tieless and open at the collar, and bellowed to a Secret Service man, "Get Dale Malinchek and Mrs. Malinchek in here"—his ranch manager and his ranch secretary—"and then fill up the car with ice and whiskey and some cups. I wanta show the Bakers my spread." I was amazed anew at the man: ten minutes earlier he'd looked and talked like a man at death's door; suddenly he was barking out commands and zipping around like the Lyndon Johnson of old. For the next couple of hours LBJ played the country squire, tooting his automobile horn as he drove among grazing cows, pointing out his irrigation system, driving up a paved road to gesture toward his restored birthplace a mile or two from the LBJ ranch house. He constantly smoked and gulped Cutty Sark; throughout our visit he kept a portable bar handy. Once, when he saw me looking at him as he again dipped into the Cutty Sark, he grinned and said, "Now don't start givin' me a lecture like Bob Kerr used to do. I think the only reason ol' Bob didn't like whiskey was because he didn't own any whiskey factories."

Later in the afternoon we sat on the patio, overlooking the Pedernales River, watching several workmen install new sod in the yard; our discussion soon drifted to politics.

"Leader, what do the think of Nixon as president?"

LBJ said, "He's treated me with respect—and that's more than I can say for a lot of Democrats. Half of 'em, you know, they've turned my picture to the wall. President Nixon's sent Henry Kissinger to brief me, he

consults with me personally. I've made it a point to refrain from express-
ing my opinions and beliefs since I left the White House. No president
needs a former president lookin' over his shoulder or second-guessin'
him and poppin' off. The only time I got a little hacked with President
Nixon was when he called me and said, 'Lyndon, I've got an old friend of
yours in my office. I've asked him to be my secretary of the Treasury and
he's accepted. I'll let you speak with him.' And then he put John Connally on the line. Well, I thought that was a little too cute. As close as
John and I had always been, I thought I should have been consulted
before the fact. By both of 'em."

I asked whether he missed the presidency.

"Bobby, the presidency is worse than being in jail."

I said, "I kinda doubt that, Mr. Leader."

LBJ's cheeks colored slightly at my personal reference, but he didn't
otherwise acknowledge it. He said, "When everybody was riotin' in the
streets over Vietnam, I got as many as five hundred death threats a
week. We kept it out of the papers, but more than twenty people scaled
that big high fence at the White House trying to get to me. If I wanted to
go to mass with my daughter, Luci, I had to go at two o'clock in the mor-
nin'—sneaking around like a tire thief so some nut wouldn't kill me. It's
a terrible feeling knowing that so many people want to hurt you, when
you're doing the best you know how for your country. Any president of
any political party has my sympathy and my prayers. I miss the action
sometimes—but I don't miss the office."

Johnson crossed his legs and hoisted his empty glass as a signal that
he needed another drink mixed, and I half expected a ghostly band
somewhere in the background to go into the strains of *"Seems like oooo-lll-
ddd times . . ."* Mrs. Malinchek took his glass while Johnson—who now
was warming to political talk and actually appeared a decade younger—
continued to hold forth. He said, "President Nixon called me into his office when Lady Bird and I went back to the White House for a Billy
Graham service, and he said, 'Lyndon, why did you keep all those
damned Kennedy appointees after your overwhelming defeat of Barry
Goldwater in '64?' He said, 'I can understand, you were trying to hold
the country together after the assassination, but why in hell did you keep
'em on after you'd won the presidency in your own right?' And I said,
'Mr. President, the longer you're in this office the more you'll come to
understand that you aren't as powerful as you think you are.' Dick Nixon
shot me a kinda hard look, a suspicious look—you know, that look he
always has like somebody's about to steal his pocketbook, and he said,
'What do you mean?'

"I said to him, 'Mr. President, I diligently sought to persuade Donald

Cook, who was president of American Gas and Electric, to be my secretary of the Treasury. He was probably among the ten most competent men in America, he'd been chief counsel and then chairman of the SEC, and I knew I could depend on his work. But he wasn't a wealthy man and he would lose a two-million-dollar pension and stock option guarantee if he resigned.

"And I offered a cabinet post to Dr. Frank Stanton of CBS, another can-do man, another old friend I trusted. But he had the same problems. I failed to persuade a half dozen top-notch men. They didn't want to give up their big salaries and pensions and then during senate confirmations have their peckers inspected in public. No sensitive man wants to see his reputation tarnished by headline-seeking senators and be picked at by the media, just because he's made a little money and is trying to serve his country.'

Nixon nodded like he agreed with me and I said, 'Before you get to be president you think you can do anything. You think you're the most powerful leader since God. But when you get in that tall chair, as you're gonna find out, Mr. President, you can't count on people. You'll find your hands tied and people cussin' you. The office is kinda like the little country boy found the hoochie-koochie show at the carnival, once he'd paid his dime and got inside the tent: 'It ain't exactly as it was advertised.' "

As dusk began to settle over the hill country and the ranch workmen headed for their homes, LBJ began to ruminate about his own cabinet. "I'll always love Dean Rusk, bless his heart. He stayed with me when nobody else did. You know, Rusk came to me and said he was gonna have to resign and I asked him why. And he said that his daughter was gonna marry a Negro and it might embarrass the administration. It was the only time I ever got mad at Dean Rusk. I told him, 'This is the most progressive administration in the civil rights field in history, and you're gonna quit it over *that*? You better start thinkin' right. I want the Johnson administration to practice what it preaches.'

"Bob McNamara started out being a good man. But he got worried he was on the wrong side of the war after his Kennedy friends turned against it, and so he started wrigin' his hands and flip-floppin'. Stewart Udall, he was always kissin' up to Lady Bird but sometimes I couldn't count on him when I needed him—or even find him. He'd be off floating down a goddamn river or watching some tame Indians dance. Willard Wirtz, my Labor man, got to liking the Georgetown crowd too much. You know, ol' Harry Truman said his biggest mistake was appointing Tom Clark to the Supreme Court. Well, *my* biggest mistake was appointing Tom's son, Ramsey, as my attorney general. He couldn't make up his mind about a fish fry. Wanted to go around preachin' bleeding-heart stuff, but he never *did* a damn thing. I heard Dick Nixon made a campaign speech against Ramsey Clark one night and I had to sit on my hands so I wouldn't cheer it.

"Hell, even some of my old staffers let me down. Bill Moyers, I made that kid. Then he took up with the Kennedys and got to the point where he knew ten times as much as I did. George Reedy went off and wrote a book that made me sound like a mad king without even mentioning my name. It's funny—the only one of my old hands that has much to do with me is Walter Jenkins. And, hell, even Walter won't pick up the telephone and call me. I always got to call *him*."

I could see that LBJ was getting into one of his self-pitying moods, and I tried to head him off at the pass. "Leader," I said, "what does your heart truly say to you about George McGovern?"

"Bobby," he said, "I despise the S.O.B."

We had left the ranch house as this conversation began; LBJ drove toward an old farmhouse on the hill near his private airstrip. He seemed restless and couldn't be still. Johnson thought about my question for a moment and said, "Well, he's my party's nominee. But understand one thing, Bakes: I didn't invite McGovern to the ranch. Sargent Shriver, and I genuinely like him and respect him, called and asked if he and Senator McGovern could visit me here at the ranch. I invited 'em to lunch. And goddamn if they didn't arrange a big press conference without consulting me! I was so pissed off I came within a inch of cancelling the luncheon. But Lady Bird said, 'No, Lyndon, it would create havoc within the party.' And I decided, 'Well, no use in me creating a big stink. The Democratic ticket's already in so much trouble it's a bad joke.'

"Bobby, I can't understand why Marvin Watson and George Christian and those other boys of mine joined John Connally's Democrats for Nixon movement. John's a damn fool to turn on the party that elected him governor as long as he wanted it. He's gonna regret it one day. George McGovern, why, he couldn't carry Texas even if they caught Dick Nixon fuckin' a Fort Worth sow. There just wasn't any need for John to get out front. It's embarrassing to me. Now, hell, John could sneak around and vote Republican—but he didn't have to beat his breast and yodel like Tarzan."

That evening, during dinner, my mind flashed back to other trips I'd made to the LBJ Ranch. Once, years earlier, while flying to Texas I'd met a comely woman seatmate; the two of us had persuaded a cooperative airline hostess to be generous in her rations of drink. By the time we'd reached Dallas, where I changed for an airplane to Austin, my seatmate and I had become chums. I'd bragged a bit of who I was and what I was and had foolishly given her the LBJ Ranch private number with airy instructions to "Call me anytime." The next night during dinner, with Senator Johnson holding forth, that private line rang. LBJ, well known for having telephoneitis, had installed a phone under the dining room table near his customary seat. He interrupted whatever story he'd been telling, barked "hello" into the phone, and as he listened his face took on thundercloud qualities. Finally he said into the phone, "Lady, *you* may think Mr. Baker is cute, but right now I don't think he's cute worth a damn." I wanted to sink under the table as all eyes swivelled my way. LBJ handed me the telephone, which had a long cord, and icily said, "Here, lover boy. Say hello to your airplane lady." I mumbled a few meek "uh-huhs" and one "sorry-I-got-to-go-now," and then bent over my plate in embarrassment while Lyndon Johnson looked a hole through me. "Them that can't hold it," he finally said, "ought not to drink it." Now, these years later, our dinner was more convivial; Lady Bird Johnson, who'd returned from her Austin shopping spree, was charming as always. LBJ kidded her about her well-known frugality and bargain hunting: "Bird, did you wear out another four dollars worth of shoe leather shoppin' around to save a dime?" He also joked that she was going to be famed for being "the prettiest and the richest widow in the world."

After dinner, in the warm October evening, the former president and I walked alone under the Texas stars. As we stood on the banks of the river he said, "Bobby, I am not going to be in this world long. I have great regrets about three people who have always been loyal to me and who gave me their full measures: John Connally, Walter Jenkins, and yourself. I wanted John to be my chief of staff at the White House but he refused because he didn't think that [Preston Smith] the lieutenant governor was capable of running our state and so he insisted on running for another term. What happened to Walter Jenkins was a tragedy that neither he, nor I, shall ever get over. And you had been an invaluable friend and adviser and when you fell on hard times there was no one to replace you. How I needed you three men in the White House! I've often thought how much easier my burdens might have been."

I said, "Well, leader, I'd a damn sight rather have been in the White House than in the big house."

Lyndon Johnson said, "All that was within me wanted to come to your aid. But Bobby Kennedy would have crucified me, the Republicans would have crucified me, the press would have crucified me. If there was any way in the world I could have turned off the investigation when I became president, I'd have gladly done it. But I knew it would be politically disastrous, and perhaps even legally disastrous. Many times I wanted to call you, to sit down over a drink with you, but conditions just didn't permit it.

"You know, J. Edgar Hoover came to me shortly after I became president and said he had electronic evidence that you were mixed up with a bunch of Las Vegas gamblers. He warned me against lifting a finger to help you. I felt helpless. My heart told me one thing and my head told me another. I know you went through very difficult years, and I'm sorry I couldn't do more. You know, after Nixon became president and you went to prison I approached John Connally and I said, 'John, I think Bobby Baker's trial was a political trial and he went down because, for one thing, he'd been so close to me. No Democrat could pardon Baker. The press and the Republicans would scream to high heaven. But Nixon, a Republican, *could* pardon him. I want you to explore that possibility with the president.' But John later said it was no dice. He raised the question with Nixon but Nixon wouldn't hear of it."

I said, "Leader, it's worse than you know. Not a month ago Bebe Rebozo put pressure on me to deliver dirt on Larry O'Brien and other prominent Democrats. The Justice Department is harassing my ass. I don't want to go back to jail. I know that you and Bebe Rebozo get along well"—LBJ earlier had said that he was sympathetic to Rebozo because any private citizen close to a president was a marked man and fair game—"and it could help me immeasurably if you'd telephone Bebe and put in a kind word for me."

Lyndon Johnson suddenly had no more pretty speeches or apologies to make. He ducked his head, pulled an ear, and said, "Well, uh, Bobby, I don't know. It might hurt you more than it could help. Democrats are threatenin' to sue Republicans over this Watergate case, and, uh, it's very partisan. You just don't know who you can trust. If Bebe Rebozo told President Nixon I was sticking my nose into it, or, uh, if the press got ahold of it, then it'd be in big black headlines and I don't think it would help either one of us."

There was an embarrassed silence. The former president gazed toward the moon as if maybe he wished one of us were on it. I was so furious I found myself shaking. Had he not been so sick, so obviously not long for this world, I might have turned on my heel, claimed my wife, and driven off without looking back. I was afraid if I said anything I would say too much, and so I said nothing. LBJ picked up the conversation as we strolled back to the ranch house, but I couldn't tell you what he talked about if my life depended on it. One thing: it wasn't about my troubles or anything approximating them.

I had trouble sleeping that night. While Dorothy breathed beside me, I lay big-eyed and thought that when it got down to the licklog, friendship with Lyndon Johnson was a one-way street. It had always been that way. It always *would* be that way. Sure, when you could do something for

"But the prodigal son . . . had only returned through the back door. I was sad . . . and wanted to get away." In better days, with my 'devoted friend' as his inscription says. (*Ransdell Inc.*)

LBJ then he would extend flattery guaranteed to motivate you to do more. If you couldn't put something helpful in his poke, however, then he concentrated on more useful targets. I should have known better than to ask him for so personal a favor, and I hated myself for having done it, for having left myself wide open to rejection and disappointment.

I've cooled off since, of course, but that night, tossing in bed at the LBJ Ranch, I made harsh evaluations of my old mentor. I rethought just about everything he'd told me during the afternoon and evening, realizing that most of it had touched on how people had let *him* down: *not a word of his own faults or failures; not a word of his own backing and filling.* No, when Lyndon Johnson told it, it always was someone else's fault that things had gone wrong. He'd mocked Hubert Humphrey for being "gutless" during Humphrey's campaign for the presidency because he'd backed off somewhat from LBJ's hard-line position on Vietnam; he'd pilloried Senator Fulbright, Senator Gene McCarthy, Senator McGovern, Congressman Mo Udall, and others who'd "turned tail" when the going got rough; he'd complained that Democrats at the 1968 convention had treated him as "a nonperson, like Khrushchev became when the Russians threw him out"; he'd gone strangely silent when I wondered why his old friend and mine, Abe Fortas, had suddenly grown so cold to me. At one point he'd astonishingly charged that "the Communists" may even have infiltrated his White House staff and possibly had subverted his former loyalists and old friends. He was afraid, even as he sensed that death crept up on him, to make one simple telephone call that might have gotten the Nixon monkey off my back. He was an old man, a scared man, a bitter man, a dying man—and, even in my anger, I wanted to weep for him.

Lyndon Johnson slept late on the final day of my visit. Despite having spent a largely sleepless night, I arose with the sun and jogged several miles on the runway of his private landing field—a holdover habit from prison. Taxpayers had been spared no expense in constructing the LBJ airfield and installing the latest in technical improvements. Many a small-town airport I'd visited had not been half so fine.

Walking around LBJ's acres to cool out after my jogging, I thought of how Johnson's presidency had enhanced the value of his holdings. Hundreds of thousands of dollars' worth of improvements had been made on his property in the name of national security; the mere fact of his presidency had driven up land values throughout the hill country; the closer one's land happened to be to the LBJ Ranch, the higher its worth on the market. There had been hard feelings between LBJ and his neighbors over land adjoining his properties. Friends of LBJ had attempted to buy up those adjoining parcels to establish a Lyndon B. Johnson State Park; some neighbors resented being pressured to sell and others had infuriated the former president by asking what he thought to be excessively high prices. "You'd have thought some of 'em descended from Jesse James," LBJ had grumbled of such neighbors.

Inspecting the showcase LBJ Ranch, I mulled over the differences in money attitudes of the Lyndon Johnsons and the Jack Kennedys. Actually, there had been one spendthrift—Jackie Kennedy and LBJ—and one pennypincher—Jack Kennedy and Lady Bird—in each family. More than once I'd heard President Kennedy grumble of his wife's loose spending habits; I think he was worried about more than the political consequences of her image as a rich big spender who cast aside expensive gowns after one or two wearings. JFK himself carefully cultivated an image of fiscal frugality and was pleased when stories appeared to the effect that he seldom had a dollar in his pocket; I always got the impression that he thought this endeared him to the common man. LBJ, though more careful of his private funds than of tax funds or political money he permitted to be spent on himself, often seemed amused by Mrs. Johnson's parsimonious instincts. When he had been in the Senate and the vice-presidency, before Air Force One was at his command, Lady Bird habitually flew tourist class on commercial flights. "Bird says the tourist part of the plane lands at the same time the first-class cabin does," Johnson chuckled. "I think she's got the first nickel she ever made."

The former president was still abed when I returned from my walk. As I showered, I again thought ruefully of his refusal to make a helpful call to Bebe Rebozo. Might I not have been better off, years earlier, had I indicated a willingness to talk before the Senate investigating committee rather than take the fifth amendment? Wouldn't the good senators have been eager to shut down the hearings and sweep everything under the rug had I begun to name names and tell all I knew of loose campaign money, outright bribes, conflict-of-interest investments, sex habits, and so on?

Once I had started it, however, it's doubtful if the press or a few self-advertised reformers would have permitted the corruption issue to die. I'm certain that some senators might have chosen not to run for reelection or might have been defeated had I originally named them even as marginal business partners. Certainly many senators would have found themselves in highly embarrassing circumstances, to say the least. Lyndon B. Johnson might have incurred a mortal wound by these revelations. They could have denied him the presidency, or driven him from office as later happened to Richard Nixon. Many times in the intervening years, friends have said, "Bobby, you made a mistake in keeping silent and becoming the fall guy. You should have chirped like a canary." I've had moments when I thought that myself, though I doubt I would have liked myself very much had I turned informer.

Lyndon Johnson joined me, Lady Bird, and Dotty for a midmorning brunch. Mrs. Johnson then modeled the new clothes she'd bought in Austin a day earlier. During this impromptu fashion show LBJ, as always, was firm in his opinions about what his wife wore. "I like that one," he'd say as Lady Bird preened in her new finery, "the color looks good on you." Or, "No, that one makes you look short and fat. Send it back." I often had known LBJ to dictate the outfits, hair styles, and shades of makeup to be worn not only by his wife and daughters, but by his secretaries. In that particular he did not change to the end: if it was there, then Lyndon Johnson was going to run it, command it, shape it, take charge of it.

About noon, as we walked across a pasture among wildflowers, LBJ gave me a sideways look and said, "Bobby, what's gonna be in that book I hear you're writing?" I responded that I was still in the outline and research stage, that the book hadn't yet been fully formed in my mind. We walked a few steps more and he said, "Is it gonna be one of those kiss-and-tell books?" Perhaps I was getting even for the night before when I answered, "Well, leader, they tell me that's the kind of book that sells."

Clearly, LBJ was not eager for me to rush into print with my recollections; he recommended that I take my time, be sure I understood things in perspective, and so forth. "I found in doing my own book that your memory can play tricks on you," he said. "Something that you'd swear had happened didn't happen at all, or happened differently, according to the documentation. It's easy to get dates and places and people mixed up." He also said of *The Vantage Point,* "You know that book of mine just barely broke even. Lady Bird's book, now, it sold real well. She teases me about hers doing better than mine did, but I'm happy for her. Hell, the money all goes in the same pot."

Lyndon Johnson stopped time and again to inspect the state of his grasslands, feed crops, cattle, the level of the water in the river. His eyes searched the land and it was obvious that he loved it. I'd read that in retirement he often startled tourists by appearing unannounced at his restored birthplace farmhouse, or the house in Johnson City where he had grown to manhood. LBJ, some writer once said, appeared to be searching in the sand for his boyhood tracks. I asked him why he so compulsively revisited his boyhood homes.

He said, "I guess it's what old men do. We try to go back. You know, I'll probably die just a few miles from where I drew my first breath. That would have seemed like a horrible prospect to me, back when I was young and ambitious and gonna set the world on fire. But there's comfort in knowing you're gonna go full circle, end up where you started out. I've said before that I want to live my last days where folks know when you're sick and care when you die. I just hope I don't drop dead on a trip away from home. Right over yonder"—and he pointed toward a big live oak tree in the distance—"is the family cemetery and that's where they'll lay my bones down. You know, Bakes, I put myself and my family's health history on a computer a year or two ago and it told me I won't live another year. I've got my business in good shape and my will made out. Lady Bird and my daughters won't be left with a tangle."

I said, "Leader, I don't wanta sound like Senator Kerr—but if you'd hold the line on cigarettes and whiskey you might beat that computer."

"No," he said. "A computer can tell you within a few yards of where a spaceship will land on the moon." Johnson remained a fatalist about his death; he was methodical in preparing for it not only in terms of tidying up his last will and testament: I've since learned that he prepared a list of thirty-odd people he wanted to see, and make some degree of amends with, before he died; he reportedly got around to seeing almost half the people on that list.

After our walk we returned to the patio overlooking the river and the low-water bridge near the entrance to the LBJ Ranch. Johnson again resumed his political commentaries. He went through a long, arm-waving defense of the Vietnam War and again damned those who'd "turned tail." He gave the impression of disliking Senator Fulbright with an intensity that was frightening. I'd had a few drinks and so I said, "Well, you and Senator Fulbright are strong-willed men. I was always proud that my friendship with Fulbright's staff members made it possible for you two to maintain a friendship. We worked problems out. I wish I'd been around when your relationship became unraveled. Maybe I could have helped." LBJ threw me a hard look and said, "It wasn't *you* and it wasn't *me*. It was *him*." Mrs. Johnson, seeing his growing irritation, began to chatter of Betty Fulbright as one of the ablest and kindest of Senate wives. "Betty always remembered," she said, "that Senator Richard Russell was a lonely bachelor and she often shopped for him at Christmastime." She continued in that light pattern until LBJ grunted, changed the subject, and the dangerous moment had passed.

Of the Kennedys he said, "Well, they're all dead except Ted and I never knew him well. He's still the fair-haired boy where the national press is concerned. You know, if I'd killed a girl like he did then they'd have wanted to send me to the electric chair. Jack Kennedy always treated me fairly and considerately. Mrs. Kennedy did too. When I was vice-president, Jackie sent me a handwritten note asking my help in getting funds for her restoration of the White House. I helped her all I could and she was truly warm and good to me—right up until Jack was assassinated. After that, I don't know, it seemed like she and the other Kennedys seemed to somehow blame me for it. Maybe it was because it happened in Texas. We invited her to the White House and tried to do all we could for her but we didn't get much of a response." Again, Lady Bird injected soothing words about the character and strength of the Kennedy women. LBJ sat silently, puffing a cigarette. He seemed jittery and impatient and soon broke in to suggest that his wife show my wife her flower beds.

When we were again alone, Johnson returned to the subject of what he called "the pitiful inadequacy" of Ramsey Clark as attorney general. I said, "Leader, pound for pound, Edward Bennett Williams was the ablest lawyer in Washington and he definitely wanted to be a part of your team. He'd have jumped at the chance to be your A.G." LBJ looked startled and said, "Then why in hell didn't he tell me? Why didn't *you* tell me?" I refrained from saying that LBJ hadn't been noted for his attempts to contact me during his White House years. Instead, I said, "Well, it's difficult for a man to seek an office that you've filled with the son of an old friend." Johnson said, "I wish I'd known of Ed Williams's interest. But a president is surrounded by so many problems, and has so many people grabbing at him, he seldom has time to sit back and think. You wind up *re*acting, when you oughta be acting on a positive plan, because there's seldom time to think things through. You run around puttin' your fingers in the leaks, trying to patch this up or that up, but it's all too hully-gully.

"You know, I often think it's a good thing that Hubert Humphrey never got to be president—for his own good as well as the good of the country. He can't say no to anybody about anything, he hasn't got much more spine than a small girl, and he runs his mouth ninety miles an hour without thinking about what he's saying. Hubert, he'd have promised a half-dozen people to appoint 'em to the same office and then he never would have slowed down long enough to appoint any one of 'em. He'd probably had a crisis in the White House about every two hours and I think the office would have driven him absolutely crazy."

I was uneasy at such raw talk against Humphrey, whom I'd always considered with affection, and presumed to change the subject by injecting, "Leader, how's old Judge Moursund these days? Is he still trying to beat you at dominoes?" Judge A. W. Moursund had been LBJ's closest

Texas pal for years: they'd hunted together, played dominoes, incessantly talked politics, and had been partners in cattle, ranching, and banking operations. The judge had been trustee of all Johnson's investments while LBJ was president.

The former president looked as if he'd just bitten into a green persimmon and snapped, "Don't know. Don't see him anymore." I could have kicked myself, but I truly had not known that the two old cronies had ripped the friendship blanket. I'd several times been a guest in Judge Moursund's Johnson City home and had visited with him at the LBJ Ranch and in Washington. A warmer, more relaxed friendship than his and Johnson's I'd seldom seen. It was inconceivable they would have experienced an irrevocable falling out.

I later learned that Lyndon Johnson and Judge Moursund had gotten crossways about a land deal and matters at the Johnson City bank, in which they were investors. LBJ would die without repairing the friendship. It seemed ironic that although Lyndon Johnson had been on top of the world, had come out of the Texas outback to achieve all to which a country boy possibly could have aspired, that even as he tried to balance his psychic and personal books before death he could not quite pull it off—he remained isolated from many old friends, could not quite reach out for the ultimate handclasp. I wondered what it was he had to fear, what final pride or stubbornness or illusion or reservation held him in emotional check. My old leader looked old and forlorn as he sat with his thoughts, gazing out across his familiar acres, gulping scotch long before the sun had come over the yardarm.

As our twenty-four-hour visit approached its end, Lyndon Johnson perked up to sign copies of his book for us, warmly inscribe photographs with flattering personal messages, and make gifts of the personalized trinkets—cuff links, ballpoint pens, matchbooks; all branded "LBJ"—he'd always handed out by the carload. There was something almost childlike in this high ceremony of handing over gifts which I had once ordered by the gross and had stuffed my pockets with so that he might turn to me and claim them when he felt called upon to press them on others. I knew that within ten minutes of having awarded such baubles, no matter his enthusiasm of the moment, he would not be able to recall who had received them. Yet, he seemed to expect me to accept them with boundless gratitude.

I really wanted to say during those final rituals at the LBJ Ranch, *Hold on, dammit, we haven't touched each other. Reach out. Don't draw back. This is a sham! Fuck your trinkets and your smiling ceremonies.* But, of course, there is no way to say such things and I did not say them. I tamely acted out my part of the charade, mumbling pleasantries, and acting as if nothing lay unrepaired between us.

The moment closest to the good old times had occurred when, showing me around his acreage on the first day of my final visit, LBJ had suddenly blurted, "Bobby, what was jail like?" I had tried to impart to him something of the sense of isolation, of the uncertainty, of the feeling of worthlessness, of the frustration, of the fear, and of the guilt and shame of simply *being* there. But it was difficult to transmit. There had been a few moments when Lyndon Johnson sat uncharacteristically still, nodding and not interrupting, his attention fully focused. At a given point, however, he suddenly had injected, "See that bull there? He's a real prize winner. Wayne Morse or Clint Anderson never had one that could touch him." And that was that.

As Dorothy and I passed through the front hall of the Johnson ranch house, taking our leave, I paused at the guest book LBJ kept on a small table. I had signed it, or one like it, many times in the past: LBJ had always been careful to record his visitors, and sometimes double-checked to make certain they'd written down the correct date. Now, I noticed, the last person to sign it—only a few days before—had been Abe Fortas. I stood there until it became too obvious that my old leader did not intend to invite my signature. *So the prodigal son had not returned all the way home. He was welcomed only by the back door.* Even as Lyndon Johnson gave me one last, seemingly warm embrace, I suddenly and desperately wanted to get away.

Driving toward the low-water bridge, trying to sort out my jumbled feelings, I looked back hoping to catch a glimpse of Lyndon Johnson as he stood on his ranch house porch. But he was gone. Vanished. I next would see him three months later as his body lay in state in the rotunda of the U.S. Capitol Building. It was the first time I'd been back to Capitol Hill since resigning a decade earlier.

Chapter Eighteen

Reflections of a
Political Has-Been

*Most of the people on top in government haven't
experienced serious adversity or they never would
have arrived there.*

I T SEEMS eons ago that I came out of the South Carolina hills,
gourd green, to chase the American Dream—only to discover that dreams sometimes turn into nightmares. I am no longer the
boy wonder of politics, but a man close to his fiftieth year; by all conven-
tional reckonings I guess you could call me a "has-been." Presidents don't
seek my advice these days; indeed, only within the last couple of years
have working politicians started to greet me in public without first looking around to make certain that photographers aren't recording the
event. Invitations to Capitol Hill social functions again are coming my
way, and bids to speak to gatherings of political groups or newsmen. I
don't accept many of these; the public arena no longer is my natural
place. I have developed a quieter and more private lifestyle. It is nice,
however, no longer to be thought of as some dangerous form of wildlife.

My problems with investigators or the highly placed who tried to in-
timidate me didn't end until after the Nixon gang got off my back—and
they didn't get off it until the desperate scramble to save their own asses
gave them no time to create mischief for others. I try not to hate people,
or even to carry around more grudges than can be lifted, but I confess to
a mean little shudder of joy on the day that a grand jury labeled my self-
righteous prosecutor, William O. Bittman, as an "unindicted co-
conspirator." Bittman had lied under oath about acting as a middleman
between the Nixon White House and his client, Watergate burglar, E.
Howard Hunt, in the matter of hush money paid to keep the lid on that
historic case of constitutional malfeasance.

I was forced to walk a tightrope during the Watergate investigation.

Probers for the special prosecutor's staff called me in to ask why I had
been trading telephone calls with Bebe Rebozo. I could not afford to say
that I'd been sought out and asked, under the implied threat of going to
jail again, to make a fall guy of Larry O'Brien or other Democrats.
Perhaps I should have done so, but I knew it would explode into another
headline-making nightmare for me. I'd had my fill of that. I also feared
that the Watergate gang might prevail: remember, it was much later that
the "smoking gun" tapes resulted in the resignation of President Nixon,
much later that a grand jury returned indictments against thirty-odd politicos who still held the reins of power, much later that Nixon would be
named as part of the cover-up or that the House Judiciary Committee
would vote articles of impeachment. I was still on parole, and wanted
nothing to happen that might cause anyone in high places to even *think*
of revoking it.

Consequently, when the special prosecutor's staffers asked me why
I'd trafficked in conversation with Bebe Rebozo I said, "I've known him
for years. We've been social friends and we've talked over potential business deals. No law against that, is there?" Did I recall what we'd specifically talked about within recent weeks? "Listen, when you have as many
problems as I have it's hard to remember what you had for breakfast yes-
terday." Had we discussed Watergate in any fashion? "No." Then I decided to take the offensive: "Now *I* have a question: How did you know
that we'd talked at all? You've got several dates there on a piece of paper.
For reasons of public relations, or politics, we used fake names when
calling each other. Sometimes we called from pay telephones. My God, is
no phone in America safe from electronic snooping? I don't intend to
answer another question until I get some answers." The investigators, on
the defensive, soon decided to leave me alone. Exactly what I wanted.
The last thing I needed was to get caught in a squeeze between the
Nixon administration and its political investigators: once bit, twice shy.
Perhaps it was a reaction to having been tapped and bugged by so many
government agencies in my own right, but at any rate I got word to Bebe
that the prosecutor's boys might be listening in on his calls.

Senator Howard Baker of Tennessee, a Republican member of the
Ervin committee, sent word that he would like to see me at his home dur-
ing the Watergate hearings. Though I did not know Senator Baker well,
I long had been a friend of his wife, Joy, the daughter of the late Senator
Everett Dirksen of Illinois. After we'd had a drink, Baker suggested we
take a stroll in his rose garden. We walked for a bit and he said, "Bobby,
I wanted to get out of the house because I can't be certain it's not bugged.
With everything we're learning about the FBI, the CIA, and even the
White House itself—well, I just don't know whom to trust." He went on

to ask whether I'd picked up anything from my Democratic contacts that might indicate what Watergate had been all about in the first place: "What in the name of God did they think they would find in Larry O'Brien's office? Why did they take that foolish risk when they already had the election won?" I told the senator I was as puzzled as he was, and had not even a helpful rumor to pass on.

This was shortly after Alexander Butterfield had astonished the world by revealing the existence of the White House taping system: that President Nixon had gone so far as to bug himself, and anyone who had contact with him. "It seems too pat, too set," Howard Baker said. "Butterfield's rumored to have been a CIA man. The Watergate burglars had CIA connections. CIA tracks turn up everywhere we look." Did President Nixon have such dirt on the CIA that its top dogs feared he'd destroy them, and did they in turn "accidentally" reveal the White House tapes through Butterfield? Again, I pled that I had no special information. I was puzzled by why Senator Baker had asked to see me: what could I know of the CIA? Probably he knew I'd been in contact with Bebe Rebozo and maybe he'd heard I'd been subjected to pressures by figures involved in the Watergate investigation and cover-up. Was he, then, attempting to extract information that might honestly aid him in his investigative deliberations? Or, conversely, could he as a leading Republican be conducting a fishing expedition for the Nixon White House in an attempt to learn what damaging or embarrassing things I might have heard? I asked myself these questions as we walked in the senator's tree-lined neighborhood. I feared to say anything of substance, though I've never found Senator Baker to be anything but friendly, considerate, and a gentleman. I simply had seen so much of intrigue, illegal wiretaps, perjury, double crosses, and threats that I had reached an advanced stage of paranoia and confusion which left me wondering—just as Senator Baker wondered—whom to trust. So I said nothing then— and, indeed, until now—to indicate any contact with Watergate characters.

If my potential criminal problems disappeared with the ultimate exploding of the Watergate mess, I continued to have civil problems with the Internal Revenue Service and the Justice Department. The latter, in 1969, had filed a suit for $108,968 it claimed I had received in six separate influence-peddling cases while secretary to the Senate majority. In 1974, on advice of counsel and to begin to clear my legal decks, I settled that case by paying the government $40,000. After months of dispute and negotiations, I paid the District of Columbia $22,000—after its tax agents dropped demands for penalties and interest—on the sale of the Carousel Motel. Since this transaction had occurred in Maryland, and I had paid taxes on it there, I felt I owed no tribute to the District of Columbia. Because I was "domiciled" in Washington, however, the District's tax agents got their pound of flesh. I still am in dispute with IRS. The feds have claimed that I owed as much as $1.3 million in back taxes, much of which was interest and penalties accumulated on disputed accounts going back as long as fifteen years. Only recently have the federal tax authorities admitted that they have never found any evidence that I received $150,000 from the insurance man, Don Reynolds, and agreed to drop attempts to collect it plus a boatload of interest and penalties. Other disputed items are being negotiated by lawyers. If the tax people can't see it as I see it, I'll see them in court. I also expect to file law suits against the government, and the individuals involved, for having planted a paid spy in my home to steal my private documents and for having employed illegal wiretaps against me; and I plan suits under the Freedom of Information Act to attempt to discover what other unlawful acts may have been performed against my constitutional rights. Certainly I am bone-weary of court, and of exhaustive attorneys' fees—but I am more weary of outlaws wearing badges, or holding commissions as prosecutors, who use the protective coloration of officialdom to advance their personal careers or causes while breaking the law in the name of the flag. Enough is, by God, enough.

It may seem strange that Bobby Baker, a bag man and scam artist in the eyes of much of the world, would deliver morality lectures. Yet, I feel uniquely qualified for the role. More than most, I've seen the system in operation at the highest level and at the lowest. I fancy that the scales dropped away from my eyes some years ago, and that I've had a clear—if highly personal—view of the system's warts and moles. I'd also like to think that I've grown more introspective and perhaps even a tad wiser than when riding high in the glory days: a fine irony, that, and one that I'm afraid holds true across the board for almost everyone who rises to a position to run things at the higher levels.

Most of the people on top in government haven't experienced thirty minutes' worth of serious adversity or they never would have arrived there. They get to the top without understanding life on the underside, or having any special compassion or feeling for those less fortunate than themselves. They are blinded by ambition; the royal treatment they receive leads them to take for granted that they are of a special few with unusual prerogatives: the confining rules are meant for others. They come to embrace the notion that they are among the chosen. They become elitist, walking cases of the old doctrine of "manifest destiny." Their arrival at high stations is all the proof they need of their natural superiority.

It is but a thoughtless hop, skip, and jump to the allied notion that one's personal beliefs, goals, whims, or opportunities are synonymous with the sacred, and must be preserved at all costs. Given this mind-set, it is easy for officials to cut corners, wink at the law, bend it or shatter it—all in the name of some great vague larger good. There is an unspoken conspiracy among officials within the system to live and let live, to make each other look good, so that in the end the system will appear, at least, to have effectively functioned toward its natural end.

It gets to be a simple game of Us against Them. That is why investigators, prosecutors, judges, and wardens can lend themselves to chicaneries ranging from unwarranted searches and seizures to the suborning of perjury to one-way rulings from the bench to inhumane treatment of the jailed—and manage not only to sleep well, but to feel righteous in their conduct. Maybe you have to be arrested, charged, indicted, tried, and even convicted to fully understand how frozen is the pattern, and how rigid are the people, when all within the system get to chasing the same rabbit. I doubt whether this condition ever will be corrected, for we are talking of no less than tribal instincts brought into play to insure self-perpetuation and self-promotion. I know of no law, God's or man's, strong enough to deal with the problem. Such constitutional care as may be taken reposes solely with private citizens called to serve as jurors or grand jurors, most of whom lack enough knowledge of the lawful processes—or how effectively to employ them—to slow down runaway prosecutors and judges hell-bent on seeing that the state has its way.

When private citizens come into the courthouse to function as jurors they are under the supervision of the state from the moment of their arrival: they may be herded, instructed, fed, bedded, transported, and to some extent entertained by officials of the court, and, in effect, they often wind up being led around by their noses. The trappings of officialdom—robes, flags, badges—seem to embody respectability itself, while one who has been charged or indicted is automatically considered suspect. The notion prevails that where there's smoke there must be fire; jurors largely find it more comfortable to identify with the state than with someone presented to them as a wrongdoer or outcast. In such conditions, most advantages repose with the state. Its agents can pretty well do as they please.

Nor do I know any effective, practical way to eliminate injustices involved in plea bargaining, a process by which the state puts the screws to one troubled soul to convince him, or her, to turn state's evidence against another—usually a presumably larger fish. Those who defend the plea-bargaining system plead that (1) court dockets would become irrevocably jammed without the ability to make deals, and (2) many big offenders never would be brought to justice without the cooperation of smaller fish who must be given incentives to testify against them. As to the first argument, I claim that (1) jammed court dockets are a lesser evil than hasty railroadings, and (2) the plea bargainer is a puppet whose eagerness to serve his own cause obviously constitutes a conflict of interest against the lawful rights of the man he accuses.

Though the law prohibits the state from rewarding its stool pigeons by making specific promises in return for their testimony, this law is more routinely violated than the one calling for New Yorkers to curb their dogs during calls of nature. Anyone who believes there are no specific trades must also believe in werewolves, moon cheese, and leprechauns. *Give us Mr. Baker and you won't be indicted, Mr. Bromley . . . Give us Mr. O'Brien and you won't go back to jail, Mr. Baker . . . Give us Mr. Baker and you won't be tried, Mr. Pollock . . .*

A plea-bargaining witness may be willing to have his memory improved in order to satisfy those who hold his future in their hands. With the enthusiastic encouragement of the prosecution, he may be likely to remember in great detail many things that never happened. Threaten a man with loss of his liberty and all that liberty implies beyond the breathing of free air—career, reputation, family life, worldly goods, sex, leisure time—and usually he'll jump through a hoop just like any trained dog. So great is the average man's fear of being locked in a cage, outcast and forgotten, that he'll chirp in notes he didn't even know he could reach. Clever prosecutions exploit even these fears by crude jokes reminding their targets of their darker prison fantasies: sexual assaults, losing their jobs or their wives, hard labor, brutal guards.

Those of us who've been through criminal trials are united in our belief that plea bargaining is among the more insidious practices of ambitious prosecutors. After John Connally was charged with accepting a $10,000 bribe from a lobbyist for the Associated Milk Producers of America, in exchange for influencing the Nixon administration to increase federal milk price supports while himself a cabinet member, he began a crusade against the plea-bargaining system. For months he told audiences, friends, and anyone who would listen—and told them accurately—that his accuser, one Jake Jacobsen, also accused of embezzlement and conspiracy to defraud Texas financial institutions with which he was affiliated, had traded a potential forty years in prison and fines of up to $100,000 for a mere *two* years: turn state's evidence against John Connally, and all save one small charge would be dropped. That was the sweet deal the prosecution made Jacobsen, and that was the way it happened that Connally was indicted and tried in a Watergate atmosphere.

During his trial, as before, John Connally grabbed every lawyer and journalist within shouting distance to rail against the vicious plea-bargaining system and to enlist their support toward prohibiting it. Since the government produced little or no corroboration of Jake Jacobsen's story that he'd bribed Connally with corporate cash, the former Texas governor and Nixon cabinet member was acquitted.

If John Connally has since made a single public appearance or utterance, or has even so much as written a letter to aid the reform of the plea-bargaining system, then I don't know of it. Those of us who were convicted, however, remember our grievances longer: Jimmy Hoffa, up until the moment he was presumably snuffed out by mobsters, was active against plea bargaining and in behalf of other judicial and prison reforms. I broke a self-imposed rule against appearing on television or granting interviews, not long after leaving prison, because Hoffa asked me to join in seeking reforms. I did so because I had become convinced that virtually nobody in the "straight" world knew, or cared, about the desperate need for such reforms. I thought it would be healthy when possible to force society to look the ugly problem in the eye.

Tighter campaign finance laws and conflict-of-interest laws are on the books than formerly, and probably it is more difficult to wheel and deal in the old Bobby Baker style nor are leaders in Congress, or their top aides, as free to exercise unilateral powers as in the old days. The newer breed of politician expects to be more of a working partner in the legislative processes and is quicker to rebel against the taut rein. This, I think, is good for the system though sometimes it appears that the congressional leadership drifts and procrastinates more than makes an old firehorse comfortable.

Many of the highly touted reforms Congress voted within past years have been more illusory than real. Not until more than a dozen years after my operations allegedly shook political Washington to its roots did Congress vote meaningful reforms; even then, it was reluctant to apply to its members the same rigid rules and standards it has written for its employees, the executive branch, the judiciary, or the general public. For example, though Congress has passed laws forbidding sexist or racial discrimination in both the public and private sectors, it has not made itself subject to those laws. So long as every congressman and senator insists on running his own office as a private grand duchy, and conducting himself as no less than a prince, Capitol Hill will continue to be a sociological backwater with elitest rule.

I remain skeptical enough to believe that for all of Congress's advertised preoccupation with official morality within the past few years, that somewhere—at this moment—a politician or a lobbyist or a hungry-eyed

young aide is carefully searching those laws for loopholes and for ways
to subvert them. The laws may be tougher than previously, but I doubt
whether the people to whom they are intended to apply are significantly
better in their instincts. There always will be those who seek the advantage without excessively worrying about how they gain it.

Just because I lost some key struggles to the system, or find much to
criticize in it, do not think that Bobby Baker has become a radical who
wants to smash it. I basically believe in the system. At the hazard of
sounding candy-assed, I know of no country or no government I would
be willing to trade for ours. I continue to be fascinated with the legislative and the political processes; if I could be granted one wish, it would
be that I might once more have the opportunity to come to Washington
as a wide-eyed kid capable of the old thrills and expectations, the juices
and the challenges. That being impossible, I guess I'd settle for being
back in the political trenches on a daily basis, even if aging and somewhat
jaded. But that, too, is beyond the realities.

Contrary to old rumors that Bobby Baker long has lived off the fat of
a fortune he once stashed in foreign banks, I am no longer even a paper
millionaire. There was a time, with all due thanks to the Internal Revenue Service, when so many tax liens were filed against my properties that
it was next to impossible to accomplish routine business. Indeed, there
were stretches and patches of time when, had it not been for the
kindness of loyal friends, I might not have eaten regularly. It was ironic
that though good credit sources remained available, I could not take advantage of them because everything I owned was worthless as collateral
so long as the government maintained its liens.

Those old problems have been resolved, however, and life now is better. Though it's doubtful I'll ever be the business whizbang I once
thirsted to be, I still enjoy putting deals together and making something
from nothing. Capitalism excites me. Accumulation acts on me like a
drug. Taking a flyer, rolling the dice, running the risk—these are tonics.
I like to dream.

Though no longer a budding tycoon, I trust that no one ever will be
required to hold a benefit for me. I've managed to hang onto a few
stocks and bonds, enjoyed a good capital gains profit from the sale of the
Carousel, and with my children grown I recently sold the big house in
Spring Valley for a neat profit. I'm a partner in a corporation operating
a Howard Johnson motel-restaurant near Charlotte, North Carolina,
and if you're passing through, then bring money and tell them Bobby
sent you. The Mecklenberg Corporation also builds and rehabilitates
rental properties in Washington. I own land in Maryland, Washington,

Delaware, West Virginia, and the Carolinas. Those looking for industrial, commercial, or residential developments are invited to get in touch.

If my lifestyle isn't as flamboyant as it once was, that's less important
to me than formerly. I still enjoy an occasional outing to the racetrack or
to the Washington Redskins football games, and seashore weekends in
Ocean City. There was a time, with pressures besetting me from all sides,
when I developed something of a drinking problem. I've licked that
problem now, if not by a knockout in the early rounds then at least by a
split decision. If the gremlins will stay out of my life I doubt whether I'll
die unattended and unshaven in a doorway. I've again got a good
woman, Doris Myers, at least a modicum of hope for the future, and free
air to breathe. Not everyone does.

Index